T0301250

Clusters in Times of Uncertainty

Clusters in Times of Uncertainty

Japanese and European Perspectives

Edited by

Luciana Lazzeretti

Professor of Economics and Management, Department of Economics and Management, University of Florence, Italy

Tamane Ozeki

Associate Professor, Graduate School of Urban Management, Osaka Metropolitan University, Japan

Silvia Rita Sedita

Professor of Management, Department of Economics and Management, University of Padova, Italy

Francesco Capone

Associate Professor of Management, Department of Economics and Management, University of Florence, Italy

 Edward **Elgar**
PUBLISHING

Cheltenham, UK • Northampton, MA, USA

Published by
Edward Elgar Publishing Limited
The Lypiatts
15 Lansdown Road
Cheltenham
Glos GL50 2JA
UK

Edward Elgar Publishing, Inc.
William Pratt House
9 Dewey Court
Northampton
Massachusetts 01060
USA

A catalogue record for this book
is available from the British Library

Library of Congress Control Number: 2024930568

This book is available electronically in the **Elgar**online
Economics subject collection
http://dx.doi.org/10.4337/9781035315765

ISBN 978 1 0353 1575 8 (cased)
ISBN 978 1 0353 1576 5 (eBook)

Printed and bound in Great Britain by TJ Books Limited, Padstow, Cornwall

Contents

Contributors

Jun Akabane, Faculty of Economics, Chuo University, Hachiouji, Tokyo, Japan.

Futoshi Akiba, Faculty of Business Administration, Ryukoku University, Kyoto, Japan.

Roberto Antonietti, "Marco Fanno" Department of Economics and Management, University of Padova, Padova, Italy.

Josep-Maria Arauzo-Carod, Departament d'Economia (ECO-SOS & IU-RESCAT), Universitat Rovira i Virgili, Reus, Spain.

Filippo Baldetti, Poste Italiane S.p.A., Roma, Italy.

Paola Beccherle, Department of Economics and Management, University of Florence, Florence, Italy.

Silvia Blasi, Department of Management, University of Verona, Verona, Italy.

Mattia Buggio, Department of Economics and Management, University of Padova, Padova, Italy.

Francesco Capone, Department of Economics and Management, University of Florence, Florence, Italy.

David Fanton, European Central Bank, Frankfurt am Mein, Germany.

Pablo Galaso, Facultad de Ciencias Económicas y de la Administración, Universidad de la República, Montevideo, Uruguay.

Niccolò Innocenti, Department of Economics and Management, University of Florence, Florence, Italy.

Hiroki Kamata, Professor Emeritus, Kyoto University, Kyoto, Japan.

Hirotoshi Kishi, Nomura Research Institute, Chiyoda, Tokyo, Japan.

Luciana Lazzeretti, Department of Economics and Management, University of Florence, Florence, Italy.

Anna Lis, Faculty of Management and Economics, Gdańsk University of Technology, Gdansk, Poland.

Marta Mackiewicz, Collegium of World Economy, SGH Warsaw School of Economics, Warsaw, Poland.

Atsuko Maeda, Center for the Study of the Creative Economy, Doshisha University, Kyoto, Japan.

Keizo Matsumura, EXPO 2025 Osaka Pavilion Association, Osaka, Japan.

Lucrezia Maria Mecenero, Distretto Veneto della Pelle, Arzignano, Vicenza, Italy.

Yoshio Mochizuki, Mayor Arida City, Wakayama, Japan.

Stefania Oliva, Department of Economics and Management, University of Florence, Florence, Italy.

Moet Onodera, Nomura Research Institute, Ltd., Chiyoda, Tokyo, Japan.

Tamane Ozeki, Osaka Metropolitan University, Osaka, Japan.

Sergio Palomeque, Facultad de Ciencias Económicas y de la Administración, Universidad de la República, Montevideo, Uruguay.

Andrea Porta, PhD candidate, Program Tourism and Leisure, Universitat Rovira i Virgili, Vila-seca, Spain, and Fondazione Santagata for the Economics of Culture, Turin, Italy.

Masayuki Sasaki, Osaka City University, Osaka, Japan and Kanazawa Seiryo University, Kanazawa, Japan.

Yuho Sasamori, Nomura Research Institute, Ltd., Chiyoda, Tokyo, Japan.

Masako Sawayanagi, President, Sense LLC, Arida, Japan.

Silvia Rita Sedita, Department of Economics and Management, University of Padova, Padova, Italy.

Giovanna Segre, Department of Economics and Statistics "Cognetti de Martiis", University of Turin, Turin, Italy, and CNR-IRCrES, Research Institute on Sustainable Economic Growth, Turin, Italy.

Italo Trevisan, Dipartimento di Economia e Management, Università degli Studi di Trento, Trento, Italy.

Anna Wendt, Faculty of Management and Economics, Gdańsk University of Technology, Gdansk, Poland.

Jin-ichiro Yamada, Graduate School of Management, Kyoto University, Kyoto, Japan.

Vincenzo Zampi, Department of Economics and Management, University of Florence, Florence, Italy.

Foreword

The world is undergoing a profound transformation, driven by the convergence of digital technologies and the imperative for sustainable development. This era of digital and green transformation presents both opportunities and challenges for cluster research, particularly in the aftermath of the COVID-19 pandemic. As we navigate this new landscape, understanding the complexities and implications of cluster dynamics becomes paramount for fostering resilient and sustainable economies.

Clusters, defined as geographic concentrations of interconnected companies, institutions, and support organizations, have been recognized as catalysts for innovation, productivity, and regional development. However, the emergence of the digital age, accelerated by the pandemic, has disrupted traditional models and reshaped the dynamics within and around clusters. Moreover, the urgency to address environmental challenges and transition towards a greener economy adds an additional layer of complexity to the research and development of clusters.

We aim to highlight the challenges faced by cluster research in the age of digital and green transformation in a post-corona world. By addressing these challenges, we can better comprehend the intricacies of cluster ecosystems and identify strategies to harness their potential for sustainable growth and societal well-being.

The rapid advancement of digital technologies such as artificial intelligence, big data analytics, cloud computing, and the Internet of Things has significantly impacted clusters. Digital transformation has the potential to drive productivity, innovation, and competitiveness within clusters, but it also raises questions regarding the adaptability of traditional cluster models. Researchers must grapple with understanding the role of digital technologies in shaping cluster dynamics, assessing the digital divide within and across clusters, and exploring the implications of virtual collaboration and remote work on cluster functioning.

The COVID-19 pandemic has challenged the traditional notions of proximity and physical co-location that have been central to cluster theories. Remote work, virtual collaboration, and digital platforms have blurred the boundaries of clusters, allowing for virtual connections and the formation of new types of cluster networks. Cluster research must explore how these changes impact innovation, knowledge sharing, and social interactions within and between clusters. Furthermore, the role of digital platforms and virtual ecosystems in supporting cluster development and collaboration needs to be examined.

As the urgency to address climate change and environmental degradation grows, clusters must adapt to a greener and more sustainable future. The research on clusters must focus on understanding how clusters can contribute to the green transition by promoting clean technologies, circular economy practices, and sustainable supply chains. Examining the role of clusters in fostering innovation for environmental sustainability and exploring the challenges of integrating green practices into cluster ecosystems are crucial areas of investigation.

The digital and green transformations should not exacerbate inequalities within and between clusters. Cluster research needs to address the potential risks of technological disruptions, such as job displacement and the digital divide, and explore strategies for inclusive and equitable development. This involves understanding how clusters can foster skills development, support entrepreneurship, and promote social inclusion, ensuring that the benefits of digital and green transformations are shared by all stakeholders.

We think arts and crafts play a significant role in developing the creative cluster within the digital and green transformation age. Here are some key ways in which arts and crafts contribute to the development of creative clusters in this context.

Arts and crafts are deeply rooted in cultural traditions and provide a means of expressing and preserving cultural identity. Within creative clusters, incorporating arts and crafts can help establish a unique cultural presence, distinguishing the cluster from others. This can attract creative individuals and businesses, fostering a vibrant and diverse creative ecosystem.

Arts and crafts are often associated with innovation, creativity, and out-of-the-box thinking. By integrating arts and crafts into a creative cluster, it can inspire new ideas, approaches, and design thinking. The unique perspectives and techniques employed in arts and crafts can stimulate innovation and cross-pollination of ideas among different industries within the cluster.

Arts and crafts emphasize the human touch, craftsmanship, and attention to detail. These principles can be valuable in the digital and green transformation age, where human-centered design is increasingly emphasized. By incorporating arts and crafts, creative clusters can foster a focus on user experience, aesthetics, and sustainability, resulting in more user-friendly and environmentally conscious products and services.

Arts and crafts can contribute to the development of experiential and creative tourism. By showcasing local arts and crafts, visitors can engage with the creative process, participate in workshops, and gain insights into the cultural heritage of the cluster. This can attract tourists, generate economic opportunities, and enhance the overall appeal and vitality of the cluster.

Arts and crafts often involve collaboration and knowledge sharing among artists, artisans, and craftsmen. This collaborative spirit can extend to the creative cluster as a whole, fostering a culture of cooperation, shared resources, and collective learning. The exchange of ideas and skills across different creative disciplines can lead to the emergence of new collaborations, interdisciplinary projects, and the development of a rich ecosystem within the cluster.

In the green transformation age, sustainability is a crucial consideration. Arts and crafts have a long history of using sustainable materials, recycling, and repurposing. By incorporating arts and crafts within a creative cluster, it can promote and inspire sustainable practices in other industries. This can contribute to the overall green transformation and environmentally friendly initiatives within the cluster.

Overall, the inclusion of arts and crafts within creative clusters in the digital and green transformation age can enrich the cultural fabric, foster innovation and creativity, promote sustainable practices, and enhance the overall attractiveness and competitiveness of the cluster.

The age of digital and green transformation, coupled with the impacts of the COVID-19 pandemic, has propelled cluster research to the forefront of understanding the dynamics of innovation, sustainability, and economic development. Japan and Europe, two regions with distinct characteristics and approaches, offer valuable insights into the challenges and opportunities of cluster research in this transformative era. A comparative study of Japan and Europe can shed light on their respective experiences, policies, and strategies, fostering cross-regional learning and identifying best practices for effective cluster development in the age of digital and green transformation in a post-corona world.

Comparing the cluster policies and governance mechanisms in Japan and Europe provides a deeper understanding of how each region approaches the challenges of digital and green transformation. By examining the strategies, incentives, and support mechanisms employed by governments and institutions, researchers can identify successful policies that have facilitated the integration of digital technologies and sustainable practices into cluster ecosystems. This analysis can inform policymakers and practitioners in both regions, guiding them towards effective policy frameworks and governance structures that encourage innovation, sustainability, and collaboration within clusters.

Japan and Europe have distinct strengths and capabilities in technological innovation. Comparative analysis can explore the different approaches to digital transformation and the adoption of emerging technologies within clusters. Understanding the factors that drive successful digitalization efforts, such as investments in research and development, collaboration between academia and industry, and the role of government support, can contribute to the development of strategies that accelerate digital transformation in clusters. Additionally, examining the impact of digitalization on productivity, job creation, and the resilience of clusters in the post-corona world can provide valuable insights for policymakers and cluster practitioners.

Both Japan and Europe have recognized the importance of transitioning towards sustainable and green economies. Comparative analysis can reveal the strategies, initiatives, and best practices employed by clusters in each region to promote sustainability and environmental stewardship. This includes exploring the integration of renewable energy, circular economy principles, and sustainable supply chains within cluster ecosystems. Researchers can examine the challenges faced by clusters in adopting green practices, identify successful models of sustainable cluster development, and highlight the role of collaboration between clusters, academia, and government agencies in driving the green transition.

Comparing the collaboration and knowledge exchange mechanisms between clusters in Japan and Europe can provide valuable insights into the benefits of cross-regional cooperation. By examining existing cluster networks, joint research projects, and collaborative initiatives, researchers can identify successful models of knowledge sharing, technology transfer, and innovation diffusion. Understanding the barriers to international collaboration, such as cultural differences or regulatory obstacles, can inform policymakers and cluster stakeholders in both regions on how to foster effective cross-border partnerships and create synergies between Japanese and European clusters.

This comparative study of Japan and Europe on cluster research in the age of digital and green transformation in a post-corona world offers a rich opportunity for cross-regional learning and collaboration. By analyzing the cluster policies, technological innovation, sustainability practices, and collaboration mechanisms in both regions, researchers and policymakers can identify successful strategies and best practices. This comparative analysis can contribute to the development of robust policy frameworks, foster knowledge exchange, and guide the future of cluster development in the digital and green transformation era. Ultimately, it is through such collaborative efforts that clusters can thrive as drivers of innovation, sustainability, and economic resilience in the post-corona world.

In writing this preface, we seek to emphasize the significance of cluster research in the age of digital and green transformation in a post-corona world. By addressing the challenges outlined above, researchers, policymakers, and practitioners can work collaboratively to shape the future of clusters as drivers of innovation, sustainability, and inclusive growth. Through interdisciplinary approaches and global collaboration, we have the opportunity to unlock the full potential of clusters and build resilient economies that embrace digital and green transformations.

Dr. Masayuki Sasaki
Professor Emeritus, Osaka City University

Introduction to *Clusters in Times of Uncertainty*

Luciana Lazzeretti, Tamane Ozeki, Silvia Rita Sedita and Francesco Capone

Welcome to this groundbreaking book, which delves into the evolutionary trajectories of clusters and territories undergoing transformation in uncertain times. The book takes a comprehensive approach to examining the transformation of clusters, industries, and places amidst an increasingly uncertain and dynamic landscape. It explores the social, economic, green, and technological changes shaping these transformations, with a specific focus on case studies and analyses from both European and Japanese contexts.

The insights presented in this book are derived from the vibrant discussions that took place during "Rethinking Clusters", the international event held in 2022 at the Metropolitan University of Osaka in Japan. The event served as a platform for leading researchers and practitioners to share their expertise and engage in thought-provoking conversations surrounding the challenges and opportunities faced by clusters and territories in the midst of profound transitions.

Clusters, defined as geographically concentrated networks of interconnected organizations and institutions, have long been recognized as catalysts for industrial agglomeration and knowledge spillovers (Porter, 1990, 1998). They foster collaboration, specialization, and the exchange of ideas, propelling industries and regions towards sustained competitiveness and prosperity (Porter, 2000). Territorial development is crucially intertwined with the improvement of the well-being and wealth of the stakeholders of a territory, given their relations of competition and cooperation, their initiatives and their oppositions, and the dynamic of territorial innovations (Torre, 2023). Clusters and territories can be considered fundamental units of analysis for exploring sustainability and technological transition. By examining clusters, we can uncover industry-specific pathways and leverage points for innovation, while territories provide a broader context and facilitate tailored approaches to sustainable development. Embracing these units of analysis empowers stakeholders to drive meaningful change, foster collaboration, and cultivate sustainability at both local and global scales.

Clusters offer fertile ground for investigating transition as they encompass a range of interconnected actors, such as companies, research institutions, and government bodies, operating within a defined spatial area. Analyzing clusters allows us to understand the interdependencies and collaboration opportunities among stakeholders within an industry, enabling the identification of leverage points for driving sustainable practices and innovations. Territorial analysis expands the scope beyond individual clusters, emphasizing the interplay between various industries, land use patterns, ecosystems, and socio-cultural contexts. Exploring territories as units of analysis enables a holistic understanding of the complex interactions between different sectors and their impact on sustainability and technological change. It helps identify the challenges and opportunities inherent in specific geographic areas, such as urban–rural interfaces or coastal regions, and allows for tailored approaches to sustainable development that address local context and needs.

The chapters in this book address timely and crucial topics related to the transformation of clusters and places, whose process was initially described in Lazzeretti et al. (2020) and Sedita and Blasi (2021), and further developed with a focus on culture and creativity and digital transformation (Lazzeretti et al., 2023). They explore how technological advancements and environmental transitions have prompted clusters to adapt and reinvent themselves. Additionally, the book investigates the emergence of new forms of entrepreneurship and business models that contribute to cluster and territorial development. Furthermore, the role of policy, networks, and institutions in either fostering or hindering these transformative processes is thoroughly examined.

By examining a diverse range of case studies and employing rigorous analyses, this book aims to provide valuable insights and practical implications for policymakers, researchers, and practitioners involved in regional development, innovation, and economic growth. It serves as a critical resource for understanding the complex dynamics and challenges faced by clusters and territories in the face of uncertainty and transitions.

Part I of this volume takes a discerning look at clusters from a Japanese perspective, unravelling their intricacies and shedding light on their role within Japan's dynamic economic landscape. Through detailed case studies and meticulous analyses, this section delves into topics such as resilience-building strategies in the face of disasters, the rise and decline of IT entrepreneurs in Sapporo, Toyota's transformative journey towards becoming a mobility company through the visionary Woven City project, the establishment of a vibrant glass art cluster in Toyama, and the dynamics of labour transfers within Tokyo's thriving entrepreneurial ecosystem.

Part II shifts our focus to Europe, offering diverse and illuminating European perspectives on clusters. This section delves into various aspects of green transformation, technological innovation, digitalization, industry 4.0, industrial districts, patent collaboration, economic complexity, and cultural and creative industries. By examining these areas of research, the book aims to contribute valuable insights and advance our understanding of the dynamic and interconnected forces that shape regional economies and their sustainable development.

By seamlessly integrating these two perspectives, the book presents a rigorous and comprehensive understanding of cluster dynamics. This scholarly work bridges theory and practice, delivering profound insights to researchers, policymakers, and practitioners. With its meticulous research methodology and scientific rigour, the book serves as a definitive resource for scholars seeking to expand their understanding of clusters, policymakers shaping effective economic strategies, and practitioners aiming to foster innovation and collaboration within their industries.

Prepare to embark on an enlightening journey through the intricate world of clusters as we explore the nuanced perspectives, challenges, and opportunities that these dynamic ecosystems offer. In the following chapters, readers will embark on an enlightening journey that explores the intricacies of cluster transformation, shedding light on innovative strategies, sustainable practices, and policy interventions that can pave the way for resilient and prosperous clusters and territories in the years to come.

The book stands as a remarkable contribution to the field, making a lasting impact on cluster studies and inspiring further scholarship in this vital domain. The first part of the book contains five chapters and focuses on a Japanese perspective on clusters. The second part contains eight chapters and focuses on a European perspective on clusters and territorial development.

The first chapter by Ozeki, Kamata, Mochizuki, Sawayanagi and Matsumura discusses the theme of the challenge of building local resilience capacities in preparation for future disasters, particularly when the memories of past catastrophic events start to fade over time. It raises questions about how socio-economic systems can be developed to ensure smooth functioning both in ordinary conditions and during disasters. The study focuses on the implementation of resilience through a case analysis of the Kanan district evacuation base concept in Miyazaki Town, Arida City, Wakayama Prefecture.

In the Kanan district, the idea was to attract tourist facilities, starting with an Italian restaurant called TestiMone, and utilize the area as an evacuation centre during disasters. By integrating disaster preparedness into daily life and updating local economic activities, the community incorporates a mechanism to absorb the impact of a disaster. The study highlights the difficulty of finding perfect measures for disaster reduction and the risks associated with investing solely in rare, once-in-a-few-thousand-years events. It also acknowledges the challenges in establishing public–private partnerships that combine local revitalization with disaster risk reduction.

However, the study suggests that it is possible to design resilience capacities that align with economic measures. By incorporating disaster preparedness into the fabric of daily life and leveraging local resources and partnerships, communities can enhance their ability to withstand and recover from disasters while also promoting economic stability.

The second chapter by Akiba and Yamada delves into the historical case of IT entrepreneurs and clusters in Sapporo, Japan, and their significant role in the development of the Japanese PC industry during the 1970s and 1980s. The study primarily focuses on two key factors that contributed to the decline of prominent IT firms: the collapse of a major bank that provided funding to these firms, and the burst of the dot-com bubble. These factors make the IT firms in Sapporo compelling subjects for theoretical sampling.

The research methodology employed approximately 27 years of data collection, along with formal and informal interviews conducted with a variety of stakeholders, including IT entrepreneurs, officials, and engineers. While the interview approach was not strictly structured, the researchers took measures to minimize biases and ensure objectivity in their one-time interactions.

This case study aims to present the psychological characteristics and genuine sentiments of the entrepreneurs, which cannot be fully captured through econometric analysis alone. Moreover, the chapter takes a fresh theoretical perspective by distinguishing between self-sustainable and high-growth entrepreneurial ecosystems and exploring their connection to traditional industrial cluster theory. The study also identifies shortcomings in commonly used models related to high-growth entrepreneurial ecosystems. Ultimately, the chapter derives theoretical implications concerning the "stay small" syndrome observed in the rise and stall lifecycle of industrial clusters.

The third chapter by Akabane focuses on the case study of Toyota's Woven City. The chapter aims to provide insights into the background of Toyota's endeavour and discusses the significance of Woven City for the transformation of Toyota's business model. The automotive industry is currently undergoing a revolutionary transformation known as CASE (Connected, Autonomous, Shared, Electric) and MaaS (Mobility as a Service), which is leading to a rapid shift in the competitive landscape. In January 2018, Toyota officially announced its transformation from an automaker to a mobility company to adapt to the significant changes in the business environment. As part of this transformation, Toyota unveiled plans to build a fully connected prototype city called "Woven City" at the base of Mount Fuji in Japan.

The chapter aims to explore the emerging megatrend in the automotive industry and the motivations behind automakers engaging in smart city projects, considering the abundance of relevant literature on the subject. It examines the impact of CASE and MaaS, as well as the resulting changes in the value chain, competitive advantage, and business models within the industry. The chapter also discusses Toyota's current initiatives in response to this paradigm shift, tracing the company's journey of business transformation through key news stories. Additionally, it provides an overview of Woven City and explores how this project can contribute to reshaping Toyota's business model. The author highlights outstanding issues and suggests areas for further exploration in future research.

The fourth chapter by Maeda delves into the case study of the Glass City of Toyama, Japan. This study examines the establishment of a creative environment in Toyama City, facilitated by networks connecting various glass art institutions, including a vocational school, studios, and museums, with artists and designers, including students, graduates, and instructors. The initiative known as "Glass City Toyama" was initiated to generate fresh cultural resources and support the growth of the art industry. Its primary objective is to enhance urban vitality and improve the quality of life for local citizens who face challenges associated with a declining and ageing population. The research specifically focuses on the acquisition and development of creative and professional talent within a unique production system, with the aim of creating a glass art cluster in an eco-model city situated in a society experiencing significant ageing trends.

The final chapter of the first part by Sasamori, Onodera and Kishi delved into the exploration of Tokyo's entrepreneurial ecosystem and specifically focuses on the phenomenon of labour transfer from large firms to start-ups.

The objective of this study is to investigate the factors that hinder job transfers from large firms to start-ups within the Tokyo ecosystem. Previous research has identified both micro- and macro-level factors that influence personnel mobility between organizations. Micro-level factors pertain to individual decision-making processes related to careers, taking into account specific characteristics and factors relevant to young tech talent. These factors may include considerations such as "future-oriented business", "social responsibility", and "work–life balance", which can impact their inclination to switch jobs to start-ups. Macro-level factors encompass labour market dynamics and organizational factors that influence job transitions.

However, there exists a knowledge gap regarding the current situation in Tokyo. Previous studies have separately examined individual job changers' perspectives, labour market dynamics, and organizational factors without integrating these perspectives at the ecosystem level. Furthermore, the coexistence of the established labour talent market and the start-up talent market has been explored independently, with limited research on their intersection within the context of Tokyo.

The findings of this study provide valuable insights for policymakers, start-up firms, and practitioners, aiding in the facilitation of human resource inflow from outside the start-up industry and supporting the growth of start-ups in Tokyo.

The second part of the book begins with a chapter by Lis, Mackiewicz and Wendt, which focuses on investigating the role of clusters in facilitating companies' transition towards sustainability. The authors specifically examine Polish clusters through a case study approach. The primary objective of this chapter is to explore the activities of clusters in promoting green transformation, including the adoption of green practices, low-carbon approaches, and the circular economy. The authors aim to identify the main green practices implemented by cluster organizations, taking into account both the attributes of the clusters themselves and the individual organizations within them. To address this research question, a two-stage quantitative survey was conducted between 2021 and 2023, primarily focusing on Polish National Key Clusters. The survey involved cluster managers in the first stage and representatives of cluster enterprises in the second stage, using the same questionnaire. The findings highlight the crucial role of geographical proximity in fostering collaboration within clusters for green transformation. This attribute is closely associated with the most prevalent green practices identified in the study, which revolve around relationship building, learning and knowledge-sharing processes, and the promotion of innovation potential.

In the following chapter, authored by Blasi, Buggio and Sedita, the focus shifts to green innovation and its connection to B Corps. The chapter aims to provide insights into the technological landscape of B Corps that have engaged in green innovation by examining their patent activities. Three research questions are addressed: (1) What is the prevalence and diversity of B Corps involved in technological innovation? (2) How significant is the contribution of B Corps to the advancement of green innovation? And (3) Do B Corps with a focus on innovation tend to cluster in specific geographic locations? Through the analysis of 17,933 patent applications filed by B Corps worldwide, the study reveals that European countries lead in terms of patent quantity, accounting for over 50 per cent of the total, followed closely by the United States at 40.9 per cent. However, patents specifically related to environmental concerns constitute a relatively small portion, totalling only 696. Notably, one in four innovative B Corps also prioritizes green innovation, making the B Corp community a valuable resource for those seeking to promote green technology development.

Moving on, the eighth chapter by Lazzeretti, Beccherle and Oliva explores the evolving role of museums in the digital era, with a focus on the Uffizi Gallery in Italy. The chapter investigates how new technologies, introduced after the 2014 state museums reform have influenced the management strategies of the Uffizi Galleries. The aim is to understand the impact of these digital technologies on online communication, engagement, and entertainment within the museum, as well as their potential for establishing a stronger connection between the museum and its surrounding territory. The findings underscore the significant influence of digital technologies, particularly social media, in creating value within the museum. This aspect is evident in the increasing importance of digital communication strategies to effectively engage younger audiences and foster stronger relationships at the local level.

In the ninth chapter, Capone, Baldetti, Innocenti and Zampi delve into the role of Industry 4.0 (I4.0) technologies within clusters. The chapter aims to explore how firms' characteristics affect their innovation performance in the context of I4.0, focusing specifically on the concepts of breadth and depth of openness in the innovation process. The study begins with a geographical analysis of I4.0 innovation, mapping the clusters of I4.0 activities in Italy. Subsequently, data is collected through a questionnaire administered to firms located within these I4.0 clusters. The collected data is then subjected to regression analysis to examine the relationship between the openness of firms' innovation processes, in terms of knowledge sources, and their innovation performance within the realm of I4.0. The findings of the chapter underscore a significant relationship between the level of openness and innovative performance within the context of Industry 4.0 (I4.0). The study reveals that the breadth and depth of firms' openness in the innovation process exhibit a curvilinear relationship with I4.0 innovation, following an inverted U-shaped pattern.

Chapter ten, authored by Trevisan and Mecenero, focuses on the Arzignano leather Italian district. The chapter delves into the transformation of this industrial district and emphasizes its resilience as a model for local economic development. The initial section introduces the conceptual framework for this evolution. The subsequent part centres on the Arzignano leather district, examining the proliferation of tanneries in the region that led to the estab-lishment of the industrial district. It further explores the district's progression from a single-industry dominated area to an integrated system. The chapter highlights the development of ancillary industries in the region as a key factor contributing to the ongoing success of the district. Moreover, it underscores the significance of this integration as the foundation for continuous innova-tion throughout the district. In conclusion, the chapter emphasizes how the Arzignano district represents the latest manifestation of the Italian district, characterized by its integrated and innovative nature.

Chapter eleven, authored by Galaso and Palomeque, investigates patent collaboration in Europe and Asia and its influence on innovation in Latin American cities. This chapter examines the impact of connections with Europe, Asia, and North America on innovation processes in cities across Latin America. The analysis utilizes patent data from the US Patent and Trademark Office (USPTO) spanning from 2006 to 2017 to identify the top 31 Latin American cities in terms of patenting activity. The study explores their local collaboration networks and their integration into global networks, specifically distinguishing between connections with Europe, East Asia, and North America. To analyze the influence of local and global networks on innovation in Latin American cities, panel data models are employed. The results reveal that links with Europe and North America have a stronger influence on innovation in Latin American cities compared to connections with Asia. Furthermore, these effects depend significantly on the local network structures. Collaborations with Europe are found to be beneficial for cities with centralized and expanded local networks, whereas connections with North America are positive for cities with decentralized and cohesive networks. These findings have implications for future research and policy development concerning innovation networks, highlighting the importance of examining the interaction between local and global networks, as well as the direction of external linkages.

Chapter twelve, authored by Antonietti and Fanton, focuses on the relationship between economic complexity and income inequality. This chapter contributes to the growing body of literature exploring the impact of regional economic complexity on income inequality. It investigates how the level of product sophistication in a region can influence workers' occupational choices, affecting factors such as education, human capital accumulation, bargaining power, and overall earning dynamics. By empirically analyzing data from 21 Italian regions spanning the period from 2004 to 2019, the authors examine the relationship between the economic complexity index and income inequality using panel fixed effects and instrumental variables regressions. The findings of this study indicate that holding other factors constant, regions with higher economic complexity tend to exhibit greater income inequality, albeit with a lag of two or three years. Notably, a contrasting pattern emerges in the North East region of Italy, where the relationship between economic complexity and income inequality becomes negative. This finding is particularly noteworthy due to the North East region's higher levels of institutional quality and technological diversification. Overall, this study sheds light on the intricate dynamics between economic complexity, income inequality, and regional characteristics, providing insights into the temporal and spatial aspects of this relationship within the context of Italy.

The final chapter of the book, authored by Porta, Segre, and Arauzo-Carod, examines cultural and creative industries (CCIs) in Italy, with a specific focus on the inner peripheries of Italian regions as defined by the Italian National Strategy of Inner Areas (SNAI). The objective of this chapter is to analyze the spatial distribution of CCIs and assess the alignment between their presence (measured in terms of establishments and employees) and the policies implemented under the National Strategy, with the aim of promoting the development of peripheral areas. The analysis utilizes quantitative methods, including specialization indexes, as well as cartographic techniques, such as mapping, at the national, regional, and local levels. These approaches provide valuable insights into the distribution of CCIs across the inner peripheries. The findings suggest that the distribution of CCIs in the inner peripheries of Italy is comparable to that of the entire country. Additionally, the results confirm the long-standing regional disparities between northern and southern Italy. This chapter paves the way for further research to explore the alignment between the SNAI, the actions undertaken at various scales, and the actual characteristics of the economic fabric. Furthermore, it raises questions about the potential role of culture in bridging the gap between different areas and contributing to the overall success of the National Strategy.

REFERENCES

Lazzeretti L., Capone F., Caloffi A., Sedita S. (Eds.) (2020). *Rethinking Clusters. Critical Issues and New Trajectories of Cluster Research.* Routledge.

Lazzeretti L., Oliva S., Innocenti N., Capone F. (Eds.) (2023). *Rethinking Culture and Creativity in the Digital Transformation.* Routledge.

Porter M. E. (1990). *The Competitive Advantage of Nations.* Free Press.

Porter M. E. (1998). *On Competition.* Harvard Business School.

Porter M. E. (2000). Location, competition and economic development: local clusters in the global economy. *Economic Development Quarterly*, 14: 15–31.

Sedita S. R., Blasi S. (Eds.) (2021). *Rethinking Clusters: Place-based Value Creation in Sustainability Transitions.* Springer Nature.

Torre A. (2023). Contribution to the theory of territorial development: a territorial innovations approach. *Regional Studies*, DOI: 10.1080/00343404.2023.2193218

PART I

A Japanese perspective on clusters in times of
uncertainty

1. Development of the resilience capacity of people by linking disaster prevention facilities with tourism: case study analysis of 'TestiMone ARIDA', Arida, Wakayama

Tamane Ozeki, Hiroki Kamata, Yoshio Mochizuki, Masako Sawayanagi, and Keizo Matsumura

1.1 INTRODUCTION

In Japan, 27 years after the Great Hanshin-Awaji Earthquake (Oliva & Lazzeretti, 2017, 2021), 12 years after the Great East Japan Earthquake, and over 7 years after the Kumamoto Earthquake, the government has made specific recommendations on disaster prevention, disaster reduction, and national land resilience (Cabinet Security, 2022). However, although people remember the most serious disasters in the years following a major earthquake, there is concern that memories may fade over time and the sense of crisis may be lost.

Disaster health measures and evacuation drills are conducted throughout Japan in the event of a major disaster, but such activities alone will not increase the resilience capacity of people to face disasters. This is because, with climate change, disasters are becoming more intense and frequent, and piecemeal evacuation drills based on lessons learnt from past disasters are likely to be insufficient. So how can local resilience capacities be developed to prepare for unforeseen disasters that may occur in the future? How can socio-economic systems be established to enable citizens to operate smoothly during normal times and disasters?

In relation to these questions, this study analyses resilience tools as a case study of the 'Kanan Refuge' concept in Arida Mikan Kaido Road (160 m above sea level) in Miyazaki Town, Arida City, Wakayama Prefecture. Arida City has taken measures to make disaster prevention and evacuation routes widely recognised by residents as part of their daily lives and compatible with economic activities by opening an Italian restaurant, a café, and other tourist facilities in its disaster prevention centres.

Arida has agreed to allow tourist facilities, including the Italian restaurant TestiMone ARIDA, to use the area as a water supply point in the event of a disaster. In the future, Arida will also take additional measures to equip the region's resilience capacity as a device over a period of several years by signing similar agreements with businesses around the Arida Mikan Road.

Business activities interact and relate to urban and regional activities, and a mutually supportive relationship among the public sector, businesses, and citizens is essential for building resilience capacity. Disaster management begins with individual action, such as providing evacuation information to individuals, guiding them to shelters, securing and transporting relief supplies, and establishing appropriate rescue systems; however, the manner in which information is provided, the structure of buildings, co-existence with local communities, and energy policies all require collaboration among industry, government, and academia to find solutions.

1.2   PREVIOUS RESEARCH

1.2.1   The Concept of Resilience and Disaster Prevention/Mitigation

Resilience is derived from the Latin word *resilire* (to bounce back, rebound) and refers to the ability to recover from difficulty. In the context of a local economy, it is referred to as the ability of a socio-economic system to recover from shocks and disruptions (Martin, 2012). The United Nations (UN) and the Organisation for Economic Co-operation and Development (OECD) have indicated the importance of resilience and advocated specific measures following the financial crisis of 2007–2008 and the 9/11 terrorist attacks in the US (OECD, 2014). In this document, resilience is defined as 'the ability of households, communities and nations to absorb and recover from shocks, whilst positively adapting and transforming their structures and means for living in the face of long-term stresses, change and uncertainty' (Mitchell, 2013, p.6); in Japanese, it is defined in the form of a metaphor: 'like a bamboo that bends under the weight of winter snow but grows tall again in spring'. In this context, resilience capacity should include not only disaster prevention, but also mitigation, recovery, and reconstruction capacity.

Resilience has three main perspectives: the engineering, ecological, and adaptive perspectives (Martin, 2012). The engineering perspective is a concept in the natural sciences that deals with the resilience or durability of materials, the ability to return to a previous state of equilibrium following a shock, such as a natural disaster. The ecological perspective focuses on the distance from a given shock to recovery. However, the process of recovering from a shock may be explained using the concept of the economy moving to another area rather than recovering its former activities—that is, to the hysteresis of the local economy. The last adaptive perspective refers to co-evolutionary interactions between components and the ability to spontaneously rearrange internal structures. From this perspective, Martin (2012) grasped resilience as a dynamic process that determines which resources and technologies are to be acquired through the industrial development of a region and constitute a new adaptive pathway (Martin, 2012).

However, it should be noted that it is difficult to make decisions pertaining to investments in millennial and million-year disaster prevention programmes. In fact, neither the Great Hanshin-Awaji Earthquake nor the Great East Japan Earthquake could have been predicted and the scale of damage was unexpectedly severe. Although the recovery from major earthquakes in the past created new paths back to economic growth (Oliva & Lazzeretti, 2017), it is predicted that in 2023, there will likely be frequent medium-sized earthquakes in unexpected areas throughout Japan. Furthermore, around 2038, there are fears that a huge earthquake—far exceeding the magnitude of previous earthquakes—could occur and preparing for this threat is a top national priority. However, there are different opinions on the calculation of the expected scale of disasters, and it is extremely difficult to come to a unified decision regarding the scale of investment in disaster prevention.

Japan's National Land Resilience Plan includes the establishment of disaster prevention methods that utilise digital technology under the ambit of 'Digital Rural Cities'. This requires securing public services and buildings for community activities as well as a living infrastructure where information, money, water, electricity, and other resources are intermittently distributed. Temporary measures, such as evacuation drills, are not sufficient; it is necessary to create and remember different modes of behaviour from everyday life based on memories of places that have existed in the past. The knowledge base of digitalisation and artificial intelligence (AI) technologies is also expected to bring diversification to local economies (Lazzeretti et al., 2022). However, it must be noted that even if digital technologies are used to establish disaster management mechanisms, they may not have the desired effect, as digital networks may be cut off during emergencies.

1.2.2 Resilience and the Local Economy

The development of new ways to cope with sudden disasters creates substantial opportunities to develop new pathways as an initial activity to build innovative growth models for local community economies (MacKinnon et al., 2019; Pike et al., 2016). Incorporating various ways of responding to shocks into everyday life can increase the diversity of local economic development processes (Boschma et al., 2017). Further, empirically perceiving and remembering the actions that must be taken during disasters in everyday life, during normal times, can help communities to develop the capacity to absorb the shocks of a disaster. This activity of ensuring resilience is a dynamic process, the essence of which lies in qualitative rather than quantitative changes in resilience capacity. In turn, this requires the interconnection of different ideas (Boschma, 2015) and the promotion and diversification of the value created by the division of labour in each economic unit (Boschma, 2015). Resilience is not a feature or outcome of change and continuity, but a complex process that can be combined in various ways (Martin & Sunley, 2015). An excessive overlapping of competences leads to cognitive lock-in, which requires a more dynamic change in the structure of local production (Martin & Sunley, 2015).

1.2.3   Resilience and Business Activities

Corporate shared value (CSV) and sustainable development goals (SDGs) are being actively advocated nowadays and it is recommended to incorporate these concepts into corporate activities as well. This concept has also been deployed in the design of organisational collaboration, including tri-sectoral (public/private/private) partnerships. The private sector ensures resilience capacity as a form of strategic responsiveness, overcoming barriers to recurrent changes in the business environment and securing sources of competitive advantage (Demmer et al., 2011; Seki, 2021; Herbane, 2010). Transitions in regional economic clusters are driven by deliberate actions at the firm and system levels, such as policy, as well as by interaction of situational factors, such as entrepreneurial collaboration through unexpected encounters. In particular, with regard to firm-level agency, the interaction of visionary entrepreneurs, ventures, and creators provides the soil for innovative matching of different knowledge bases and rethinking of regional pathways (Sedita & Ozeki, 2021).

Further, businesses are also required to consider disaster preparedness in advance. Businesses that utilise specific local resources or private companies that rely heavily on local contacts can be devastated in terms of business continuity in the event of a crisis, and natural disasters are no exception. This is in line with Mayer (2021), who states that the protection and utilisation of natural capital is necessary for the future of business activities.

1.2.4   Resilience, Culture, and Tourism

Resilience has also been discussed in relation to local cultural resources, with the resilience of cities being concerned with re-energising and developing their own ability to respond to external pressures, thereby making the power of urban culture a source of vitality (Lazzeretti & Cooke, 2017). Tourism has also been discussed as a link between local culture and the economy, with the development of the tourism industry bringing new diversity and changing the economic structure of cities and regions to function and create 'cultural tourism' (Richards, 2011). The link between culture and tourism encourages the accumulation of a distinctive intangible cultural heritage that harnesses the power of tradition and gives a place its identity (Bellandi & Santini, 2016). The relationship between creative class occupations, employment growth and entrepreneurship has been observed at the regional level in different European countries, suggesting that creativity can enhance regional economic activity (Boschma & Fritsch, 2009). Moreover, cultural resources are expressed in a wide variety of lifestyles on their path to being transformed into tourism and, lead to the emergence of social life in places that benefit from the resulting business activities.

Further, local community systems can exhibit a high degree of adaptive capacity in response to changes in the socio-economic environment; however, these can also become unstable and locked-in when major changes occur. Bellini et al. (2017) argued in favour of smart specialisation in tourism—that is, knowledge-driven local economic growth through knowledge-driven tourism; they revealed that tourism innovation is about strengthening ecological resilience through local identity and place branding. Vegt et al. (2021) argue that the challenge of pursuing innovative approaches to the role and functioning of organisations during adverse natural or social events is important. However, there is a concern that, in general, in the aftermath of catastrophic events, tourism is vulnerable whenever threats to the safety of travellers emerge. Considering the relationship between tourism and resilience as a means of stimulating local economies, it is desirable to use the effect of tourism for other economic activities and find specific solutions for regional development.

1.2.5 Instrumentalising Resilience

Thus, resilience is strengthened by the dynamic diversification of the local economy and the interaction of its components, but how can resilience capacity be built? What are the dynamic processes of capacity building? With regard to these research questions, this study examines the measures attempted by Arida City, Wakayama Prefecture, to create an interconnection between disaster prevention/mitigation and tourism projects and make them function as a combined system. Rather than anticipating the impact of a disaster and building a system to withstand it, a system is constructed to increase resilience over time to prepare for possible future disasters, with the aim of creating a town where preparing for such shocks is integrated into daily life. Previous research does not include any case studies on a city that functions as a socio-economic apparatus or infrastructure that enables citizens to function smoothly in the event of a disaster while conducting economic activities as a tourist facility during normal times.

1.3   ANALYTICAL METHODS

Through a case study analysis of Arida City, Wakayama Prefecture, this study conceptualises the attempt to integrate disaster prevention and tourism through public–private partnerships as 'instrumentalising resilience capacity'. This is the reverse of the resilience behaviour of recovering from a shock in the event of a disaster. Arida has secured the necessary water supply facilities in the event of a disaster and worked with the tourism-related private sector to create a new pathway for economic development in the region. The presence of an Italian restaurant, a café, and other tourism facilities will enable citizens to expand their recognition of the cultural and natural environment as part of the normal spheres of activity and embed disaster preparedness behaviour in their daily lives, even before a disaster strikes.

The methodology for the analysis was implemented in the following manner. First, the business plan to establish TestiMone ARIDA in 2016 was reviewed, and then the mayor of Arida—who compiled the administrative decision-making on the contract for the water supply facilities to a restaurant called TestiMone ARIDA—was interviewed. The authors considered this activity as action research and collected and validated relevant information from several data sources, including interviews and primary data from people associated with the project, such as the Arida City Hall and the Kinki Economic Bureau. As secondary data, information on the websites of Arida City and the target companies, as well as relevant books, was used. In addition, several interviews were conducted with the former company president to confirm the post-establishment development and future prospects through narrative dialogue methods. It must be noted that instrumentalising resilience is a value-added methodology for discussing a significant initiative to prepare for the unexpected disaster of the potential Nankai Trough crisis, as argued by Kamata (2022).

A narrative approach was employed to conduct the interviews, with the aim of building theory from in-depth qualitative case studies. This approach treats research subjects as collaborators rather than informants and emphasises a collaborative process with the researcher. Narrative research is characterised by its emphasis on subjective evaluations and interpretations, personal experiences, and narratives. Researchers explore personal stories and experiences in order to understand the context and background. Moreover, researchers must be aware of their own biases and assumptions and deal appropriately with those aspects that may influence research findings.

1.4   CASE STUDY ANALYSIS: CONCEPT OF THE EVACUATION CENTRE BASE IN THE KAWAN AREA OF ARIDA CITY, WAKAYAMA PREFECTURE

1.4.1   Outline of Arida City

Arida City is located in the north-west of Wakayama Prefecture, with Arida River—whose source is Mount Koya, is a World Heritage Site—flowing through the centre of the city. To the north and south are terraced fields of mandarin oranges, the city's main industry, and to the west is Kii Channel, which is rich in fishery resources. The city covers an area of 36.83 km, has a population of 26,500, and includes 11,731 households (as of 1 May 2022).

The main industry here is agriculture, with a flourishing citrus production that is mainly constituted of Arida mandarins—approximately 90% of the farmers are citrus growers.

The region is famous for its mandarins, which are branded as Arida mandarins. In order to increase tax revenue, Arida uses a system called 'Furusato Tax Payment'. Furusato taxation is a system under which taxpayers contribute to local governments (prefectures, cities, towns, and villages) in Japan by making tax payments. Specifically, Japanese citizens donate to the area of their choice (hometown) and the government uses the funds to develop projects to revitalise the area. Arida City uses this system to increase tax revenues by treating Arida mandarin oranges as return gifts. Since the system was introduced in 2014, the hometown tax system has spread rapidly. Under this system, tax credits for income tax and inhabitant tax are available, depending on the amount of the donation.

Arida City also has a thriving fishing industry, and a rich variety of fish is brought here to be sold, mainly from Minoshima Fishing Port, one of the leading coastal fishing bases in western Japan. Minoshima boasts the largest catch of swordfish in Japan. In addition, the Mikan Kaido Road, with its spectacular view of Kii Channel and Yuasa Bay below, is ideal for driving and walking.

Furthermore, the city has been home to an oil refinery called ENEOS Wakayama Refinery for the last 80 years and, although the refinery had announced its intention to withdraw by October 2023, in September 2022, the city announced plans to build a large-scale solar power plant on approximately 78,000 sq. mts. of unused land to create a mega solar power station, with a maximum output of approximately 8.5 megawatts, all of which will be sold to the Kansai Electric Power Group to cover the annual electricity consumption of approximately 2,600 ordinary households. In November 2022,

Source: GSI Maps https://www.gsi.go.jp/kihonjohochousa/multilingual.html. Mikan Kaido Road, TestiMone ARIDA. Photos taken and elaborated by the author.

Figure 1.1   *Overview of Arida City, Wakayama Prefecture and TestiMone ARIDA*

the company also announced its intention to establish a joint venture with Total Energy to convert its Negishi refinery (Yokohama) into a Wakayama refinery that will recycle aviation fuel from cooking oil and other waste oil. Furthermore, the company also manufactures mosquito coils in the city, which is home to the headquarters of Dainippon Pyrethrum (KINCHO) and is known as the birthplace of mosquito coils.

In addition, Arida City could be severely damaged in the event of a Nankai Trough earthquake because of its location. The crust of the Japanese archipelago is in a phase of change, and a Nankai Trough earthquake is predicted to occur around 2035 (± five years), possibly in 2038 (Kamata, 2022).

Nankai Trough earthquakes occur on the Nankai Trough fault zone, which runs along the Pacific Ocean side of western Japan. This fault zone is a vast undersea geological feature that extends from Suruga Bay in Shizuoka Prefecture to off the Hyuga-nada coast in Kyushu, and it has multiple epicentres, including those for the Tokai, Tonankai, and Nankai earthquakes. The Nankai Trough fault zone has experienced major earthquakes in the past, including the Nankai (1946) and Tonankai (1944) earthquakes; the next major earthquake is estimated to be 10 times greater in magnitude than the Great East Japan Earthquake of 11 March 2011 (Kamata, 2022). In other words, due to the tremendous hazards posed by the possibility of these earthquakes, approximately 320,000 people could die, 2.39 million seaweed beds are estimated to be destroyed or burnt down, and tsunami damage is likely to occur over a vast area. In addition, the inundated area is estimated to be approximately 1000 km^2 and affect 60 million people, which is approximately half of Japan's population (Kamata, 2022). The economic damage would also likely be enormous, with the Nankai Trough earthquake estimated to cost 220 trillion yen (compared to 20 trillion yen for the Great East Japan Earthquake), which is equivalent to approximately a quarter of the Japanese government's tax revenue. In addition, damage to infrastructure would likely last for 20 years after the disaster, with total damage estimated to reach 1410 trillion yen (Kamata, 2022). The dangers are unpredictable due to the predicted magnitude of the damage and casualties, the existence of unknown active faults, the possibility of a major earthquake anywhere in the Japanese archipelago, and the fact that the period of change is likely to continue for over 20 years (Kamata, 2022).

Furthermore, Arida is also exposed to flooding. In 1953, the Great Kishu Flood (Southern Kishu Torrential Rainfall) occurred, causing massive river flooding, landslides, and mountain tsunamis; in 2016, the central settlements around Arida River were destroyed. Damage was caused mainly along River Arida and throughout Wakayama Prefecture. In 2011, Typhoon No. 12 and heavy rains caused the Kii Peninsula floods, which led to flooding and landslides that made it impossible to enter isolated settlements. Much damage occurred throughout the course of these floods.

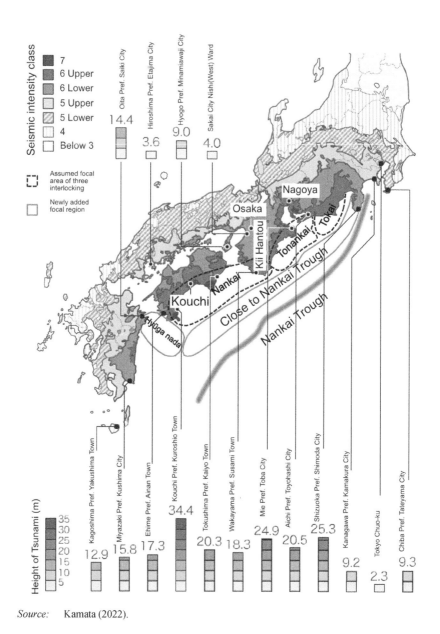

Source: Kamata (2022).

Figure 1.2   *Geographical risk: projections for possible damage to the*
                 Nankai Trough

It is the substantial perception of residents that flooding is a repeated crisis in the region and residents have developed a fear of floods; however, awareness of the dangers of major earthquakes is waning. In the years following the Great East Japan Earthquake, there were memories of the worst disaster, but the memories have faded with time and the sense of crisis has diminished. Therefore, rather than devoting effort to maintaining a sense of crisis that fades with time, it would be preferable to imprint in people's memories what they should do when a crisis occurs in their daily lives, even during times of normalcy. In fact, during the 2011 floods, numerous people drove to the Mikan Road in the middle of the night to evacuate the area of the floods, causing traffic jams. Thus, it is also important to secure transport routes from disaster management centres to the affected areas for rescue and relief and the transport of emergency supplies and equipment as part of the emergency response immediately after a disaster.

1.4.2 Agreements with Evacuation Centres

Against this background, Arida City established an emergency heliport landing site on Mikan Kaido Road, which was designated as an emergency evacuation site and a wide-area operation base for self-defence forces and firefighters. There are concerns that the city could be inundated by a tsunami over a wide area in the event of a Nankai Trough earthquake, thereby causing major flood damage. Thus, a plaza for approximately 3,000 people has been created along the designated road as an evacuation site to accommodate a large number of people.

In developing this infrastructure, Arida utilised the Emergency Disaster Prevention and Mitigation Project Bonds, which are municipal bonds based on the Emergency Disaster Prevention and Mitigation Project Bond System. Based on the lessons learnt from the Great East Japan Earthquake, the bonds are intended for projects of local governments that contribute to urgent and immediate disaster prevention and disaster mitigation projects nationwide, such as evacuation of residents, maintenance of administrative and social functions, and development of disaster-resistant towns. In addition to ensuring the seismic upgradation of public and official facilities that will serve as disaster response bases in the event of a disaster, the project also encompasses the relocation of public and official facilities located in the expected tsunami inundation zone, which are positioned as requiring relocation from the perspective of tsunami countermeasures in regional disaster management plans.

In addition, Arida used the funds raised through the 'disaster prevention project bonds' for the construction of a water storage tank and the installation of water supply facilities. The amount allocated for local government bonds in relation to the amount of projects to be implemented—that is, the debt ratio (the percentage of the amount to be voluntarily set aside), is fixed; however, since they are bonds, they must be repaid within a certain period of time. The local government usually sets aside the amount to be repaid from its budget, but a certain portion of the appropriation ratio—known as the 'local tax grant appropriation ratio'—is subsequently granted by the state as a local tax grant, which reduces the municipal tax burden (municipal budget) by less than half.

In this manner, an agreement (signed on 25 January 2016) on the use of the site as an evacuation facility and the effective use of the site as an evacuation base was concluded between TestiMone ARIDA and Arida City as the contracting parties. In a location with two potential strengths (resources)—geographical landscape and high ground close to the flood zone—the need for a common condition of 'drinking water supply' made it possible to develop water supply as a common element and effectively attract private operators such as restaurant and café to utilise the disaster prevention base.

1.4.3   Tourist Base: TestiMone ARIDA

The first tourist base on this mandarin road was the Italian restaurant TestiMone ARIDA. The restaurant offers a service that makes the most of the natural resources of the region and enriches everyday life. Various economic activities have been developed around the region's varied geographical vitalities, such as the abundance of agricultural and fishery products harvested as well as tourist facilities and disaster-prevention infrastructure.

The restaurant also aims to add to people's lives by making these economic activities more accessible on a daily basis, an anomalous event that is not too specific. Moreover, the restaurant's proximity to the disaster management centre implies that the restaurant's customers will gradually feel a sense of familiarity with the location. This is achieved by increasing the sensitivity of the population to the geographical vitality of the location and developing their ability to absorb new local shocks that may occur. Further, residents who become familiar with facilities available to mitigate shocks in the event of a major disaster will likely develop an experiential mindset in disaster response, thereby leading to a gradual recognition of their newly built resilience capacities.

Here, in order to attract tourists and other visitors from outside, the natural culture of the region is linked to materials such as the sea, fisheries, and scenic areas. There is a focus on identifying business models that utilise local culture and local products. However, the aim is not to seek luxury but to develop accommodation facilities that encourage tourists to stay longer and maintain a comfortable living environment. Nevertheless, the strategy for utilising fresh materials as tourism resources alone has its limitations, and new value creation based on deep insights into local culture is required.

In this context, the Osaka-Kansai Japan Expo has turned its attention to a world event to be held in Japan in 2025. It will be held for 184 days from 13 April 2025 to 13 October 2025 at Yumeshima, Osaka, as the main venue. The theme of the expo is the sustainable development goals (SDGs), which are international goals given by the UN to be achieved by 2030 with the aim of realising a sustainable society. In relation to this, eight clusters have been established, including 'Environment and Energy', 'Society and Health', and 'Future and Frontiers'. They are positioned as places where visitors can share ideas and actions to solve global problems as well as experience, learn, and empathise. During the event, pavilions, exhibitions, and symposia from various countries and regions will be held, thereby aiming to attract numerous visitors from home and abroad. Accordingly, the number of tourists from abroad is expected to increase. Arida City, which is close to Kansai International Airport, is also expected to witness a corresponding increase in tourists during this time. Thus, TestiMone ARIDA will also take these developments into account in its business activities.

1.5   EXAMPLES OF DEVELOPMENT AS TOURIST DESTINATIONS: KUMANO KODO AND CAMINO DE SANTIAGO

Arida City is located near Kumano Kodo. Kumano Kodo was included as a World Heritage Site in 2004 and is a pilgrimage route to the Kumano Sanzan (Kumano Hongu Taisha, Kumano Hayatama Taisha, and Kumano Nachi Taisha), spanning Wakayama, Mie, and Nara Prefectures; Kumano Kodo is steeped in ancient Japanese beliefs and culture. In addition to historic sites such as pilgrimage routes and post towns, Kumano Kodo is also rich in natural attractions such as clear streams, waterfalls, and mountains. Kumano Kodo is also the place of origin for numerous cultural beliefs and legends as well as a diverse range of cultural assets created by the beliefs of pilgrims. Further, there are two main routes to the Kumano Hongu Taisha shrine, the terminus of Kumano Kodo—the Saikai Route and the Tokaido Route. The Saikai route begins from Shingu City, Wakayama Prefecture. The distance from Arida City to Kumano Hongu Taisha is approximately 25 km and is characterised by mountainous landscapes dotted with shrines, temples, inns, and other historical buildings.

After the opening of TestiMone ARIDA, contrary to prior expectations, numerous tourists from Spain began to visit the area. The reason for this is that Kumano Kodo has a strong historical affinity with Camino de Santiago (the pilgrimage route to Santiago de Compostela) in Spain. In Spain, it is customary for parents to give their children an eventful gift when they come of age, and new Spanish adults who are familiar with Camino de Santiago occasionally visit Kumano Kodo in Japan with their parents.

Camino de Santiago is a Christian pilgrimage route spanning 800 km, through Galicia in northwest Spain to Santiago Cathedral in Santiago de Compostela. Considered one of the most important pilgrimage routes in medieval Europe and still traversed by numerous pilgrims and travellers, it is believed to have been instituted in honour of the Christian saint Santiago Matamoros, who was martyred in Spain in the ninth century. Today, it is visited not only by Christians but also by people of different faiths and cultural backgrounds for self-exploration and spiritual experiences.

1.6   CONSIDERATIONS ON INSTRUMENTALISING RESILIENCE

1.6.1   Balancing Disaster Prevention and Tourism—Transforming Content

In summary, the case analysis presented in this study reveals the following policy and coordination aspects of disaster management in Arida town as a whole. The policy aspect involves the continuous strengthening of infrastructure, such as the construction of water pipes and the establishment of a disaster management centre. Complementing this is the cooperation of local authorities, relevant agencies and community associations in disaster response and recovery. In the case of TestiMone ARIDA, this involves supporting the establishment of a disaster management centre, maximising local tourism, and supporting the distribution of local foodstuffs, thereby balancing local development and disaster management.

Further, disaster prevention and mitigation bonds are issued to establish facilities and equipment that are prepared for any eventuality; thus, these facilities and equipment do not play an active role in daily life but are a source of funds that create value by demonstrating their effectiveness in the event of a disaster. In Arida, a disaster agreement has been concluded between the public and private sectors to develop evacuation centres and ensure water supply so that water facilities are not interrupted in the event of an unexpected disaster. If the water is also used to support private economic activity, it will be effective in stimulating the economy. This mechanism was established because the mayor of Arida functions as a system-level institution and Masako Sawayanagi functions as a business-level institution, and policies and new projects have been conceived through collaboration between the two (Sawayanagi, 2017).

The addition of the resource of water to the tourist base has created compatibility between the public–private business model of disaster prevention and tourism. The residents of Arida want a quiet life and are not in favour of expanding tourism, building luxury facilities, or altering the scenic landscape. Therefore, it is necessary for the administration to act, while ascribing top priority to making the town a comfortable place to live for its 26,000 inhabitants.

1.6.2 Hazard Awareness among the Residents of Arida City

The citizens of Arida oppose two hazard measures. One is flood damage caused by typhoons and torrential rains, which potentially occur every year. The extensive damage caused in 2011 is particularly fresh in the collective memory, thereby causing residents to be rather risk averse. However, very few residents have a sense of crisis regarding the impending Nankai Trough earthquake in 2038, partially because they were not directly affected by the 2011 Great East Japan Earthquake. Indeed, many people know that a disaster could be catastrophic, but only a minority are aware of the need to prepare for a major earthquake on a daily basis.

In this context, it is important to view resilience as an apparatus—an infrastructural facility that absorbs crisis situations and their impacts—and to create a narrative to integrate disaster preparedness into everyday life. It is difficult to create a budget and promote understanding among the population if the establishment of a disaster management centre entails huge costs and its effectiveness can only be measured in the event of a disaster. It is also important to make residents aware of the positive aspects of such an effort, such as the revitalisation of the local economy and international exchange through tourism, as well as integrating these aspects into daily life and ensuring that they associate the mandarin road as being a place of refuge during an emergency.

Therefore, although TestiMone ARIDA aims to raise disaster awareness and serve as an evacuation centre, it does not emphasise that it is a disaster management centre. Rather than making it a full-fledged disaster management centre, where food is stockpiled, it has established its raison d'être as a disaster management centre by constructing a helipad and accepting food from other areas in the event of an emergency. Thus, Arida is attempting to promote understanding among the local population by ascribing a resilience function to a complex and valuable facility. Conversely, the emphasis on disaster management centres has led to numerous restrictions, such as their use only in emergency situations, which make it difficult to manage these centres flexibly, including private economic activities. Based on the minimum water requirements in the event of a disaster, this centre provides a sense of security for the entire community.

1.7   CONCLUSION

This study sets out the research questions of how to prepare local resilience against possible future unexpected catastrophes and how to build
a socio-economic system that enables citizens to function smoothly while preparing for a disaster in normal times. In this chapter, the concept of an evacuation centre was discussed using the Kawan area of Arida Mikan Kaido (Arida
Mikan Road), which extends into Miyazaki Town, Arida City, Wakayama
Prefecture, as a case study. Specifically, it was agreed to attract an Italian
restaurant, TestiMone ARIDA, and other tourist facilities to Arida, which
would then be used as evacuation centres in the event of a disaster. In addition,
a water reservoir has been established on Mikan Kaido Road that will serve as
a water source for the surrounding facilities, and an agreement has been made
to allow restaurants, cafés, and accommodation facilities that use this reservoir
to be used as evacuation centres.

There are no perfect disaster prevention measures against the possibility of
major earthquakes in the future. It is risky for governments to invest in disasters that have an extremely low probability of occurring, such as those that may
occur once in 1,000 years or once in 10,000 years. Public–private partnerships
and economic measures that link disaster prevention to regional revitalisation,
as in Arida City, are difficult to implement; however, it is important to incorporate the functions required in the event of a disaster into daily life. It is also
important to note that this has the effect of imparting knowledge (anchoring)
regarding disaster prevention among various age groups, as opposed to only
the age group that participates in disaster drills.

Further, the creation of new disaster management centres requires cooperation with the private sector and indicates the importance of local administration, political and social contacts, and digital technology. In addition to
stimulating the local economy, Arida aims to link disaster prevention and
tourism to make residents more aware of the risks associated with disasters.
Therefore, this study conceptualised the simultaneous development of the
local economy and disaster preparedness as being instrumental in creating
resilience. Previous studies on regional resilience have mainly focused on the
perspectives of co-existence with the local community and continuation of
business activities. Although the perspective of regional resilience through the
development of economic activities in disaster prevention centres has thus far
never been discussed in extant literature, this study provided a new perspective
in this direction.

In addition, this study explored the concept of establishing a base for
implementing resilience functions by linking disaster prevention facilities and
tourism, using TestiMone ARIDA, Arita, Wakayama Prefecture, as a case

study. Although the value of this facility as a new environmental hub has been recognised and has attracted much attention since its inception, more time is needed to develop the base on the Mikan Kaido Road, which limits the approach of this research. This research needs to be reviewed, restructured, and strengthened as attention is drawn to the dynamic progress of this endeavour, which is a process of building capacity for resilience in the face of natural disasters.

REFERENCES

Bellandi, M. & Santini, E. (2016). Resilience and the role of arts and culture-based activities in mature industrial districts. *European Planning Studies*, *25*(1), 88–106. doi:10.1080/09654313.2016.1268096.

Bellini, N., Grillo, F., Lazzeri, G. & Pasquinelli, C. (2017). Tourism and regional economic resilience from a policy perspective: Lessons from smart specialization strategies in Europe. *European Planning Studies*, *25*(1), 140–153. http://dx.doi.org/10.1080/09654313.2016.1273323.

Boschma, R. (2015). Towards an evolutionary perspective on regional resilience. *Regional Studies*, *49*(5), 733–751. doi:10.1080/00343404.2014.959481.

Boschma, R., Coenen, L., Frenken, K. & Truffer, B. (2017). Towards a theory of regional diversification: Combining insights from evolutionary economic geography and transition studies. *Regional Studies*, *51*(1), 31–45. doi:10.1080/00343404.2016.1258460.

Boschma, R. & Fritsch, M (2009). Creative class and regional growth: Empirical evidence from seven European countries. *Economic Geography*, *85*(4), 391–423. doi:10.1111/j.1944-8287.2009.01048.x.

Cabinet Security. (2022). *Annual Plan for National Land Stewardship 2022*. National Land Stewardship Promotion Office, kakuteihonbun.pdf (cas.go.jp).

Demmer, W. A., Vickery, A. K. & Calantone, R. (2011). Engendering resilience in small- and medium-sized enterprises (SMEs): A case study of the Demmer Corporation. *Journal of Contingencies and Crisis Management*, *19*(3), 5395–5413. doi:10.1080/00207543. 2011.563903.

Herbane, B. (2010). Small business research: The need for a crisis-based view. *International Small Business Journal*, *28*(1), 43–64. doi:10.1177/0266242609035080.

Kamata, H. (2022). *Living intellectually in the shaking land*. Kadokawa Shinsho Series K-401, Kadokawa Shoten.

Lazzeretti, L. & Cooke, P. (2017). Responding to and resisting resilience. *European Planning Studies*, *2017*, *25*(1), 1–9. doi.org/10.1080/09654313.2016.1270911.

Lazzeretti, L., Oliva, S. & Innocenti, N. (2022). Unfolding smart specialisation for regional economic resilience: The role of industrial structure. *Journal of Regional Research*, *54*, 5–25. doi.org/10.38191/iirr-jorr.22.015.

McKinnon, D., Drury, S., Pike, A. & Cambers, A. (2019). Rethinking path creation: A geographical political economy approach. *Economic Geography*, *95*(2), 113–135. doi:10.1080/00130095.2018.1498294.

Martin, R. (2012). Resilience, hysteresis and recession shocks in regional economies. *Journal of Economic Geography*, *12*(1), 1–32. doi:10.1093/jeg/lbr019.

Martin, R. & Sunley, P. (2015). On the notion of regional economic resilience: Conceptualization and explanation. *Journal of Economic Geography*, *15*(1), 1–42. doi:10.1093/JEG/LBU015.

Mayer, C. (2021). *Prosperity: Better business makes the greater good*. Oxford University Press.

Mitchell, A. (2013). Risk and resilience: From good idea to good practice. *OECD Development Co-operation Working Paper*, WP 13/2013, December 2013. doi.org/10.1787/22220518.

Oliva, S. & Lazzeretti, L. (2021). Unravelling the sustainable resilient region: Exploring regional resilience in sustainable transition. In S. Sedita & S. Blasi (Eds.) *Rethinking clusters*, Springer, 3–16.

Oliva, S. & Lazzeretti, L. (2017). Adaptation, adaptability, and resilience: The recovery of Kobe after the Great Hanshin Earthquake of 1995. *European Planning Studies*, *25*(1), 1–21.

Organisation for Economic Co-operation and Development (OECD) (2014). *Guidelines for resilience systems analysis*. OECD Publishing.

Pike, A., Rodriguez-Pose, A. & Tomany J. (2016). *Local and regional development*, 2nd edition. Routledge.

Richards, G. (2011). Creativity and tourism: The State of the Art. *Annals of Tourism Research*, *38*(4), 1225–1253. doi.org/10.1016/j.annals.2011.07.008.

Sawayanagi, T. (2017). *Restaurants with a population of 30,000*. Thesis, Graduate School of Creative Cities, Osaka City University.

Sedita, S. R. & Ozeki, T. (2021). Path renewal dynamics in the Kyoto kimono cluster: How to revitalize cultural heritage through digitalisation. *European Planning Studies*, *30*(6), 1–19. doi:10.1080/09654313.2021.1972938.

Seki, S. (2021). Entrepreneurial activity process of small and medium-sized enterprises in a crisis situation: An approach to entrepreneurship research to construct an analytical framework. *Social Science Research*, *50*(4), 177–195. doi:10.14988/0002805.

Vegt. G. S. van der, Gerben, S., Essens, P., Wahlström, M., & Gerard, G. (2021). Guidelines for resilience systems analysis, how to analyse risk and build a roadmap to resilience. *Academy of Management Review*, *46*(3), 421–430. doi.org/10. 5465/amr.2021.0180.

2. "Stay small" syndrome in the rise and stall lifecycle of industrial clusters: evidence from Sapporo Valley cluster

Futoshi Akiba and Jin-ichiro Yamada

2.1 INTRODUCTION

Drawing inspiration from Bahrami and Evans (1995), this study endeavors to harmonize cluster theory and entrepreneurial ecosystem theory by spotlighting both low-growth and high-growth entrepreneurs, thereby presenting an authentic portrayal of information technology (IT) cluster entrepreneurs' narratives.

Our investigation shifts away from independently examining the components of entrepreneurial ecosystems. If we scrutinize the entrepreneurial ecosystem from the perspective of productive entrepreneurs, our deductions echo the insights gleaned from existing entrepreneurial networking rather than from the entrepreneurial ecosystem, rendering the study incomplete in the context of a region or cluster. Presumptions regarding the stunted growth of most low-growth entrepreneurs within clusters, such as capability and social integration, are rarely explicitly discussed within the framework of clusters and entrepreneurial ecosystems.

To capture entrepreneurial behavior within IT clusters, we posit the existence of two entrepreneurial ecosystems: one catering to high-growth entrepreneurs and the other catering to the remaining entrepreneurs. Additionally, we employ the concept of small business orientation to understand the actions of low-growth entrepreneurs (Section 2.2). By collating a plethora of narratives from entrepreneurs and support entities within the IT cluster, including those of low-growth entrepreneurs (Sections 2.3 and 2.4), we aim to construct a realistic picture of the IT cluster (Section 2.5), bridge the existing gap between the entrepreneurial ecosystem, cluster, and reality, and draw theoretical inferences.

Through case studies, we discovered that entrepreneurs within IT clusters prefer to consciously keep their organizations small, in response to environmental fluctuations. Even though the term 'cluster' encompasses both low and

high-growth entrepreneurs, we identify the coexistence of two distinct entrepreneurial ecosystems: a high-growth entrepreneurial ecosystem propelled by
the venture capital (VC) business model and a self-sustainable entrepreneurial
ecosystem bolstered by external economics (Sections 2.6 and 2.7).

2.2   THEORETICAL BACKGROUND

2.2.1   Industrial Districts, Clusters, and Entrepreneurial Ecosystem

Three salient trends currently dominate the academic discourse on regional
and entrepreneurial research. First, the investigation of industrial districts
(IDs) constitutes a principal avenue of exploration (Markusen, 1996; Belussi
& Sedita, 2009). This research stream meticulously scrutinizes IDs, as initially defined by Marshall (1920), extending its purview to their geographical
placement, institutional features, and the dynamism and evolution of the entire
region. The second focal trend is the examination of industrial clusters (Porter,
1998), emphasizing the peculiarities of diverse industries and sectors. Third,
there is research on entrepreneurial ecosystems. Despite the increasingly neb-
ulous demarcation between industrial district and cluster (Grandinetti, 2019),
a paramount distinction persists—the extent to which each approach integrates
entrepreneurship as a fundamental concept. However, while numerous studies
have been conducted, the concept of entrepreneurial ecosystems continues to
suffer from challenges (Stam & Van de Ven, 2021; Isenberg, 2016; Rocha &
Audretsch, 2022).

Research on entrepreneurs and their attempts to produce high-growth firms
continues the lineage of previous entrepreneurship research. For example, the
elements of the entrepreneurial ecosystem and the organic relationships among
them have been studied in various forms even before the concept received
much attention (Van de Ven, 1993; Kenney, 2000). Bahrami and Evans (1995)
emphasize that in the study of Silicon Valley, which serves as both a high-tech
cluster and a prototype for the entrepreneurial ecosystem concept, the demise
of one company leads to the establishment of another, suggesting that it contributes to supporting the local ecosystem through entrepreneurial "flexible
recycling." This study specifically examined the contribution of failed entrepreneurs, a factor that has been overlooked in high-growth entrepreneurial
ecosystem studies. While there have been some discussions on the nested
structure of the entrepreneurial ecosystem, these discussions have remained
largely conceptual (Wurth et al., 2021) or have only explored specific aspects
(Spigel, 2022) of the ecosystem.

The variation of elements presented in previous entrepreneurial ecosystem
studies (Stam, 2015; Spigel, 2020) is not significantly different from early
Silicon Valley studies (Bahrami & Evans, 1995; Kenney, 2000; Cohen, 2005).

Since then, a wealth of case studies have emphasized the importance of each of these elements: universities, talent pools, entrepreneurship, support infrastructure, venture capital, formal and informal networks, and government.

Against the backdrop of the failure of Silicon Valley's cloning policy (Isenberg, 2010, 2016), a new entrepreneurial ecosystem theory emerged around 2010, attracting many researchers by placing the "ambitious entrepreneur" at its core; Autio et al. (2014) focused on the entrepreneurial innovation context synthesizing previous studies, and Stam (2015) attracted attention by presenting a comprehensive framework of entrepreneurial ecosystems centered on the importance of "ambitious entrepreneurs" whose goal is entrepreneurial growth rather than the number of startups. The effect of the entrepreneurial ecosystem on economic growth has gradually shifted focus from average to high-growth entrepreneurs, as evidenced by research trends (Cao & Shi, 2021; Wurth et al., 2021).

A significant policy advantage of adopting the entrepreneurial ecosystem concept rather than the industrial agglomeration or cluster concept is that it eliminates the need to assume the given conditions of the accumulated sectors in a region.

Entrepreneurial ecosystems, which are based on the sector-agnostic creation of new businesses by entrepreneurs, are interpreted as constructible in many regions. The focus of the research is on elucidating positive causal relationships. Therefore, the policy dimension has become much stronger, with research designs (Stam & Van de Ven, 2021; Nicotra et al., 2018) that index and compare entrepreneurial ecosystems at the city level. Similarly, it is also considered policy relevant that entrepreneurs in the entrepreneurial ecosystem are given role expectations that contribute to the interests of the entrepreneurial ecosystem as a whole (Spigel, 2020).

Progress has been made in elucidating various constituents and their interrelationships within the entrepreneurial ecosystem. However, an inherent challenge is the empirical observation of these relationships and their synergistic operation as a comprehensive system (Bruns et al., 2017). This presents a notable conceptual divergence from IDs and sectors where boundaries and industrial scales are relatively tangible.

In a social network-oriented study, Motoyama and Knowlton (2017) scrutinized 16 entrepreneurial enterprises in St. Louis and discovered that entrepreneurs employ many strategies to gain insights via networking. Conversely, Breznitz and Taylor (2014) explored why Atlanta struggled to retain burgeoning enterprises within the IT sector. Their analysis revealed that, notwithstanding Atlanta's conducive social conditions, a distinct lack of a social framework fostering entrepreneurial growth persists. While significant in dissecting the complex relationships within the entrepreneurial ecosystem, these investigations tend to echo the familiar conclusion that thriving entrepreneurs are adept at cultivating and optimizing their network connections.

Pioneering studies that incorporate entrepreneurship into the conceptual framework of clusters and IDs, such as Pitelis (2012) and Grandinetti (2019), predominantly restrict themselves to institutional explanations of regional entrepreneurial behavior. However, they largely overlooked the psychological dimensions of entrepreneurs that drive this behavior. Furthermore, these studies exhibit a notable dearth of attention toward the influence of industry-specific traits and external forces on entrepreneurial endeavors.

While IDs and clusters serve as conceptual constructs inclusive of low-growth firms, primary emphasis is placed on the aggregate features and evolutionary phases of a region or sector. This results in a somewhat constrained body of research that directly addresses entrepreneurial activities. The sector has continuously contended with the predicament of path dependency, largely attributable to its analytical predilection toward the manufacturing sector (Belussi & Sedita, 2009). In contrast, entrepreneurial ecosystems are uniquely poised to be home to high-growth entrepreneurs, as socially anticipated (Shane, 2009). This focus paves the way for policy dialogues to alleviate path dependency in many areas. However, a concentrated examination of the relationships between high-growth entrepreneurs and various actors or components introduces challenges that blur the lines that distinguish them from traditional entrepreneurial networking studies.

This review highlighted three significant theoretical aspects of lacunae. First, Bahrami and Evans' (1995) perspective that flexible recycling leads to ecosystem revitalization has been missing from recent studies of high-growth entrepreneurial ecosystems. The idea that unproductive entrepreneurs, who are unexplained variables in entrepreneurial ecosystem studies, play a demanding role is important when considering the lifecycle of a cluster.

Second, extant theories on entrepreneurial ecosystems argue that high-growth entrepreneurs maximize their utilization of external resources through networking. However, these theories do not explain why other entrepreneurs within the same region do not similarly adopt networking or exhibit an absence of growth-oriented behavior. While studies on IDs and clusters propose that institutional integration (Granovetter, 1985) might inhibit entrepreneurial activity, this contention might not stand up to scrutiny for low-growth entrepreneurs in sectors marked by a lean division of labor and less rigorous institutional constraints. This particularly applies to sectors such as the IT industry, which deviates markedly from the manufacturing sector.

Third, if they are not oriented toward high growth, why do they become entrepreneurs and not just employees? IDs and clusters have external economies that significantly reduce the copycat entrepreneurship risk. However, the entrepreneurial ecosystem theory does not assume external economies and emphasizes factors that promote rapid growth rather than risk reduction. Is reducing risk and increasing the number of entrepreneurs desirable to achieve regional economic growth? Is it desirable to support only those entrepreneurs who have achieved growth? Or are both necessary? Based on empirical evidence, we believe that it is necessary to consider the aforementioned research gap.

The high-growth entrepreneurial ecosystem and the cluster lifecycle theory carry social expectations because most entrepreneurs do not grow (Bosma & Levie, 2010). However, in both scenarios, whether organizational evolution targets growth represents a multifaceted causal outcome resulting from entrepreneurial behavior. Japan has a low entrepreneurship rate based on global standards, low human resource mobility, and strict layoff regulations. The fact that entrepreneurs who do not aim for growth form and maintain IT and industrial clusters in the country are a significant departure from the premise that entrepreneurs pursue opportunities. Focusing on low-growth entrepreneurs, who tend to be neglected when focusing on the relationship between regions, and entrepreneurs (who make up a large percentage) is likely to lead to a deeper understanding of the lifecycle of clusters.

2.2.2   Small Business Orientation

Runyan and Covin (2019) attempt to link entrepreneurship and small business management from a new perspective. Their conceptual design is suited for empirical studies on entrepreneurial orientation but remains a developing concept with few followers. They define small business orientation as the mindset of individual managers that promotes organizational behavior comprising universalism and benevolence.

Runyan and Covin's exploratory and theoretical study takes cues from Schwartz's (1994) theory of personal values namely, self-transcendence, which includes universalism and benevolence, and self-direction, which includes openness to change. Exploration of entrepreneurship along these lines is worthy of attention.

Kanai (2005, 2006, 2012) identified two factors that contributed to the need for growth in the Sapporo IT cluster: the absence of a social platform for entrepreneurial activities and the amateurism of Sapporo IT entrepreneurs. Although chain spin-offs by entrepreneurs have been observed in Sapporo; they seldom experience significant growth. Kanai stated that this is not due to the difficulty of growth but rather the intention of the entrepreneurs themselves. He called this phenomenon "Stay Small Syndrome."[1] We believe the "Stay Small Syndrome" accurately captures IT entrepreneurs' focus on self-direction and stimulation.

The discussion of small business orientation and the "stay small syndrome" suggests a bias that excludes low-growth entrepreneurs in studies of entrepreneurial ecosystems. Research focusing only on productive entrepreneurs who increase employment may limit our understanding of ecosystem functions. If an entrepreneurial ecosystem functions through the complex and organic interaction of diverse actors, it is natural to assume that low-growth entrepreneurs, who constitute the majority, play a role in the entrepreneurial ecosystem.

In this context, these two concepts prioritize self-determination over the traditional bias of valuing entrepreneurs as subsistence or low-growth entrepreneurs in terms of social imperatives. The current research lacks such a perspective, which makes applying conceptual models to real-world cases challenging.

2.3   RESEARCH QUESTION AND METHOD

2.3.1   Research Question

This research explores the ensuing inquiries:

(1)   In what manner do entrepreneurs interpret and adjust their entrepreneurial orientation in reaction to environmental shifts within IT clusters, considering these clusters as units within the tangible economy?

(2)   What is the propensity of IT cluster entrepreneurs toward growth?

(3)   How do entrepreneurs with high and low growth profiles perceive their respective roles?

(4)   Which psychological elements and impediments shape entrepreneurs' predispositions toward growth?

2.3.2   Subjects of Research

Our research focuses on the IT cluster in Sapporo City, which spontaneously emerged from the development of BASIC software and various hardware at the dawn of the PC industry, and the two support activities for forming industrial clusters.

These research subjects had the appropriate characteristics for theoretical sampling. There are good records of active interactions among entrepreneurs, government agencies, business organizations, IT engineers, and citizens. The abundance of documents and publications on activities that supported the creation of industrial clusters also allows us to clarify the outlines and progress of these activities.

2.3.3   Data Collection

Our research employs a qualitative methodology underpinned by Alvesson's (2003) interpretive approach to interviews. Over 27 years, we accumulated a diverse dataset, primarily focusing on entrepreneurial realities in local-level business creation and spin-offs. Central to our approach were over 67 direct interviews conducted by the authors through snowball sampling (Atkinson & Flint, 2001), both formal and informal, which offered a nuanced understanding of entrepreneurial reality.

In addition, we deepened our data through archival research of the internal documents of the core companies studied, providing historical and cultural contexts and insight into their processes. Complementing this, we performed a content analysis of emails associated with product development, revealing the subtleties of communication, decision-making, and partnership collaboration—aspects that might otherwise be elusive.

Finally, we supplemented the dataset with observational surveys at selected executive-level meetings, enriching our understanding of real-time decision-making, power dynamics, and negotiation strategies. Our comprehensive methodology integrates longitudinal, multisource, and multimethod data collection. It allows us to chronicle a detailed account of a firm's evolution over 27 years and capture its growth, dynamics, and operational processes.

2.4   CASE STUDY: SAPPORO IT CLUSTER[2]

2.4.1   Spontaneous Emergence of the Sapporo IT Cluster and its Role in the Japanese PC Industry

Around 1976, with the release of microcomputer chips, the *Hokkaido Microcomputer Study Group* was established as a private study group by Yoshinao Aoki, a professor of the Faculty of Engineering at Hokkaido University. In that study group, he built his PC at the same time as Apple Computer. In 1978, when practical spreadsheets and word processors were no more than a shadow of their former selves, Hudson, a leading software company in Sapporo, developed and sold its first PC game software in Japan.

In the early 1980s, several engineers from the Hokkaido Microcomputer Study Group and the engineering department almost single-handedly created BASIC, which executed faster than Microsoft BASIC, for Sharp (1982), Sony (1982), Fujitsu (1984), and Nintendo (1984) hardware. Major computer manufacturers relied on engineers at Sapporo for much of the development of BASIC (basic software) for PCs.

In 1982, the Hokkaido Software Association requested financial assistance from Sapporo City to purchase a large general-purpose computer. A related survey by Sapporo City revealed that approximately 160 information-related companies were already located in the city at the time.

2.4.2   Effect of NES on the Sapporo IT Cluster

The Nintendo Family Computer (released in the U.S. in 1985 as the Nintendo Entertainment System or NES) was launched in 1983, and by 1991, had sold a total of approximately 16 million units. In 1984, Hudson joined the NES platform as its first third-party game vendor.

Hudson's sales grew rapidly from 1.53 billion yen (about US$ 11.8 million; 130 yen to the dollar) in 1984 to 43 billion yen (US$ 330 million) in 1991, cementing its significant presence in the budding IT cluster at Sapporo. At the same time, much of the development was outsourced, along with db Soft and B.U.G. (specializing in cutting-edge technology, three of the spin-off companies went public), which also grew significantly, spawning numerous spin-offs and had a major effect on the formation of the Sapporo IT Cluster (Figure 2.1).

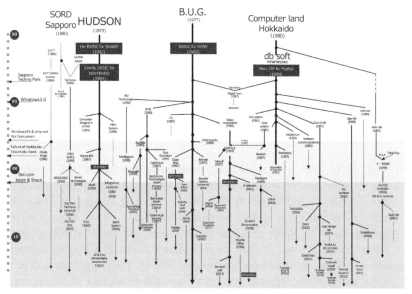

Note: If there is no official English translation of a company name, and the domain name of the company's website is phonetically identical to the Japanese name, that domain name is used as the English equivalent of the company name.
Source: Prepared by the author with new information added based on Hokkaido Information Industry History Edito1ittee (2000).

Figure 2.1   *Spin-off tree from major four IT ventures*

According to a report by a research organization in the year 2000, there were approximately 300 IT companies in the entire city of Sapporo, with approximately 30 companies located in the Sapporo Station area. However, according to our interview, there were 150–200 IT companies in the Sapporo Station area alone.

2.4.3 Overview of Sapporo IT Cluster Business in the 1980s–1990s and its Decline

In the 1980s–1990s, the PC industry had significant business opportunities. In addition to the development of games for the NES, which had begun to rapidly expand across countries, there was localization (porting) of software for the non-standardized PCs of various companies and a gradual shift to digitalization in the publishing and broadcasting industries. The trigger for this major change in the business environment was the standardization of the DOS/V standard in 1990, which allowed Japanese-language support to be completed entirely through software, and the massive influx of inexpensive PCs from overseas into the Japanese market.

The launch of Windows 95 also brought PC/AT-compatible machines to the Japanese market, uprooting the business of localizing PC software to different

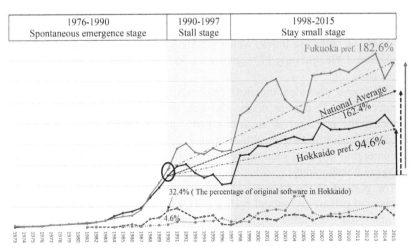

1976-1990	1990-1997	1998-2015
Spontaneous emergence stage	Stall stage	Stay small stage

Note: The reason for the seemingly rapid recovery from 1997 to 1998 is a change in the sampling method of the survey. Direct comparisons are therefore difficult.
Source: Prepared by the author based on data from the Ministry of Economy, Trade and Industry (1985–2015).

Figure 2.2   Trend comparison of IT sales in Fukuoka and Hokkaido, 1981–2015

standards, which had once been important for IT ventures and entrepreneurs in Sapporo. In a business environment, where the possibility of a gradual decrease in work is predicted, it is inevitable to focus on ordered software, which ensures cost recovery. The 1997 collapse of Hokkaido Takushoku Bank, Hokkaido's largest bank, which played a central role in providing funds to IT companies, was a symbolic event during Hokkaido's economic crisis.

The sales growth rate of the IT industry in Hokkaido, whose prefectural capital is Sapporo, from 1990 to 2015 is significantly lower than that of Fukuoka Prefecture, which has a similar population. This is also significantly lower than the national average. The sales ratio of the original software requiring initial development costs in 1990 was 32.4%, seven times higher than in Fukuoka Prefecture. This was an exceptionally high percentage, even according to the national standards. However, this ratio declined sharply in 1997, and most of the software sold in the cluster is ordered. The stall of the Sapporo IT cluster is mainly due to the loss of the original software, as shown in Figure 2.2. Given the unique characteristics of Sapporo's IT cluster, the impact of the collapse of a large financial institution was significant.

2.4.4   Capital Market Revival and Stagnation with the Dot-com Boom

Around 1997, large financial institutions failed not only in Hokkaido, but also in other regions of Japan, and the timing proved inauspicious for business confidence. Meanwhile, the stock market began to rise suddenly in mid-1999. The NASDAQ Composite Index, which mainly tracks U.S. startups, fell to 1343 in October 1998, but only 17 months later, in March 2000, it rose by about 3.8 times to 5132.

This move provided the next opportunity for the IT entrepreneurs in Sapporo. Some IT entrepreneurs, who were on the cutting edge of technology, attracted the attention of securities firms and investors. These companies suddenly began making headlines around 1998 for technologies essential to the emerging Internet, such as the world's fastest Voice over IP and Internet encryption technology.

The plateau of the Sapporo IT cluster in 1991 sparked the formation of public and private communal bodies in Hokkaido. The Network Community Forum (NCF), established in 1996, includes 800 participants from every corner of Hokkaido. They have been involved in various Internet-focused technology initiatives to reinvigorate local communities. In 2000, the Sapporo Biz Café was launched to nurture entrepreneurial talent, and it managed to capture significant attention, especially from core members of the NCF and eminent IT entrepreneurs on the verge of going public. Interestingly, this café also served as a launchpad for Japan's first independent local venture capital firm, which was established after the implementation of the Venture Fund Law in May 1998.

In 1994, Hokkaido Electric Power Company (HEPCO), Hokkaido's largest company, kickstarted activities to establish a future-forward industrial cluster within the region. Consequently, the NOASTEC Foundation was established as an organization dedicated to supporting cluster formation, and it started providing extensive aid for commercialization with a specific focus on the food industry, one of Hokkaido's cardinal sectors. This initiative was a concerted action endorsed by many economic entities in Hokkaido.

Nonetheless, the bursting of the dot-com bubbles abruptly halted these activities. The U.S. NASDAQ Composite Index fell sharply by one-fifth of its value by the end of 2002. Japan's capital markets were also severely affected, with prominent IT companies and entrepreneurs in Sapporo that went public around 2000 could not continue their growth, leading to a wave of reluctant restructuring, acquisitions, and mergers that drew considerable public attention.

Sapporo Biz Café was closed in 2002. Hokkaido Venture Capital invested in 12 companies, but Sapporo Biz Café did not continue to produce entrepreneurs. While it retained its name, the establishment was entrusted to another operator.

Despite these setbacks, the entrepreneurial assistance provided by the NOASTEC Foundation, underpinned by the Hokkaido Electric Power Company, endured. However, the anticipated outcome of a chain reaction by entrepreneurs leading to growth into an industrial cluster did not materialize. In this regard, the person in charge at the time stated that only a limited number of entrepreneurs within the food sector of the province pursued autonomous growth after obtaining funding. Unfortunately, they had little interaction with entrepreneurs who aimed for high growth.

2.4.5   Social Network in Sapporo at that Time

Numerous individuals associated with Hokkaido industrial clusters and development initiatives engaged in shared communities and activities and were familiar with each other's work. Sapporo's urban layout, characterized by a close-knit downtown, commercial, and government sectors, promotes the establishment of interconnected social frameworks. However, the NOASTEC Foundation was not adept at supporting IT entrepreneurs with significant technological capabilities in a manner that responded to societal shifts. This was largely due to its adherence to industrial support strategies conceived prior to the decline of the IT cluster.

Conversely, IT entrepreneurs exhibited a minimal interest in obtaining assistance from the NOASTEC Foundation. A prevalent inclination to sidestep the business practices of previous generations was noted. Consequently, Sapporo

Table 2.1   Discourse on Sapporo IT cluster entrepreneur and support organization

Discourse on Sapporo IT cluster entrepreneurs		
(Though it appeared to be open) Many people didn't make it into the "Sapporo valley" community.	Director, Young Engineers Community
Engineers go independent because they want to do what they want to do. When a company grows, it needs management. Many people are not good at that; even if you have a company of 10 people, there are many people who later on make it smaller, and I think that is more common.	Director, Young Engineers Community
IT entrepreneurs in Sapporo often lack a strong growth-oriented mindset. There is a notable scarcity of IT companies in Sapporo that have achieved significant milestones, such as generating over 1 billion yen in sales and employing more than 50 individuals.	The first generation of famous IT entrepreneurs
Sapporo seems to lack a strong competitive atmosphere, and there is a prevailing perception that engineers prioritize personal satisfaction over competitiveness. Despite growing up inspired by companies like Namco and Konami, it is unfortunate that local businesses have not shown an interest in learning from or collaborating with my company.	Hudson (biggest game development company), President (Newspaper report)
It could be seen as unfortunate for Sapporo that it became overly dependent on commissioned software development. During that period, simply advertising software development services would lead to immediate job offers. It's not surprising that people eventually stopped putting in extra effort, given the easy availability of work.	Well-known top IT engineer

Discourse on Entrepreneurial Support Organizations		
	IT is just a tool. (Hokkaido's core industry is agriculture.)	Cluster Support Organization Executives
	In the Cluster Division, our primary focus was on providing support for commercialization efforts. We were actively involved in offering hands-on assistance to entrepreneurs. The frequency of hand-offs or transferring tasks to others was relatively low. It was notable that there were only a limited number of entrepreneurs.	Cluster Support Organization Manager
	The individuals involved in Biz Café were predominantly in their 30s or 40s, representing a younger generation characterized by their strong individualism. The fundamental idea behind the café was to establish a remarkable and legendary space. I got a strong impression that the young individuals who initiated the café were driven by a deep determination to accomplish something significant.	Manager, Entrepreneurship Support Organization
	We believed that we had made a significant contribution to the preparation of that plan, but the personnel proposal that was disclosed after the secretariat transitioned to the NOASTEC Foundation was completely different from our original intentions.	The first generation of famous IT entrepreneurs
	For us, Biz Café was not a relaxed environment. The individuals present were primarily entrepreneurs, not IT engineers. The main emphasis was on profit-making, and there was a questionable atmosphere surrounding it.	Director, Young Engineers Community
	I didn't appreciate the fact that establishing business connections seemed difficult if you weren't a part of the golf or nightclub community. That's why I felt it was important to create a space like Biz Café, where business discussions could take place openly, allowing anyone to participate. The intention behind it was to move away from environments where older individuals held all the power.	Founder, Entrepreneurship Support Organization

Biz Café, a favored hub for budding entrepreneurs, and the NOASTEC Foundation, overseen by a prominent incumbent infrastructure company, failed to collaborate despite sharing the mutual objective of cluster formation.

2.5   FACT-FINDING

First, IT entrepreneurs in Sapporo value Schwartz's (1994) self-direction. One interviewee explained that he spun off his company to "do what I want to do without being bound by an organization," which occupied a central narrative in many of his explanations (Table 2.1). From the historical spin-off tree, IT firms in the Sapporo IT Cluster can be seen as having valued or tolerated the self-determination and welfare of individual engineering entrepreneurs over organizational growth. This corresponds to the universalism and benevolence of small business orientation proposed by Runyan and Covin (2019).

	1976-1990 Spontaneous emergence stage	1991-1997 Stall stage	1998-2015 Stay small stage
Exogenous factors influencing the IT cluster	• Global success and widespread adoption of Nintendo • Expansion of the PC industry • Attention towards Sapporo, a hub for microcomputer engineers	• Completion of software-based Japanese language adaptation • Influx of affordable foreign PCs into the domestic market • Proliferation of PC/AT compatible machines • Emergence of the Internet	• Rapid spread of the Internet • Increased investment in computer-related companies due to the dot-com boom in the United States • Collapse of the dot-com bubble
Events that occurred within the IT cluster	• Entrepreneurship stemming from university research groups • Development of BASIC by a national PC manufacturer • Spin-offs from Anchor Firm • Growth of software localization business	• Development of social communities • Bankruptcy of bank that provided R & D funding • Contraction of the original software business • Rising concerns over the economic decline of Hokkaido • Cluster formation support by electronic power companies	• Establishment of regional independent venture capital firms • Investor interest in Sapporo's cutting-edge IT startups • Establishment of Biz Cafe • Difficulties faced by listed IT ventures
	Sapporo IT cluster Self-sustainable entrepreneurial ecosystem	Sapporo IT cluster Self-sustainable entrepreneurial ecosystem	Sapporo IT cluster High-growth entrepreneurial ecosystem Self-sustainable entrepreneurial ecosystem
	As the IT cluster thrives, the various elements of the self-sustainable entrepreneurial ecosystem also develop.	The rise in self-directed entrepreneurs coincides with the development of the IT cluster. As the cluster expands, there is a corresponding increase in the pool of skilled professionals, including engineers.	The IT cluster experiences the emergence of high-growth entrepreneurial ecosystem, yet the dot-com crash prompts a significant number of venture capitalists to suspend their investments.

Figure 2.3   Transformation of the Sapporo IT Cluster

Second, it was posited that the defining characteristic of high-growth entrepreneurs may not be their individuality but rather their approach toward investors. In the Sapporo IT cluster, notable IT ventures that garnered investor attention during the dot-com bubble and its subsequent burst were occasionally compelled to undertake undesired workforce reductions and seemingly irrational mergers and acquisitions in an attempt to go public or generate profit amidst a rapidly deteriorating business climate. Entrepreneurs who receive investments under the label of productive entrepreneurs may feel obliged to act accordingly.

Third, social networks within the clusters did not operate efficiently. Despite knowing each other's goals, the interviews revealed numerous impediments, including generational differences, diverging orientations, and the policies and cultures of their respective organizations. Sapporo Biz Café, a private-sector initiative, garnered nationwide acclaim and substantial grassroots support. However, it has never established ties with the cluster development activities spearheaded by the power company. The individuals responsible for the project were aware of each other and had existing relationships with them.

2.6   DISCUSSION

2.6.1   Spontaneous IT Clusters and Self-sustainable Entrepreneurial Ecosystems

The ensuing theoretical implications buttress and expand upon the propositions of Bahrami and Evans (1995). By acknowledging the existence of various entrepreneurial ecosystems within the IT cluster, a clearer understanding of the diverse entrepreneurial behaviors within the cluster can be gleaned. One ecosystem type is characterized by high-growth and reliance on the venture capital model and investors' risk capital, while the other represents a self-sustainable entrepreneurial ecosystem deeply rooted in the cluster's external economies.

Despite the limited number of entrepreneurs seeking risk capital for high-growth pursuits, a startup's capability to retain its regional presence is likely to be influenced by its capacity to draw the required talent from the local talent pool. Contemporary theories of high-growth entrepreneurial ecosystems do not sufficiently address how regional talent pools are developed and preserved. A self-sustainable entrepreneurial ecosystem can be identified, assuming that clusters spontaneously arise and are maintained. This perspective is contingent on the calibration of the human resources sought by entrepreneurs targeting high growth. Startups requiring specialized skills may struggle to maintain growth if they fail to secure the required human resources, regardless of the availability of risk capital.

Theoretical distinction has been drawn between high-growth entrepreneurial ecosystems and clusters, positing that the former is not sector-specific for startups in sectors that demand special talent and skills. A well-functioning, self-sustainable entrepreneurial ecosystem rooted in a cluster is essential along with the development of a necessary talent pool. Theoretically, clusters encompass a self-sustainable entrepreneurial ecosystem that serves as a robust supplement to high-growth entrepreneurial ecosystems.

2.6.2   Role Expectations and the Stay Small Dilemma for High-growth-oriented Entrepreneurs

Numerous studies have demonstrated that entrepreneurs can be segmented into a select group of high-growth entrepreneurs, with the majority being low-growth entrepreneurs. High-growth entrepreneurs typically expand their knowledge base and procure resources through robust networks. Conversely, low-growth entrepreneurs often engage in small-scale operations.

Potential explanations for low-growth entrepreneurs preferring to sustain a small footprint include the escalating management expenses incurred as the organization expands and the stress and pressure associated with securing capital. These challenges are unlikely to be mitigated by the evolution of a well-functioning high-growth entrepreneurial ecosystem.

The role expectations of entrepreneurs in the high-growth-oriented entrepreneurial ecosystem are extremely high, which conflicts starkly with the entrepreneur's well-being. This is especially true for high-growth-oriented entrepreneurial ecosystems that rely on the role of venture capitalists based on the assumption of short- to medium-term exits. To be successful in a high-growth-oriented entrepreneurial ecosystem, entrepreneurs are forced to give up some of their self-direction, raise capital, make upfront development investments, and scale their business in a growing market before their capital is extinguished.

They may be forced to unconsciously play the typical character of high-growth entrepreneurs, which is convenient for investors in order to raise funds. In this case study, there was some disconnection between their true intentions and acting as growth entrepreneurs. Entrepreneurs do not only enjoy advantages from a high-growth entrepreneurial ecosystem, but they also suffer disadvantages that hinder self-determination.

Given this background, it is natural for many entrepreneurs to have a small business orientation that favors their well-being and psychological security. The current high-growth-oriented entrepreneurial ecosystem, in which productive entrepreneurship is the dominant logic, may be the product of wishful thinking.

One must strongly question whether the entrepreneurial ecosystem concept and studies focusing solely on high-growth entrepreneurship function adequately in a real-world environment. When scrutinizing micro-level testimony, numerous factors explain why the entrepreneurial ecosystem of the Sapporo IT cluster failed to work.

2.7   CONCLUSIONS AND DIRECTIONS FOR FUTURE WORK

2.7.1   Theoretical Implications

This study presents a unique approach that attempts to amalgamate cluster and entrepreneurial ecosystem theories, typically considered distinct theoretical frameworks. It proposes the coexistence of two cluster types: a high-growth entrepreneurial ecosystem that significantly relies on venture capital functions for growth and a self-sustainable entrepreneurial ecosystem that hinges on the cluster's external economies. The self-sustainable entrepreneurial ecosystem is postulated to serve as the bedrock for a high-growth entrepreneurial ecosystem.

By focusing on various entrepreneurial discourses, the study revealed that IT entrepreneurs within the Sapporo IT cluster prioritize self-governance overgrowth, demonstrating an aversion to management and avoiding organizational expansion.

2.7.2   Management and Policy Implications

This study does not definitively address whether non-growth-oriented entrepreneurs transition into productive entrepreneurs but suggests minimal likelihood. The theoretical implications of this study may resonate with researchers examining industrial regions and clusters in Japan over extended periods. Although entrepreneurs in existing clusters leverage external economies, few pursue robust growth beyond a cluster's sectoral boundaries.

An ideal high-growth entrepreneur identifies and pursues opportunities, an assumption embedded in many entrepreneurial ecosystem theories. However, most entrepreneurs tend to be self-directed. Venture capital funding places intense pressure on entrepreneurs for long-term growth, which is not conducive to their well-being. Prospective entrepreneurs and policymakers do not widely acknowledge or recognize this fact in the entrepreneurial ecosystem theory.

Self-sustainable entrepreneurial ecosystems are established in areas with existing clusters. Constructing high-growth entrepreneurial ecosystems by leveraging talent pools and components nurtured by clusters, such as consensus-building that enables new entrepreneurs and investors to infiltrate clusters, could prove effective.

2.7.3   Limitations and Challenges

Measuring clusters and entrepreneurial activities comprising diverse and numerous actors is exceedingly challenging using rigorous procedures regarding both time and cost. Accurate statistical data are often lacking. From a population sampling perspective, the effectiveness of snowball sampling is not guaranteed. Furthermore, we cannot provide a detailed account of our materials because of paper constraints.

Nevertheless, the facts revealed in this study align with those observed in other clusters in different sectors and are largely rational. Clusters generate and retain substantial managerial resources because of their historical trajectories. However, it is likely that these resources have not been fully exploited.

The progressive internationalization of venture investments portends an intensifying trend of startups incorporating within and leveraging the resources of distinct clusters to generate innovative value propositions. Such participatory observation serves as a critical foundation for enhancing our understanding of cluster lifecycle dynamics.

ACKNOWLEDGEMENTS

This research project is supported by the following research grants: Japanese Ministry of Education, *Kakenhi* (Science Foundation no.22H00878:2022–2025, no.23H00845:2023–2026, no.23H00052:2023–2027), the authors gratefully acknowledge special cooperation by all interviewees, and wish to thank four special editors for organizing Rethinking Clusters conferences and for their constructive efforts.

NOTES

1.   We have been using this term continuously in our research projects, which have been directed by Professor Kazuyori Kanai, for an extended period.
2.   Hokkaido Information Industry History Editorial Committee, ed. (2000) and our interviews.

REFERENCES

Alvesson, M. (2003). Beyond neopositivists, romantics, and localists: A reflexive approach to interviews in organizational research. *Academy of Management Review*, 28(1), 13–33.

Atkinson, R. & Flint, J. (2001). Accessing hidden and hard-to-reach populations: *Snowball Research Strategies*. Social Res Update. 33.

Autio, E., Kenney, M. & Mustar, P. (2014). Entrepreneurial innovation: The importance of context. *Research Policy*, 43. 10.1016/j.respol.2014.01.015.

Bahrami, H. & Evans, S. (1995). Flexible re-cycling and high-technology entrepreneurship. *California Management Review*, 37, 62–89. 10.2307/41165799.

Belussi, F. & Sedita, S. (2009). Life cycle vs. multiple path dependency in industrial districts. *European Planning Studies*, 17(4), 505–528.

Bosma, N. S. & Levie, J. (2010). Global Entrepreneurship Monitor 2009 Executive Report. Utrecht University Repository.

Breznitz, D. & Taylor, M. (2014). The communal roots of entrepreneurial–technological growth – social fragmentation and stagnation: Reflection on Atlanta's technology cluster. *Entrepreneurship & Regional Development*, 26(3–4), 375–396.

Bruns, K., Bosma, N., Sanders, M. et al. (2017). Searching for the existence of entrepreneurial ecosystems: A regional cross-section growth regression approach. *Small Business Economics*, 49(1), 31–54.

Cao, Z. & Shi, X. (2021). A systematic literature review of entrepreneurial ecosystems in advanced and emerging economies. *Small Business Economics*, 57. 10.1007/s11187-020-00326-y.

Cohen, B. (2005). Sustainable valley entrepreneurial ecosystems. *Business Strategy and the Environment*, 15(1), 1–14. 10.1002/bse.428.

Grandinetti, R. (2019). Rereading industrial districts through the lens of entrepreneurship. *European Planning Studies*, 27(10), 1959–1977.

Granovetter, M. (1985). Economic action and social structure: The problem of embeddedness. *American Journal of Sociology*, 91(3), 481–510.

Hokkaido Information Industry History Editorial Committee, ed. (2000). *The Birth of Sapporo Valley: 20 Years of Information Ventures*. Yellow page mook.

Isenberg, D. J. (2010). How to start an entrepreneurial revolution. *Harvard Business Review*, 88(6), 40–50.

Isenberg, D. J. (2016). Applying the ecosystem metaphor to entrepreneurship: Uses and abuses. *The Antitrust Bulletin*, 61, 564–573. 10.1177/0003603X16676162.

Kanai, K. (2005). Creation and development of industrial clusters and entrepreneurial activities: Dynamics of firm activities in the Sapporo IT Cluster formation process. *Organizational Science*, 38(3), 15–24.

Kanai, K. (2006). Evolution and innovation dynamics of Sapporo Valley: A perspective on entrepreneurial activity in the formation of industrial clusters. *The Japan Academic Society for Ventures and Entrepreneurs 9th Conference Proceedings*, 36–39.

Kanai, K. (2012). Micro-meso integration of entrepreneurial activities and regional ecosystem building processes, in Nishizawa, A., Kutsuna, K., Hibara, N., Saburi, M., Wakabayashi, N. and Kanai, K.（Eds）*High-tech Industry and Regional Eco-system*. Yuhikaku Publishing.

Kenney, M., ed. (2000). *Understanding Silicon Valley: The Anatomy of an Entrepreneurial Region*. Bibliovault OAI Repository, the University of Chicago Press.

Markusen, A. (1996). Sticky places in slippery space: A typology on industrial districts. *Economic Geography*, 72(3), 293–313.

Marshall, A. (1920 [1890]). *Principles of Economics*. McMillan.

Ministry of Economy, Trade and Industry (1985–2015; each year). *Survey of Selected Service Industries*. Ministry of Economy, Trade and Industry.

Motoyama, Y. & Knowlton, K. (2017). Examining the connections within the startup ecosystem: A case study of St. Louis. *Entrepreneurship Research Journal*, 7(1).

Nicotra, M., Romano, M., Del Giudice, M. et al. (2018). The causal relation between entrepreneurial ecosystem and productive entrepreneurship. *The Journal of Technology Transfer*, 43(3), 640–673.

Pitelis, C. (2012). Clusters, entrepreneurial ecosystem co-creation, and appropriability: A conceptual framework. *Industrial and Corporate Change*, 21(6), 1359–1388.

Porter, M. E. (1998). *On Competition*. Harvard Business School Press.

Rocha, H. & Audretsch, D. (2022). Entrepreneurial ecosystems, regional clusters, and industrial districts: Historical transformations or rhetorical devices? *The Journal of Technology Transfer*. 10.1007/s10961-022-09920-6.

Runyan, R. C. & Covin, J. G. (2019). Small business orientation: A construct proposal. *Entrepreneurship Theory and Practice*, 43(3), 529–552.

Schwartz, S. (1994). Are there universal aspects in the structure and contents of human values? *Journal of Social Issues*, 50, 19–46.

Shane, S. (2009). Why encouraging more people to become entrepreneurs is bad public policy. *Small Business Economics*, 33(2), 141–149.

Spigel, B. (2020). *Entrepreneurial Ecosystems: Theory, Practice, Futures*. Cheltenham, UK and Northampton, MA, USA: Edward Elgar Publishing.

Spigel, B. (2022). Examining the cohesiveness and nestedness entrepreneurial ecosystems: Evidence from British FinTechs. *Small Business Economics*, 59(4), 1381–1399.

Stam, E. (2015). Entrepreneurial ecosystems and regional policy: A sympathetic critique. *European Planning Studies*, 23(9), 1759–1769.

Stam, E. & Van de Ven, A. (2021). Entrepreneurial ecosystem elements. *Small Business Economics*, 56(2), 809–832.

Van de Ven, H. (1993). The development of an infrastructure for entrepreneurship. *Journal of Business Venturing*, 8(3), 211–230.

Wurth, B., Stam, E. & Spigel, B. (2021). Toward an entrepreneurial ecosystem research program. *Entrepreneurship Theory and Practice*, 46(3), 729–778.

3. The significance of a smart city for transformation of an automaker's business model: a case study of Toyota's Woven City

Jun Akabane

3.1 INTRODUCTION

In terms of business scale and profitability, Toyota is the company that most often springs to mind when one mentions the term "automaker." Toyota group's global sales equaled 10.5 million units in 2021, which ranked No. 1 worldwide and was 1 million units more than the VW group which ranked No. 2. As for the latest operating profit ratio, Toyota's was 8.1%, while VW's was just 4.9% in 2021.[1] Although the profitability of many automakers worsened from 2020 to 2021 due to COVID-19, Toyota improved its operating profit ratio from 8.0% in 2020 to 8.1% in 2021. Based on these data, Toyota could be regarded as the strongest automaker in the world.

Looking at the current trend in the automobile industry, the so-called CASE[2] and MaaS[3] revolution is evolving, and the paradigm of competition is rapidly changing (Becker et al., 2020; Akabane, 2021; Kim et al., 2022; Nasuno, 2022). Toyota officially announced it had begun its transformation from an automaker to a mobility company in January 2018 to survive the dramatic change of business environment. As part of the transformation, Toyota also announced a plan to build a fully connected, prototype city named "Woven City" at the base of Mt. Fuji in Japan.

As the technology innovations of CASE and Maas evolve in the automobile industry, the functions of a car will be dramatically diversified. For instance, apart from its major function of "run," "turn," and "stop," a car will have the functions of a power supply and a multimedia device. It will also provide us with entertainment services such as movies and games. This suggests ways that a car's involvement with our daily lives will be expanding and deepening. An automaker accordingly should consider various use cases of a car under the paradigm change. A challenge to the design of a smart city seems to be an effective approach for the manufacturer to understand the essence of the new business model since the automaker can expose itself to various use cases through the smart city project.

The purpose of this chapter is to explore the background of Toyota's challenge and discuss the significance of Woven City for the transformation of Toyota's business model. The discussion in this chapter is structured as follows. Section 3.2 outlines prior studies regarding issues such as CASE, MaaS, smart city, and the business model of an automaker. Our interest here focuses on the new megatrend in the automobile industry and the background leading to an automaker being involved in a smart city project since the number of relevant articles is countless. Section 3.3 presents our analytical framework. To understand Toyota's intention to build Woven City, what is currently happening in the automobile industry should be captured first. We examine the impact of CASE and MaaS, and then show how the value chain, competitive advantage, and the business model are accordingly changing in the automobile industry. Section 3.4 discusses current movements of Toyota and other major automakers under the paradigm change. We explain Toyota's process of business transformation and clarify its differentiation point through a comparison with the other major automakers. Section 3.5 introduces an outline of Woven City. In particular, we investigate its unique feature as an ever-evolving city. Section 3.6 discusses the significance of Woven City for Toyota's transformation. We use the perspective presented in Section 3.3 and examine how the project of Woven City will be able to contribute to the transformation of Toyota's business model. Finally, we present our overall view of the study, referring to outstanding issues and agendas to be explored in a future study.

3.2   LITERATURE REVIEWS

From the acronyms CASE and MaaS, the most critical impetus promoting an industrial revolution is the term *connected*. We can understand its importance if we consider that other factors more or less presuppose users being "connected." In particular, autonomous driving is ultimately an advanced system realized by a fully connected vehicle. It will bring dramatic changes to our lives and may well cause disruptive innovation in the automobile industry.

Previous studies seemed to concentrate on connected vehicles and autonomous driving due to their impact. A transition of the automobile sector toward innovative mobility services with a diffusion of connected autonomous vehicles looks to be a very important perspective (Alochet et al., 2021; Silva et al., 2021; Nikitas et al., 2019). How users will perceive and accept autonomous driving as part of their daily lives is another controversial point (Bonnardel, 2021; Wong & Rinderer, 2020). Moreover, sharing mobility services is also a hot issue because autonomous driving accelerates participation in a shared economy (Wong & Rinderer, 2020; Svennevik, 2019).

On the other hand, some studies focus on cutting-edge technologies' impact on the automobile industry. For instance, electrification in mobility will change focal points of competition. More specifically, natural resources will play an important role due to the relative scarcity of raw materials from which batteries are made (Jetin, 2020). Artificial intelligence (AI) is regarded as a determinant for reshaping the automobile industry (Antonialli et al., 2022). Although the digital transformation (DX) is another critical factor for upgrading the automobile industry, it is revealed that the larger automobile companies have tended to fail to make consistent progress (Sommer et al., 2021).

The impact of these technological developments on the business model has also attracted the interest of many academicians. Favoretto et al. (2022) reveal how state-of-the-art technology such as DX brings a significant revolution in the value architecture, such as value creation, value proposition, value delivery, and value capture. Loebbecke and Picot (2015) discuss how DX also reshapes business models and impacts employment among knowledge workers just as automation affected manufacturing workers. Furthermore, the business model of the automaker will also dramatically change as electric vehicle use and urban mobility services using EVs expand (Souza et al., 2022; Proff et al., 2019). Meanwhile, as network externality continues to develop due to DX, the business model with multi-actor coordination is growing in importance (Kurti & Haftor, 2015). This implies that a horizontal collaboration business model across various industries will be more effective for value creation under the paradigm shift (Riosvelasco-Monroy et al., 2023). And based on this perspective, the traditional business model with vertical integration seen in a typical large automaker cannot avoid any reform in the era of CASE.

Some of the previous studies have focused on intelligent transportation systems (ITS) in the context of a smart city and have discussed emerging technologies, use cases, and services of connected autonomous vehicles used in a smart city. For instance, AI is an indispensable infrastructure component for intelligent transportation systems in the smart city as is 5G (Nikitas et al., 2020; Guevara & Auat Cheein, 2020; Gohar & Nencioni, 2021). Unmanned aerial vehicles are also envisaged in many ITS application domains in the smart city (Menouar et al., 2017). From the viewpoint of use cases, Manfreda et al. (2021) focus on millennials and examine their adoption of autonomous vehicles since they are keen to adopt technology and new transport modes in a smart city. Campisi et al. (2021) and Kim (2022) take a more holistic approach and discuss the effects of smart city services including urban mobility with autonomous vehicles.

As for Woven City, few academic studies of it exist at the moment because the city remains under construction. Kitayama (2021) thought Toyota's challenge of Woven City could lead to negative results by referring to the taxonomy of "smart city" because Woven City does not locate the functions of local or municipal government as a gateway to public opinion.

Overlooking the literature surveys so far, we understand many studies have mentioned megatrends in the automobile industry and mobility services in a smart city, yet few studies have directly explored the impact or interaction between smart city projects and the business models of automakers. This chapter sheds light on this point through a case study of Toyota's Woven City. We will take a deductive approach because the project is still ongoing. Specifically, we first conceptualize a paradigm change in the automobile industry. Then, we define the effects of Woven City and discuss how the project will contribute to a transformation of Toyota's business model.

3.3   PARADIGM CHANGE IN THE AUTOMOBILE INDUSTRY

CASE and MaaS are symbolic acronyms explaining much of the rapid change of business environment in the automobile industry. Under this megatrend, the function of software is getting more important and ICT-related technologies play an increasingly significant role in the design and production of vehicles and the operation of mobility services. As the business environment is changing, different businesses are now entering the automobile market. Meanwhile, global warming is an urgent agenda item and carbon neutralization is becoming mandatory for all industries. Looking at the telecommunications infrastructure, the 5G network has already been developed, and now 6G is forecast to become commercialized around 2030. Therefore, CASE and MaaS seem to be irreversible trends and traditional automakers must take some major steps to shift to this new paradigm.

More specifically, the value chain, competitive advantage, and business models seem to be changing dramatically under the new paradigm. Figure 3.1 is a conceptual picture of the value chain comparing before and after the paradigm change. Before the change, the value chain consisted mainly of production, sales, and after-sale service, with financing supporting sales and after-sale service. Although some services with software were present, such as telematics, most parts of the value chain were created from the production, sales, and after-sale service of a car as an item of hardware.

By contrast, the value chain is separating into multiple lines after the paradigm change. In addition to the traditional one, new mobility services such as car-sharing, ride-sharing, and MaaS are growing in importance. Moreover, various solution services, such as autonomous driving, multimodal applications, and entertainment systems connected with the internet, are also appearing, while finance services seem to be diversifying due to the develop-

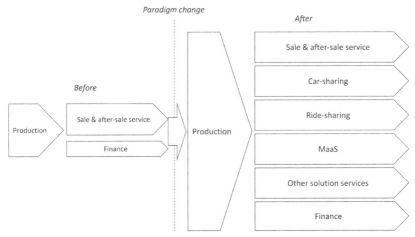

Source: Author's creation.

Figure 3.1   *Value chain in the automobile industry before and after the paradigm change*

ment of blockchain technology. The most epoch-making feature here is that most services are subject to update by means of "over-the-air" (OTA) systems, which transmit and receive data through wireless communication. Software installed in a car needs to be updated periodically and especially the role of the operating system (OS) is getting more critical.[4]

Figure 3.2 is another conceptual picture describing the comparison of competitive advantage in the automobile industry before and after the paradigm change. Traditionally, automakers have produced and sold cars as pieces of hardware. The value of a conventional car begins to depreciate after it is handed over to a user, which leads automakers to be continuously launching next-generation models. The main theme for the R&D team has accordingly been to develop an excellent car as a hardware item. In this case, automakers prioritize the manufacturing technology of hardware and the focal points of competitive advantage are the quality, cost, and delivery (QCD) of the car and those manufacturing capabilities that support a high level of QCD.

Now, automakers will not only produce and sell a physical car, but they will also provide various mobility services via the car after the paradigm change. A car as hardware will be depreciated; however, the addition of OTA-related services is likely to appreciate the vehicle's value as these features represent a resource of additional value, which is shifting the emphasis toward services. Priority should be placed on software and the focal points of competitive advantage will consist of the environmental performance of car and services,

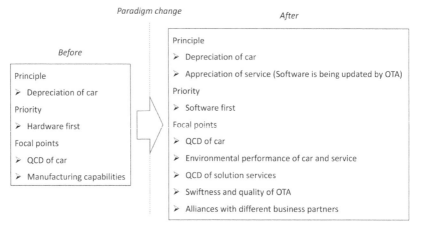

Source: Author's creation.

Figure 3.2   *Competitive advantage in the automobile industry before and*
                 after the paradigm change

the QCD of solution services, the swiftness and quality of OTA-connected systems, and alliances with different business partners, which will all add QCD to the car. Overall, a variety of business opportunities arise in the new paradigm. The capability of automakers to collaborate with external partners will be a key factor for monetization, however. For instance, car allocation service providers, public transportation authorities, travel agencies, and municipal governments will become critical partners in car-sharing, ride-sharing, and MaaS. Talking about the development of software, alliances with tech firms and communication carriers seem to be indispensable. At this moment, most technologies are still in the stage of R&D and business is still at the level of a demonstration experiment. Hence, many industries are watching vigilantly for a chance, as are the automakers.

Figure 3.3 describes a comparison of the business model before and after the paradigm change. The model before the change is organized as a set of hierarchical, exclusive, and closely connected supply chains comprising the automaker at the top and in tier 1 and tier 2, with the small parts makers, called *keiretsu*, coming below in tier 3. A car has a closed integral architecture. A careful and sophisticated integration between the parts and the main body of the car is needed and the hierarchical business model is suitable for the production system. Moreover, what should be emphasized here is that the information of the technologies and customers is concentrated on the automaker at the top, and, therefore, the automaker takes the initiative in each stage of the operation. Consequently, the supply chain represents a top-down system, and the partnership between each hierarchy is mutually cooperative and reliable. This is a kind of community bound together by a common destiny.

On the other hand, the model after the paradigm change is that the cluster of the supply chain of car production makes alliances with different business clusters. The business model before the change is hierarchically closed, whereas the model after the change is more open and horizontal. Although only three clusters have been described in Figure 3.3 due to the limitation of space, we can easily suggest other business clusters such as public transportation authorities, energy management companies, and housing builders as potential partners. In this respect, this may be a kind of business consortium rather than a business model. Talking about the characteristics of the model, the decision-making system could be more bottom-up and partnerships between the clusters more horizontal. For that reason, the partnerships are likely to be vulnerable, mutually competitive, and sometimes suspicious, as if cohabiting but living in different worlds.

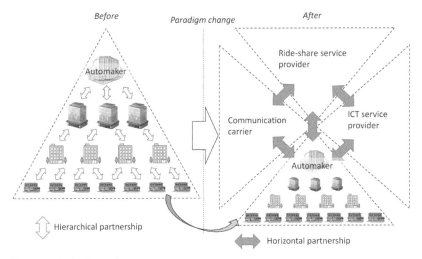

Source: Author's creation.

Figure 3.3   *Business model in the automobile industry before and after the paradigm change*

3.4   THE MOVEMENTS OF TOYOTA AND OTHER AUTOMAKERS UNDER THE PARADIGM CHANGE

Akio Toyoda was inducted as the president of Toyota in March 2009 amidst the Lehman Brothers collapse. Soon after, he had to busily deal with unexpected crises such as the 2008–2009 global recession, recall problems in the US market, and the Great East Japan Earthquake. Toyota's global unit sales also lagged from 2009 to 2011. Global sales started recovering and growing steadily after 2012, however. Although Toyota's global market portfolio leaned toward advanced countries such as the US and Japan (Akabane, 2012), Toyota especially expanded sales in emerging markets and successfully rebalanced its global market portfolio (Akabane, 2021). Toyota retrieved its No. 1 position in terms of global sales units in 2020.

Toyota also took practical steps to deal with the rapid change of business environment. For instance, the Mobility Team Concept was announced in October 2015. This is a fundamental policy of autonomous driving technology predicated on the car and the driver collaborating to achieve a high level of safety on the road. The Toyota Research Institute (TRI) was established in January 2016. Its main mission is R&D of artificial intelligence (AI), which is indispensable for autonomous driving. Moreover, in November 2017, President Akio Toyoda emphasized in a statement that, due to the impact of CASE, the automobile industry was facing a dramatic revolution occurring only once every 100 years. He then officially announced that Toyota was transforming itself into being a "mobility company" in January 2018.

After the announcement of the mobility company concept, Toyota accelerated a series of related actions. Toyota Mobility Services was established in April 2018 and KINTO, which is car-sharing and multimodal service with a subscription system, started in February 2019. Furthermore, Toyota officially declared "software first" in March 2020, which means Toyota will prioritize development of software. And then, Woven Planet Group consisting of a holding company and three operational companies was established in January 2021. Woven Alpha, one of the operational companies, oversees Woven City. As can be seen, its name does not include the "Toyota" brand. This means Woven Planet Group should remain separate from Toyota's current management so that the group can promote new innovative projects without any intervention.[5] However, the DNA of Toyota is reflected in the word "Woven," which reminds us that historically Toyota's first product was a weaving machine.

Looking at the activities of other major automakers, we understand they are different from Toyota's. For instance, US and European automakers are taking a more BEV (battery EV)-oriented strategy. They have already launched multiple BEV models, and these are currently occupying a higher market share than Toyota. The main motivation of their strategy is to differentiate their models from those of Toyota and other Japanese automakers which have their relative strengths in HEV (hybrid EV). Their national governments have also fashioned automotive and environmental policies that offer favorable treatment to the home automakers. Similar to the US and Europeans, Chinese automakers have also prioritized BEV. Sales of the new energy vehicles in China reached 5,670,000 in 2022, and BEVs represented more than 4 million out of the total sales, which means China is currently the largest BEV market in the world. Taking advantage of the market trend, Chinese automakers are rushing into development new models of BEVs, and some of these products have advanced into South-East Asian countries such as Thailand and Indonesia.

Compared to the major foreign automakers, Japanese automakers, including Toyota, may look more conservatively toward BEVs. Especially in the case of Toyota, it is devoting its development resources to other powertrains, such as HEVs, PHEVs (plug-in hybrid EVs), and FCVs (fuel cell vehicles running on hydrogen), as well as BEVs. This means Toyota is adopting a multidirectional strategy. The BEV market is rapidly expanding; however, that does not mean the demand for vehicles running on other alternative fuel systems is globally shrinking. Moreover, considering the fast pace of technological change, the dominant powertrain might be replaced by newer technology earlier than we can imagine. In this context, Toyota's multidirectional strategy makes sense.

Furthermore, the focal point of competition is not limited to kinds of powertrains. As mentioned before, the most critical impetus promoting an industrial revolution is "connected" because a connected car will have more diversified functions and accordingly create various use cases which will bring significant business opportunities to automakers and service providers. If it is to be a city operator, Toyota will be able to overlook the whole system connecting a vehicle and other devices, and place itself in a more advantageous position in the new markets. That is to say, while other automakers devote themselves to producing BEVs and the major ICT entrants are trying to take the initiative mainly in the design of vehicle operating systems, Toyota is involved in all of these segments and is additionally trying to capture diversified use cases brought by the connectivity between a car and, for example, objects that are part of the Internet of Things (IoT) through the project of Woven City.

3.5   AN OVERVIEW OF WOVEN CITY

The concept of "Woven City" was unveiled at the Consumer Electronics Show (CES) in Las Vegas in January 2020. At the CES presentation, Akio Toyoda said, "We plan to build a fully connected, digitalized, and carbon-neutral smart city." The groundbreaking ceremony for Woven City was held on February 23, 2021. The city is now being built at the old vehicle yard adjacent to the former Higashi-Fuji plant site.

Woven City is being designed by the American-Danish architecture firm BIG (Bjarke Ingels Group). Toyota has been working with BIG on the city design. Streets will have a new look to emphasize efficiency, safety, and sustainability, and residents will be able to travel on the city's main thoroughfares only in fully autonomous, zero-emission vehicles (ZEV).[6] Much of the city's infrastructure will be underground, including hydrogen fuel cells and water filtration systems, along with a network for autonomous goods delivery that connects to the above-ground buildings. Homes will be equipped with innovative technologies such as sensor-based AI to monitor the residents' health and enhance their lives (Pyzyk, 2020).

One of the epoch-making characteristics of Woven City is a laboratory city, which implies it is a never-ending or completed city. The philosophy of *kaizen* ("continuous improvement"), which is the prop of the TPS,[7] is reflected in the concept of Woven City. Through Woven City, Toyota will conduct demonstration experiments to solve various social problems such as enhancement of barrier-free mitigation of traffic jams, revitalization of shopping districts, and reduction of traffic accidents. Toyota will analyze traffic and parking data in the city and develop a system to propose the best timing of movement for residents, thus keeping traffic flowing smoothly.

Another feature of Woven City is that it is being built on Toyota's private land, which will bring two advantages to Toyota. First, as we saw from the failure case of Sidewalk Labs in Toronto, how to persuade local people and obtain their cooperation in the smart city project is a big issue for the city planner (Filion et al., 2023). Especially vexing is how their concern that their privacy is being invaded through data gathering and analysis can lead to an opposition movement. Toyota does not have to reconcile this kind of interest with residents, however. Second, Toyota can establish the whole infrastructure with perfect freedom. This is costly in one way because Toyota cannot utilize existing infrastructures, whereas it is efficient in the sense that Toyota can reflect all of the ideas they would like to try in the city design from the beginning. As mentioned below, demonstration experiments planned in Woven City will be wide ranging. Therefore, a greenfield site seems to be more favorable than a brownfield site for Toyota.

Based on Toyota Motor Corporation (2021), the essence of the experiments in Woven City can be summarized as inspired by three themes. The first theme is "traffic management by autonomous vehicles and three separated streets." Toyota will analyze traffic and parking data in the city and develop a system to propose the best timing of movement for residents and thus mitigate traffic jams. The second theme is to "make a whole city design being carbon-neutral."

This objective affects not only vehicles but also other facilities such as homes and components of the infrastructure. Especially energy management by renewable energy sources and fuel-cell generation will become core technologies. The third theme is to "enhance QOL [quality of life] of residents consisting of many generations through the latest technologies such as AI and robotics." As one of the core concepts of the city is its "human-centered" design factor, so seeking the solution of current social problems and exploring an ideal future lifestyle by applying new technologies are very important missions for the city planners. Furthermore, what should be emphasized regarding the three themes is that the gathering and analysis of big data will be a major approach. All systems in the city will be centrally controlled through the data, and solutions will also come out of the data analysis.

3.6   THE THREE EFFECTS OF WOVEN CITY

This section explores how the three themes of the demonstration experiments in Woven City will contribute to the transformation of Toyota's business model by using the frameworks presented in Section 3.3.

The three themes cover multiple businesses and various applications of the latest technologies. It is almost impossible for even Toyota to provide the necessary resources by itself. Thus, Woven City will offer an opportunity for Toyota to learn how to build a smart city and also conduct open innovation. More specifically, Toyota will be able to learn how to collaborate and reconcile interests with external partners through the projects in Woven City. Meanwhile, the company will be able to understand various use cases and user experiences through the three experiments. Previously, Toyota as an automaker understood only how drivers used cars and which cars attracted drivers. To survive and thrive through this paradigm change, however, Toyota is widening its scope to surrounding viewpoints such as distribution systems, human lifestyles, and energy management. It is expected that Toyota researchers can familiarize themselves with these unfamiliar domains and accordingly increase new contact points with customers through the projects. Furthermore, Woven City will provide Toyota with an opportunity to apply its own technologies while motivating the company to develop new software-oriented technologies. As is well known, Toyota successfully launched both the first FCEV[8] and the first HEV.[9] Besides production of EVs, these technologies are very applicable to carbon-neutral city designs. On the other hand, various connected systems and autonomous services will be installed in Woven City. Thus, Toyota will need to strengthen development of its software technology; otherwise, Toyota will lose its leadership in the projects of Woven City.

To sum up the discussion so far, the three learning points derived from the experiments in Woven City can be summarized as: (A) learn how to collaborate with different business partners, (B) experience varieties of use cases and increase contact points with customers, and (C) apply Toyota's technologies not only to automobiles but also to various domains. Most importantly, each of these effects could be conceptualized in these key words, namely "open innovation," "servitization,"[10] and "scope of economy."

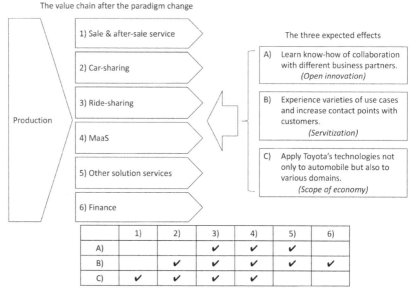

Source: Author's creation.

Figure 3.4   The three effects and the new value chain

Next, let us think how the effects will contribute to the creation of the new value chain, competitive advantage, and business model. Figure 3.4 describes the relation between the effects and the value chain. First, (3) ride-sharing, (4) MaaS, and (5) other solution services will be realized through the collaboration of the automaker, ride-sharing service providers, public transport institutions, travel agencies, and software service developers. In this respect, the effect of "(A) open innovation" enables Toyota to learn the relevant skills and know-how to make proper collaborative efforts. Second, (2) car-sharing, (3) ride-sharing, (4) MaaS, (5) other solution services, and (6) finance offer various use cases accompanied by new user experiences. For instance, how to use car-sharing, ride-sharing, and privately owned cars separately is one of the most important issues not only for users but also for automakers. With respect to MaaS, an optimized combination of car and other means of transportation presumably differs among the users, and the division of labor among the companies concerned will also be different for each use case. Moreover, as the function of a car diversifies beyond "run," "turn," and "stop," varieties of applications with a car will dramatically expand and related solution services will accordingly increase. Therefore, the effect of "(B) servitization" enables Toyota to take the initiative in the promotion of new services. Third, considering cars used in (2) car-sharing, (3) ride-sharing, and (4) MaaS will be mostly connected and autonomous EVs in the near future, Toyota's existing technology will be applied to these new mobility services as well as the traditional value chain of (1) Sale & after-sale service. The effect of "(C) scope of economy" contributes to these aspects.

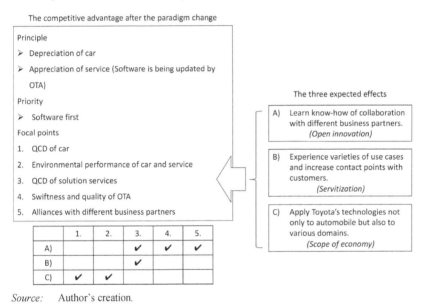

Source: Author's creation.

Figure 3.5   The three effects and the new competitive advantage

Figure 3.5 depicts the relation between the three effects and the new competitive advantage after the paradigm change. The effect of "(A) open innovation" will contribute to three focal points. First, (5) alliances with different business partners is directly promoted. Moreover, (3) QCD of solution services and (4) swiftness and quality of OTA will also be strengthened because Toyota is relatively unfamiliar with these domains and definitely needs external resources through the open innovation. As a matter of fact, Woven City is recruiting researchers involved in software from other companies, and the Woven Planet

Group is currently conducting M&A with software firms involved in the development of autonomous driving. The effect of "(B) servitization" will mainly encourage (3) QCD of solution services. Operations in Woven City will cover all processes of the human lifestyle across all genders and generations. By experiencing various use cases, Toyota can recognize which human-centered services should be operationalized, thereby enhancing its capability of product planning for solution services. Finally, the effect of "(C) scope of economy" will contribute to (1) QCD of car and (2) environmental performance of car and service. Even under the new paradigm, the QCD of a car is still very important. Toyota's technologies will be fully utilized in the development of future vehicles. More importantly, other opportunities where Toyota applies its technologies will expand because the need for carbon neutralization is becoming more urgent in various products and services. Toyota could learn methods to apply its technologies across a wide range of areas, such as home, factory, and infrastructure since the whole city design will be carbon neutral.

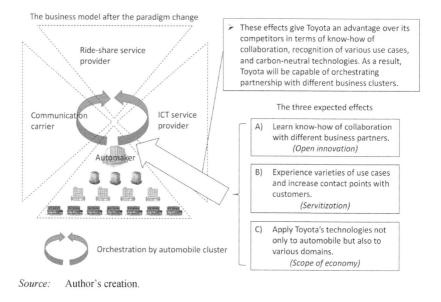

Source: Author's creation.

Figure 3.6   *The three effects and the new business model*

Based on the discussion so far, we can summarize the positive effects of the new business model as illustrated in Figure 3.6. As explained above, the new business model is a system involving the collaboration of different business clusters. Therefore, a sensitive reconciliation of interests is needed; otherwise, conflicts could easily take place among clusters. However, if Toyota is superior to other clusters in terms of know-how of collaboration, recognition of various use cases, and carbon-neutral technologies, the company will be capable of executing its leadership and orchestrating partnerships with other clusters. The three effects should give Toyota an advantage over other clusters due to these critical factors.

3.7   CONCLUDING REMARKS

In this chapter, we have first conceptualized the value chain, competitive advantage, and business model after the paradigm change in the automobile industry. We then defined the significance of Toyota's Woven City and subsequently discussed how the demonstration experiments there will contribute to the transformation of Toyota's business model.

As a result of the discussion so far, we have extracted the three effects symbolically expressed by "open innovation," "servitization," and "scope of economy," and discussed their contributions to Toyota's transformation in terms of value chain, competitive advantage, and business model. Specifically, the effect of "open innovation" directly enhances Toyota's capability to make a proper collaboration with other clusters and enables Toyota to develop its unfamiliar resources, such as software, through the collaboration. The effect of "servitization" makes Toyota experience various use cases and enables Toyota to exercise its leadership in new service-related businesses. The effect of "scope of economy" provides Toyota abundant opportunities to apply its technologies across a wide range of areas such as home, factory, and infrastructure since carbon neutralization is an urgent agenda item in the world.

The cascading effects of Woven City as Toyota's business model is transformed as described in this chapter is an ideal situation. In other words, it cannot be automatically realized. For the next study, we need to examine how Toyota should deploy practical operations in Woven City to develop its effects and utilize them for Toyota's repurposing of its resources. Verifying the process and the way Toyota operates Woven City effectively will provide a clear picture of the road to the successful transformation of Toyota's business model.

NOTES

1.   The latest information retrieval (IR) data from each company.
2.   CASE stands for connected, autonomous, electric, and sharing & service, factors regarded as a megatrend in the automobile industry and leading to a disruption of the existing business system.

3.   MaaS stands for mobility as a service and is a service concept that integrates public transport with other mobility services, such as car-sharing, ride-sourcing, and bicycle-sharing (Smith, 2020).
4.   Over-the-air (OTA) updates allow automakers to issue current and future operating system (OS) refreshes quickly, conveniently, and automatically to a car in much the same way that a smartphone receives an OS upgrade from its cellular provider (https://www.jdpower.com/Cars/Shopping-Guides/what-are-over-the-air-updates-for-cars).
5.   This is in line with Christensen's argument that an independent unit free from intervention from headquarters is necessary to promote newly innovative projects (Christensen, 2013).
6.   E-Pallet, a fully autonomous driving vehicle, will be the main means of mobility in Woven City. It has a wide and tall door, which assists those using wheelchairs or baby carriages in getting on and off.
7.   Toyota production system.
8.   Toyota launched the first-generation FCEV, Mirai, in 2014.
9.   Toyota launched the first generation HEV, Prius, in 1999.
10. The shift of product-based manufacturers toward offering business solutions and value-added services to consumers is termed as 'Servitization' (Kamal et al., 2020).

REFERENCES

Akabane, J. (2012). Study on the global market strategies of the big six. *The Bulletin of the Yokohama Municipal University Society. Social Science*, *64*(1), 13–38.
Akabane, J. (2021). Study of the global market portfolio of the big seven automakers. *The Journal of Economics*, *62*(1.2.3), 1–23.
Alochet, M., Midler, C., Shou, Y., & Wang, X. (2021). The road to autonomous mobility services: Who drives the transition, where, and how? *International Journal of Automotive Technology and Management*, *21*(4), 343–364.
Antonialli, F., Martinesco, A., & Mira-Bonnardel, S. (2022). Artificial intelligence as a determinant for reshaping the automotive industry and urban mobility services. *International Journal of Automotive Technology and Management*, *22*(3), 324–351.
Becker, H., Balac, M., Ciari, F., & Axhausen, K. W. (2020). Assessing the welfare impacts of Shared Mobility and Mobility as a Service (MaaS). *Transportation Research Part A: Policy and Practice*, *131*, 228–243.
Bonnardel, S. M. (2021). Robomobility for collective transport: A prospective user centric view. *International Journal of Automotive Technology and Management*, *21*(1–2), 99–120.
Campisi, T., Severino, A., Al-Rashid, M. A., & Pau, G. (2021). The development of the smart cities in the connected and autonomous vehicles (CAVs) era: From mobility patterns to scaling in cities. *Infrastructures*, *6*(7), 100.
Christensen, C. M. (2013). *The Innovator's Dilemma: When New Technologies Cause Great Firms to Fail*. Harvard Business Review Press.
Favoretto, C., Mendes, G. H. D. S., Filho, M. G., Gouvea de Oliveira, M., & Ganga, G. M. D. (2022). Digital transformation of business model in manufacturing companies: Challenges and research agenda. *Journal of Business & Industrial Marketing*, *37*(4), 748–767.

Filion, P., Moos, M., & Sands, G. (2023). Urban neoliberalism, smart city, and Big Tech: The aborted Sidewalk Labs Toronto experiment. *Journal of Urban Affairs*, 1–19.

Gohar, A., & Nencioni, G. (2021). The role of 5G technologies in a smart city: The case for intelligent transportation system. *Sustainability*, *13*(9), 5188.

Guevara, L., & Auat Cheein, F. (2020). The role of 5G technologies: Challenges in smart cities and intelligent transportation systems. *Sustainability*, *12*(16), 6469.

Jetin, B. (2020). Who will control the electric vehicle market? *International Journal of Automotive Technology and Management*, *20*(2), 156–177.

Kamal, M. M., Sivarajah, U., Bigdeli, A. Z., Missi, F., & Koliousis, Y. (2020). Servitization implementation in the manufacturing organisations: Classification of strategies, definitions, benefits and challenges. *International Journal of Information Management*, *55*, 102206.

Kim, J. (2022). Smart city trends: A focus on 5 countries and 15 companies. *Cities*, *123*, 103551.

Kim, J., Paek, B., & Lee, H. (2022). Exploring innovation ecosystem of incumbents in the face of technological discontinuities: Automobile firms. *Sustainability*, *14*(3), 1606.

Kitayama. (2021). Automotive-driven city of smartness: Study of compatibility between Toyota's woven city and its current business model (Master dissertation, Keio Business School (Japan)).

Kurti, E., & Haftor, D. (2015, September). Barriers and enablers of digital business model transformation. In *The European Conference on Information Systems Management* (pp. 262–268). Academic Conferences International.

Loebbecke, C., & Picot, A. (2015). Reflections on societal and business model transformation arising from digitization and big data analytics: A research agenda. *Journal of Strategic Information Systems*, *24*(3), 149–157.

Manfreda, A., Ljubi, K., & Groznik, A. (2021). Autonomous vehicles in the smart city era: An empirical study of adoption factors important for millennials. *International Journal of Information Management*, *58*, 102050.

Menouar, H., Guvenc, I., Akkaya, K., Uluagac, A. S., Kadri, A., & Tuncer, A. (2017). UAV-enabled intelligent transportation systems for the smart city: Applications and challenges. *IEEE Communications Magazine*, *55*(3), 22–28.

Nasuno, K. (2022). Progress of electric vehicles and transformation of supply chain in the Japanese automobile industry. In T. Higuchi (ed.) *Frameworks and Cases on Evolutional Supply Chain* (pp. 46–67). IGI Global.

Nikitas, A., Michalakopoulou, K., Njoya, E. T., & Karampatzakis, D. (2020). Artificial intelligence, transport and the smart city: Definitions and dimensions of a new mobility era. *Sustainability*, *12*(7), 2789.

Nikitas, A., Njoya, E. T., & Dani, S. (2019). Examining the myths of connected and autonomous vehicles: Analysing the pathway to a driverless mobility paradigm. *International Journal of Automotive Technology and Management*, *19*(1–2), 10–30.

Proff, H., Szybisty, G., & Fojcik, T. M. (2019). From electric cars to energy-efficient houses: The automotive retail sector at the crossroads. *International Journal of Automotive Technology and Management*, *19*(1–2), 55–73.

Pyzyk, K. (2020). Toyota unveils plan to build 'City of the Future' in Japan. *Smart Cities Dive*, January 8.

Riosvelasco-Monroy, G. E., Pérez-Olguín, I. J. C., Flores-Amador, J., Pérez-Domínguez, L. A., & Hernández-Gómez, J. A. (2023). Horizontal collaboration business model towards a sustainable I4.0 value creation. In H. Gholami, G. Abdul-Nour, S. Sharif

& D. Streimikiene (eds.) *Sustainable Manufacturing in Industry 4.0: Pathways and Practices* (pp. 157–185). Springer Nature Singapore.

Silva, J. P. N. D., Vieira, K. C., Sugano, J. Y., Pedrosa, G., & Oliveira, C. C. D. (2021). Factors of diffusion of innovations: Analysis of the literature of autonomous vehicles. *International Journal of Automotive Technology and Management, 21*(1–2), 29–52.

Smith, G. (2020). Making mobility-as-a-service: Towards governance principles and pathways (Doctoral dissertation, Chalmers Tekniska Hogskola (Sweden)).

Sommer, S., Proff, H., & Proff, H. (2021). Digital transformation in the global automotive industry. *International Journal of Automotive Technology and Management, 21*(4), 295–321.

Souza, J. V. R. D., Mello, A. M. D., & Marx, R. (2022). Barriers and drivers to implement innovative business models towards sustainable urban mobility. *International Journal of Automotive Technology and Management, 22*(4), 485–505.

Svennevik, E. M. C. (2019). The existing and the emerging: Car ownership and car sharing on the road towards sustainable mobility. *International Journal of Automotive Technology and Management, 19*(3–4), 281–300.

Toyota Motor Corporation (2021). *Magazine Toyotimes*. Sekaibunkasha.

Wong, A., & Rinderer, P. (2020). Customer perceptions of shared autonomous vehicle usage: An empirical study. *International Journal of Automotive Technology and Management, 20*(1), 108–129.

4. Urban policy and securing talent toward realizing an international creative environment: Glass City Toyama, Japan

Atsuko Maeda[1]

4.1   INTRODUCTION

From the present social view of culture and economics (Throsby 2001), sustainable development of a creative environment that utilizes local cultural resources necessitates the creation of facilities and the development of talent while promoting the arts and related industries (Maeda 2021, 2022). For the arts and culture that symbolize a region to contribute to the eco-production system with the aim of realizing sustainable development, how should we develop the talent and facilities that internationalize the region's unique cultural strengths?

First, the relevance of this study is examined by a brief review of the literature. Piore and Sable (1984) advocated the "flexible specialization" of craft production systems, through which production processes are constantly reorganized by rearranging production factors and specialized knowledge is acquired. In the case of second-generation and later generations of family run businesses, after completing specialized education and training at university, craftsmen accumulate knowledge and experience in the home environment. However, Markusen (2006) concluded that the craft production system consisting of family-run businesses, which forms an industrial cluster in a given area (Piore and Sable 1984; Yamada and Ito 2013), is limited in terms of internationalization of the production system, employment stability, and research and development capability. Moreover, Markusen (2006) suggested that the creative social activities of local artists may be able to overcome these challenges. Meanwhile, according to Lazzeretti et al. (2008), creativity is a cross-sectional phenomenon that spreads and develops across industries, and in Europe, creativity is realized in two main ways. One is technology-driven, which is common in northern Europe and manifests as the creative class

(Florida 2002) and as creative industries such as digital art and design. The other is heritage-driven, which is common in central and southern European countries as well as in Japanese cities such as Kyoto and Kanazawa (Sasaki 2020; Maeda 2021) and is more directly related to studies on cultural economics (Throsby 2001; Ikegami et al. 1998) and to cultural industries. As an application of these two approaches, the present study explores the process and factors in successfully establishing a creative environment focused on glass art as a new local cultural resource, based on the manufacturing spirit of glass bottles used in the pharmaceutical industry as well as rich communications with stakeholders in advanced glass art cities in Europe and the United States. According to Toshimitsu (2019), both a comprehensive craft-art design education curriculum that enhances creativity and practical professional training are prerequisites to promote the wide-ranging social activities of studio glass artists who make glass works at their own studios and also do design work for corporations. The German Bauhaus system of education and training has been greatly admired as an advanced model for fostering flexible and innovative glass artists and designers worldwide since the early 20th century.

Next, the social background of this study in terms of the need for specialized and adaptable talent from all over Japan and overseas as well as facilities is discussed. Since the end of the 20th century, more and more open-call exhibitions, art festivals, and trade fairs have been held worldwide, and in Japan, these events have had large economic effects in terms of inbound cultural tourism (Todate 2016; Maeda 2021). Partly due to this trend, the techniques, designs, and final products of glass artists have become diversified and reflect an international influence. Additionally, young artists and designers who are active in the cutting-edge field of glass modeling are emerging from technical research institutes (e.g., vocational schools, studios, and related facilities) clustered in Toyama City (Maeda 2022). In other words, artists, designers, and entrepreneurs of various generations, nationalities, and professions have been drawn to this creative environment where they now contribute to the realization of a vibrant international creative environment. During the COVID-19 pandemic, glass artists in their 30s and 40s who graduated from glass vocational schools a generation ago (about 10 years ago) and have opened their own studios are on track to become self-sufficient and are as active as they were before the pandemic because they have attended various forms of exhibitions and sold their work online. In addition to glassmaking, they also contribute to the promotion of the creative glass environment by researching new designs, developing the market, and tapping new sales channels.[2]

Against the academic and social background described above, this study identifies the process and factors in successfully establishing a creative environment where international educational and research institutions with a high level of openness and flexibility can operate. In particular, this study explores how the strengths of local culture manifest on the global stage, thereby bringing sustainable development to the city and region, with a focus on relationships among a glass vocational school, a glass studio, and a glass art museum in Toyama City. The method involves extracting the names of persons, facilities, and systems involved in promoting individual career development, organizational exchanges aimed at internationalization and localization, and support for regional settlement that lead to realizing a sustainable production system as well as securing and fostering international professional talent. The persons, facilities, and systems that are repeatedly identified are considered to be factors underlying the success of realizing a new production system with new cultural resources, including human resources and infrastructure.

4.2 CONCEPT OF GLASS CITY TOYAMA

Toyama City, the capital of Toyama Prefecture, is located next to the Sea of Japan, which faces Russia and China, on the central coast of Japan's main

Source: Toyama City.

Figure 4.1 Location of Toyama City, Japan

island and is about two hours from Tokyo by Shinkansen bullet train (Figure 4.1). The population of Toyama City is about 410,000 and that of Toyama Prefecture is around 1,000,000 (Appendix 4.1). The main industries of Toyama City are pharmaceutical manufacturing and handicrafts. However, since the end of the 20th century, Toyama City, like other Japanese cities, has seen shrinking and aging of its population and has also seen declines in manufacturing (Appendix 4.1). Toyama City has responded to these issues by implementing a compact city strategy aimed at increasing urban functionality and attracting residents from suburbs by using decarbonized trams (light rail transit) to reduce the need for cars and counter urban sprawl, thereby allowing citizens to lead high-quality lives downtown, where they can walk around and enjoy art and cultural facilities (Nakajima et al. 2020). Toyama City's efforts to solve various problems caused by climate change as well as Japan's declining birthrate and aging population have led to its selection as one of five advanced "Compact Cities" by the Organisation for Economic Co-operation and Development in 2012, one of the Rockefeller Foundation's 100 Resilient Cities in 2013, and an "Eco-Model City" and a "SDGs FutureCity" by the Japanese government in 2008 and 2018.[3]

As Table 4.1 shows, following the formulation of the "Toyama City Comprehensive Plan" in 2007, the inbound effects of the opening of the Hokuriku Shinkansen in 2015 and the Tokyo Olympics held in 2021 over-lapped with urban policies and accelerated the promotion of a project aimed at enhancing urban functionality and enticing residents from the suburbs to relocate to the city center. Cultural tourism facilities were gradually built in redevelopment areas. Then, the "Toyama City Cultural Creation City Vision" development policy was implemented in 2016, with the aim of enhancing cultural resources in order to enrich the lives of local citizens, who make up a shrinking and aging population. For these reasons and based on the values of diversity, potentiality, internationality, and locality, glass art was selected to be a new local cultural resource through the mayor's leadership as well as public–private professional partnerships.[4] Here, "diversity" refers to the various techniques, forms, and uses of glass; "potentiality" refers to market development and the creation of production bases not bound by traditional distribution systems and forms of activity; "internationality" and "locality" refers to the coexistence of international contemporary glass art and the local glassware manufacturing industry inspired by traditional glass bottles. In 1988, the "Glass Village" initiative (Table 4.1) was launched and in 2012 it was renamed "Glass Art Hills Toyama." Starting in 1996, the project was expanded to the city center as part of the "Glass City" initiative. In 2015, a glass art museum was opened, using "glass" as a new means of communicating art and culture in which people, towns, and nature can coexist in harmony and work toward achieving SDGs. The two projects have been consolidated under the

Table 4.1   Glass city making and related urban strategies

Year	Urban strategy on Glass City Making	Achievement (cultural resources (Infra.& H.R.)) and process (methods/systems) for Glass City Making
1988	**"Glass Village" initiative**	**Glass School Establishment Committee established**
1991		Glass School **(TIGA)** opens
1992		**1st Open Workshop** by P. SIGNORETTO **(TIGA, stakeholders, residents)**
1994		Glass Studio **(TGS)** opens
		1st Citizen workshop (TGS, residents)
		Open Workshop by L. TAGLIAPIETRA **(TIGA, TGS, residents, stakeholders, tourists)**
1996	**"Glass City Making" initiative**	**Glass Installations on Streets (City with TGS, TIGA, stakeholders, residents, tourists)**
1997		Rental Solo-Studio opens **(TGS, residents); Graduate exhibition in Civic Hall (TIGA, residents, tourists, stakeholders)**
1998	**"Glass Village" "Glass Museum" concept**	
1999	Int'l Conference Hall opens	Public Glass Salon opens **(TIGA, TGS, Int'l Conference Hall, residents, tourists, stakeholders); R&D starts for new unique colors (TGS, stakeholders)**
2000		**10 years' commemorative exhibition (TIGA, Int'l Conference Hall, residents, tourists, stakeholders) exchange program tie-up** with Australian National University, Canberra **(TIGA)**
2002	**Compact City Strategy established**	**Triennale Open Call Exhibition starts in Civic Hall (TIGA, TGS, residents, tourists, stakeholders)**
2004		Rental Studio and Gallery open **(TGS, residents, tourists, stakeholders)**
2006	**Compact City embodied: LRT opens**	
2007	**Toyama City Comprehensive Plan**	
2008	**Announcement of TGAM establishment**	**TIGA transfers to division under mayor's direct control**
2009	**Master plan "Glass City Making" created**	**Accredited as** specialized training college **(TIGA)**
2010	**Policy put for the TGAM establishment**	Student dormitory **(TIGA) and** artist accommodation open **(TIGA, TGS); artists-in-residence starts (TIGA)**
2011		Café gallery opens **(TGS, visitors)**

Year	Urban strategy on Glass City Making	Achievement (cultural resources (Infra.& H.R.)) and process (methods/systems) for Glass City Making
2012		**From "Glass Village" to "Glass Art Hills" by public offering** Studio for citizens and tourists opens **(TGS, residents, tourists)**
2013	**Urban redevelopment project commences**	**Exchange program tie-up** with Academy (University) of Art, Architecture, and Design in Prague **(TIGA)**
2014		**20 years' commemorative public workshop (TGS, community)**
2015	**Hokuriku Shinkansen bullet train**	Glass Museum (TGAM) opens **Cooperative production** by D. Chihuly **(TGAM, TGS, TIGA, stakeholders, residents, tourists)**
2016	**"Cultural Creation City Vision"**	**Graduation exhibition held at TGAM (TIGA, residents, stakeholders, tourists)** **Annual exchange program tie-up** with Australian Canberra Glass Studio **(TGS)**
2017	**2nd Toyama City Comprehensive Plan**	**Exchange program tie-up** with Gerrit Rietveld Academie (Art University) in Amsterdam **(TIGA)**
2018		**Int'l Open Call Exhibition starts (TGAM, residents, tourists, stakeholders)**
2020		**New R&D accomplishments (TGS, local artists, city, customers)**
2021	**Tokyo Olympics**	**Int'l Open Call Exhibition (TGAM, residents, tourists, stakeholders)** **30 years' commemorative exhibition (TGAM, TIGA, residents, tourists, stakeholders)**
2022		**Cooperation tie-up** with the Corning Museum of Glass **(TGAM)**

Note: The key actors of Glass City Toyama are TGAM, TIGA, and TGS, while those of Glass Art Hills Toyama are TIGA, TGS, and related facilities. The bold terms enclosed in parentheses indicate the organizers or key actors of glass art projects or events. Bold words intend new policies, projects, systems, or methods. Underlined words intend new or impacted facilities and human resources. LRT, light rail transit.
Source: Toyama City, TIGA (Toyama Institute of Glass Art), TGS (Toyama Glass Studio) and TGAM (Toyama Glass Art Museum); *30 years of Toyama Institute of Glass Art* (TGAM 2021).

"Glass City Toyama" master plan, which was developed in 2009 as a part of Toyama's City Comprehensive Plans (2007 to present).

Subsequently, the "Glass City Toyama" concept has developed into a new production environment by reorganizing local resources and actors, resulting in an art and culture cluster (Piore and Sable 1984).

4.3   TOYAMA CITY AS A CLUSTER OF GLASS ART

As described in Sections 4.3.1 and 4.3.2, the "Glass City" concept, which started as "Glass Village," has come to embody an international hub for professional exchange, citizen exchange, regional industrialization, tourism, and leadership through the manufacture, exhibition, and the sale of studio glass artwork/craft glassware as well as education and research, facility development, and citizen participation program. As a result of these efforts over the last 30 years, Toyama City has built the infrastructure and developed the talent for simultaneous internationalization of human resource development (glass vocational school), industrialization promotion (glass studio), and art promotion (glass museum, public gallery) and has attracted highly skilled professionals from all over the world.

4.3.1   Key Actors of Glass City Toyama

This section introduces basic information about the three key actors that form the base of Glass City Toyama and describes their interrelations.

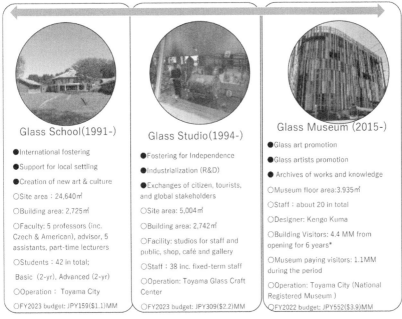

Glass School(1991-)
- International fostering
- Support for local settling
- Creation of new art & culture
○ Site area : 24,640㎡
○ Building area: 2,725㎡
○ Faculty: 5 professors (inc. Czech & American), advisor, 5 assistants, part-time lecturers
○ Students : 42 in total; Basic (2-yr), Advanced (2-yr)
○ Operation : Toyama City
○ FY2023 budget: JPY159($1.1)MM

Glass Studio(1994-)
- Fostering for Independence
- Industrialization (R&D)
- Exchanges of citizen, tourists, and global stakeholders
○ Site area: 5,004㎡
○ Building area: 2,742㎡
○ Facility: studios for staff and public, shop, café and gallery
○ Staff : 38 inc. fixed-term staff
○ Operation: Toyama Glass Craft Center
○ FY2023 budget: JPY309($2.2)MM

Glass Museum (2015-)
- Glass art promotion
- Glass artists promotion
- Archives of works and knowledge
○ Museum floor area:3.935㎡
○ Staff : about 20 in total
○ Designer: Kengo Kuma
○ Building Visitors: 4.4 MM from opening for 6 years*
○ Museum paying visitors: 1.1MM during the period
○ Operation: Toyama City (National Registered Museum)
○ FY2022 budget: JPY552($3.9)MM

Note: * Including the long-term closing period and admission restrictions due to the COVID-19 pandemic; USD 1 ≈ JPY 140.
Source: Photos by the author. Financial and Business Reports, and Official Publications of Toyama City, Toyama Institute of Glass Art, Toyama Glass Studio, Toyama Glass Craft Center, and Toyama Glass Art Museum.

Figure 4.2   *Production networks that formalize a new ecosystem of institutes in Glass City Toyama*

As Table 4.1 and Figure 4.2 show, the Toyama Institute of Glass Art (TIGA),[5] which is the first public glass vocational school, was established in 1991. It later moved to a division under the mayor's direction in 2008, where it has played a key role in realizing the aforementioned "Glass City Making" master plan developed in 2009 (a. b. c. in Section 4.3.2).

Adjacent to TIGA, the Toyama Glass Studio (TGS)[6] was established in 1994 to train glass artists, most of whom are top graduates of TIGA or have achieved an equivalent technical level, with the aim of facilitating research and development (R&D) of new glass designs and businesses,[7] as well as providing social education to residents and tourists of all ages.[8] TGS has studio spaces, a gallery café, and a shop that supports young artists and designers by giving them space and opportunities to gain practical experience. Furthermore, TGS established individual and rental studios[9] in 1997 and 2004, respectively, to support the independent activities of young artists, from all over the country to continue pursuing their creative activities even after graduation. Together, TIGA and TGS make up the facility known as Glass Art Hills Toyama.

About a 20-minute drive away, in the city center, is the Toyama Glass Art Museum (TGAM),[10] which along with the Toyama City Library, was opened in 2015 as Toyama Kirari, a complex built in a space that had been hollowed out by suburban sprawl. The name "Kirari" symbolizes urban redevelopment and the vitality of the city and its citizens. Toyama Kirari was designed by Kengo Kuma, who used local wood and metal for a design meant to represent the steepness of the Tateyama Mountain Range that symbolizes the region. In the first six years since its opening in August 2015,[11] the total number of visitors to Toyama Kirari, including the free spaces of the museum, the library, the café, and the museum shop, was 4.4 million, while TGAM had 1.1 million paying visitors during the same period, which includes the period it was closed due to the COVID-19 pandemic. As a symbol of Glass City Toyama, TGAM serves as an international creative hub for artists, designers, stakeholders, citizens, and tourists, as well as a venue for graduation exhibits by TIGA students, thereby promoting contemporary glass art and local culture.

In just over 30 years, Toyama City has become the only city in the world with three public facilities—a vocational school, a studio, and a museum—dedicated to glass art. These three facilities have developed in a new production system involving art, culture, industry, human resource development, and local society built through mutual collaborative relationships as well as domestic and international exchanges in an eco-model city based on a compact city strategy.

4.3.2   Social Roles of Education and Research Institutes

According to the "Toyama City Cultural Creation City Vision" development policy (Toyama City 2016), the social roles of TIGA, which are fulfilled in cooperation with TGS and TGAM, are as follows: a. international fostering of glass artists and designers, b. attracting a diverse pool of talent from all over Japan and overseas, and c. creating both vitality as well as new international art and culture. To fulfill these roles, the following actors, systems, and facilities have emerged and endeavored to create glass art.

a.   **High-level international exchange programs carried out by a small number of select talent, using various approaches**

The faculty are modeling artists who are active on the frontlines of the field and have high academic achievement, teaching careers, and rich networks with overseas professionals:[12] there are five full-time faculty members, including one each from the Czech Republic and the United States with contracts lasting up to four years; five full-time assistants with contracts lasting up to three years; and eight part-time staff members. The total number of students eligible for the two-year basic course, two-year advanced course, and research programs is 42. Additionally, the following major international programs are available (Table 4.1): annual artists-in-residence programs and workshops, which accept mainly foreign artists; international exchange programs lasting up to several months with the Australian National University School of Art & Design in Canberra, the Academy of Arts, Architecture and Design in Prague, and the Gerrit Rietveld Academie[13] in Amsterdam; and summer training courses at the Pilchuck Glass School near Seattle and the Corning Museum of Glass in Corning, New York. By implementing a multi-layered curriculum involving collaboration with specialists who have maintained networks with the world's most advanced glass education and research institutes, participants can experience the rich glass art culture of Europe and the United States, including their various techniques and designs.[14]

Perspectives gained from these relationships among the diversity, potentiality, internationality, and locality of glass have helped Toyama City to promote the development of an environment that facilitates the creation of world-class art and culture projects, thereby securing leaders who share the aims of "Glass City Toyama."

b.   **Incubation facilities and support systems in collaboration with TGS and TGAM**

Over 50% of the students and assistants involved in TIGA courses are university graduates and 90% come from outside Toyama Prefecture. Both young talent with high aspirations and leading professionals in the field migrate to the

Glass Art Hills neighborhood in search of the abovementioned international and diverse education and research programs as well as a creative environment with abundant networking opportunities. Although the local settlement rate of TIGA graduates (currently n=570) is 50% immediately after graduation, just over 20% of all graduates had opened private studios.[15] This is partly due to the limited employment opportunities and competition for securing a livelihood, leading some graduates to go abroad in search of work.[16] However, according to the aforementioned Czech faculty member at TIGA,[17] the 20% settlement rate of the glass artists who establish their own studios is quite good for the following reasons.

Incubation facilities and other systems for promoting glass art in Toyama have been supported by the Toyama City government in cooperation with TGS. In addition, Toyama City has promoted local settlement from other regions in order to secure the necessary human resources that will sustain and enhance the vitality of the region. For example, there are student dormitories with production spaces available for trainees as well as accommodation and production facilities for artists staying long-term.[18] After graduation, it is possible to rent a glass studio, sell one's work in shop, and get orders (note 2). Furthermore, if a graduate or other artist is hired as a technical staff member at TGS, they can participate in R&D projects and collaborate with local governments, universities, and companies, provide technical guidance on popularization and enlightenment projects for citizens and tourists (note 8), and expand sales channels through social media (note 7). Also, over 120 artists, most of whom are TIGA graduates, live in the city, and are studio entrepreneurs. When studio owners who have more than 10 years of professional experience hire young artists, a public support project provides funds to subsidize part of the labor costs, thereby encouraging both employers and employees to settle in the community.[19] As described above, support for establishing and operating individual studios locally and building personal connections has been continuously provided by the mutually complementing organizational functions of TIGA and TGS in Glass Art Hills Toyama.

Meanwhile, TIGA's graduation exhibition is held every year in collaboration with TGAM. The effect of this collaboration is that a wide range of information is continuously disseminated to both domestic and international stakeholders as well as local residents and tourists. This is made possible by the network established through TIGA's international exchanges and TGAM's international exhibitions. In addition, the collaboration between TIGA and TGAM creates a value-creation channel for glass artists that can help many of them feel a sense of accomplishment and gain recognition as professionals.

c.   **Cooperation with creative professionals and institutes all over Japan and overseas**

New cultural projects, employment, industrialization, high-level professional exchanges, and local vitality are realized through cooperation between glass education and research institutions as well as networking with creative environments in Japan and overseas. The professional career data[20] of local artists demonstrate their notable achievements in open-call exhibitions, museum exhibitions, and gallery exhibitions in Japan and overseas, their involvement in a wide range of regional collaboration art projects, and their status as employees and artists-in-residence at institutions overseas.

TGAM has hosted an international open-call exhibition every three years since its inception. It has also organized special exhibitions in cooperation with the world-renowned Corning Museum of Glass and master artists with connections to glass art schools such as the Pilchuck Glass School near Seattle, the Art & Design School of Australian National University in Melbourne, and Academy of Arts, Architecture, and Design in Prague. These open-call exhibitions attracted 1,110 submissions from 46 countries and regions for the first international competition in 2018 and 1,126 submissions from 51 countries and regions for the second competition, with around 75% of the submitted works coming from well-known artists, experienced instructors, and college students of overseas (TGAM 2018, 2021). In addition, faculty members and graduates of TIGA and TGS often participate in these art exhibitions.

Moreover, the multi-layered support systems and presentation opportunities have greatly benefited the entrepreneurs who graduated from TIGA and have opened and manage their own studios and galleries and are responsible for everything from production to sales. One such example is Taizo Yasuda,[21] who was born in Kobe, studied at TIGA, and spent a total of six years at TGS, first as a student and later as a technical staff member. After that, Yasuda turned an old house in Toyama City into an individual studio and a gallery, using it as a base from which to spread new kinds of knowledge, designs, and techniques to the local glass art culture and to work with younger local artists through individual activities and collaborative projects. These creative achievements also contribute to the development of the tourism industry and create a vitality that supports the internationalization and sustainability of the city.

Their achievements are made possible and supported by the individual international and local activities of TIGA faculty members and graduates as well as through organizational relationships with TGS, TGAM, and other education and research institutes in Japan and overseas, including the abovementioned art universities, museums, and vocational schools.

4.4   GLASS CITIES: PRAGUE, THE CZECH REPUBLIC AND CORNING, THE UNITED STATES

Although Toyama is the only major "Glass City" in Japan, an advanced counterpart can be found overseas in the Czech Republic, namely, Prague, whose Academy of Arts, Architecture, and Design, contemporary art museums, research libraries, and glass studios have fostered a unique glass art cluster since the middle of the 20th century. Prague's success as a "Glass City" is due to the following three factors (Petrova 2005). First, the tradition of Bohemian handmade glass dates back 800 years and was supported by governments including the Holy Roman Empire and Habsburg Dynasty. Local techniques have been passed down from generation to generation, fostering craftsmen at vocational schools and factories in production clusters located north of Prague. Second, the unique current education system fosters various kinds of specialists, techniques, designs, and "creativity" in both glass art and glassware production, from hands-on glass practice in elementary school to comprehensive art research in academics and production of studio glass art in the graduate school of an art university. Šára, the Czech faculty member at TIGA,[22] is a typical example of someone who has received education through this system. He had hands-on experience with general art at a hobby school in his elementary school days and later specialized in glass studies in a high school of applied arts and glass in Kamenický Šenov followed by a vocational school of applied arts and glass in Nový Bor, both in well-known glass production clusters in the western part of the Czech Republic. He also studied art theory, applied art, and design involving natural materials and graduated with a Master of Art from a university of applied art and design. After that, he began his professional career as a studio glass artist and designer. He has collaborated with well-known studios and workshops and has led many educational programs at his own studio as well as world-class glass facilities such as the Academy of Arts, Architecture, and Design in Prague, the Pilchuck Glass School, and the Corning Museum of Glass. Third, the Academy of Arts, Architecture, and Design,[23] which has introduced much innovation in art and design, has been engaged in professional development influenced by the theory and practical exercises of the German Bauhaus art school since the 1940s. The new concept of producing glass in glass studios was popularized mainly by professors and graduates from the Academy of Arts, Architecture, and Design, and eventually spread to other education institutes in Europe, the United States, Australia, and Japan (e.g., TIGA). Studio glass art is glass art that is produced in an individual studio. Before the advent of such studios, glass art and glass crafts were generally produced in glass factories or group studios. The curriculum and approach to fostering young talent at TIGA were modeled on the theories and methods of the Academy of Arts, Architecture, and Design, and the Pilchuck Glass School. For this reason, TIGA has invited many Czech and American artists who are familiar with these techniques, expressions, theories, and networks to serve as faculty members or to participate in artists-in-residence and workshop programs.

The results of social collaboration among education and research organizations, local industries, governments, and glass artists have built a sustainable "creative environment" where international and regional characteristics intersect and fuse, thereby fostering individual learning, producing artwork materials, and facilitating R&D (Saxenian 1994; Lazzeretti et al. 2021).

Another "Glass City" is Corning City, New York, where the headquarters of the pioneering glass company Corning, Inc. is located. The Corning Museum of Glass,[24] with which TGAM jointly organized an exhibition in 2022, was founded in 1951 to commemorate the company's 100th anniversary. The museum is a not-for-profit organization dedicated to the art, history, technology, and science of glass materials. The museum is home to one of the world's most important and innovative collections, which covers 3,500 years of glass history up to the present, and brings together world-class artists, including former TIGA faculty members, designers, craftsmen, researchers, tourists, patrons, and citizens. The glass museum has galleries for a diverse array of exhibits, and a school studio for artists-in-residence, demonstrations, and lectures. It also has an innovation center for hands-on exhibits in the science and technology of glass as well as a research library with 260,000 objects. So, the Corning Museum of Glass itself promotes both regional and international glass art, culture, and industry. Similar to TIGA, TGS, and TGAM, the Corning Glass Museum also engages in talent development, research and development, and dissemination of knowledge, and thus has huge operating expenses, massive spaces, and a large staff.

The activities of the museum are supported by the company and the local government as well as patrons of art, design, technology, and history and have helped to establish a global creative environment for collaboration and exchange through human resources development, R&D, tourism, and programs open to the public, bringing attention to the strengths of art and culture that symbolize the city, despite having a population of only 10,000. The industrial glass company Corning and its glass art museum are icons that symbolize this glass city.

4.5   DISCUSSION

This study examined the case of Toyama City as a glass art cluster. Table 4.1 presents the names of new cultural resources (facilities and human resources) and processes (methods and systems) that reflect the achievement of the Glass City Making concept in realizing public-private professional partnerships.

By promoting itself as an international glass art hub built on a new local cultural resource rooted in the tradition of glass manufacturing while developing talent, Toyama City has been able to secure talent and leaders from all over Japan and overseas as well as develop infrastructure in the form of educational and research facilities in just over 30 years from the start of the "Glass Village" initiative to the present. Toyama City set the goal of becoming a Glass City, aiming to enhance the cultural quality of life and realize a sustainable vitality in an aging society. This goal was achieved through the cooperation among local government, education and research institutes, corporations, citizens, and glass artists and designers from all over Japan and overseas.

The realization of the "Glass City" concept is attributable to the enthusiasm and activities of the professionals involved. It also reflects the aims of comprehensive urban plans and compact city strategies to realize an "Eco-Model City" and a "FutureCity" by emphasizing the coexistence of people, cities, and nature (discussed in Section 4.2, Table 4.1). These efforts are not limited to cultural activities nor are they dependent on the economic policies recommended by experts in a wide range of fields.

Meanwhile, a vocational school (TIGA) now exists as a major actor that provides an open and tolerant space, which Florida (2002) argued, was necessary to realize creative clusters, through mutual complementarity between related external organizations (TGS and TGAM) and affiliated human resources. TIGA has carried out international exchanges with high-level stakeholders that develop human resources at high technical levels in cooperation with TGS and TGAM, thereby achieving Piore and Sable's (1984) ideal of "flexible specialization."

Various support systems that help glass artists develop skills, find work, and secure studio space have led many of these artists to settle in the area as studio entrepreneurs, which in turn has helped to establish a new production system, human resources development, and the facilities necessary to form a glass art cluster that continues to attract professionals, citizens, and tourists. This has also had spillover effects such as spreading new techniques, designs, knowledge, and human exchanges (Table 4.1, discussed in Section 4.3).

4.6   CONCLUSION

The "Glass City Toyama" concept has developed into a new urban production environment by reorganizing local resources and actors, resulting in an art and culture cluster (Piore and Sable 1984).

The success of Glass City Toyama can be attributed in part to the fact that the local government established TIGA, TGS, and TGAM and then entrusted the organizational management and training projects to experts who play an active role in various fields both in Japan and overseas (discussed in Section 4.3, Table 4.1). As a result, business planning and human resource development are carried out by artists and other specialists who continue to create pioneering art achievements that reflect high knowledge of artistry and design, thereby producing cultural, economic, and social spillover effects (Throsby 2001) in the region. Although this chapter does not quantify the economic ripple effects on cities, it is important to note that the establishment and operation of vibrant art museums, vocational schools, and studios internationally has increased the number of cultural exchange events through multi-layered activities involving highly skilled professionals and local citizens in the city (Table 4.1). Thus, the enrichment of urban functions through increased human exchanges involving local citizens from the suburbs as well as visitors from outside the city will clearly amplify the economic ripple effects.

That is, the balanced synergistic effects between sustainability-oriented innovation and techniques (e.g., Lazzeretti et al. 2021), which are realized by artists, designers, and stakeholders as well as complementary networks between education and research institutes, local government, entrepreneurs, industry, and the local community, are the most important factors in successfully building an international art cluster using local cultural resources, as opposed to an industrial cluster.

The case study presented in this chapter suggests that innovation and development of artistic cultural clusters require an international, diversified, and attractive production system based on social cooperation among education institutes, local government, corporations, local society, and affiliates in order to secure young talent and instructors to settle locally while working on a global stage. Accordingly, further academic and practical surveys comparing similar cases involving overseas glass art clusters, such as the Glass Cities of Prague and Corning, which have served as models of education and research institutes in the field of glass, are necessary (as noted in Section 4.4). TIGA, TGAM, TGS and related professionals (faculty members and graduates) have maintained mutual networks with leading overseas professionals, and these networks have contributed to the realization of organizational and regional exchanges in glass art. Such networks can also facilitate human resources development and the realization of new high cultural resources and methods to enhance urban vitality and enrich the lives of local residents, from children to seniors, through hand-made glass production in an ecosystem as opposed to digitalization.

ACKNOWLEDGMENT

This chapter is a development of the Toyama Glass City study (2022) "Policy and Human Resource Development for a Sustainable Creative Environment: Glass Art Hills Toyama and Ceramic Valley Mino, Japan," *Cultural Economics*, 1, 43–56. This study was supported by a grant from the Japan Society for the Promotion of Science (JSPS22K13023). Finally, I would like to express my sincere gratitude to all those who cooperated in this research, specifically the faculty, alumni, and staff of the Toyama Institute of Glass Art, the staff and alumni of the Toyama Glass Studio, and the director and staff of the Toyama Glass Art Museum.

NOTES

1. On January 1, 2024 (Japan's biggest national holiday), a magnitude 7.6 earthquake hit Noto Peninsula, Ishikawa Prefecture (prefectural capital is Kanazawa). Many died in Noto region and are also seriously affected in Toyama, Niigata, and Fukui as same as Ishikawa. Here, I express my deepest sympathy to all disaster victims.
2. Confirmed with the Chief Professor of TIGA and the Director of TGS (November 5, 2021). Also, TGS glassware sales were not affected by the pandemic and ranged from JPY64MM ($457K) to JPY99MM ($708K), according to annual reports released by Toyama Grass Craft Center (FY2018–2022). The yen against the dollar has fallen by up to 30% over the two years from 2021. USD 1 ≈ JPY 140.
3. See "future-city.go.jp," Japanese Cabinet Office. Concept Of FutureCity Initiative *FutureCity Eco-model City*, future-city.go.jp and "FutureCity," Toyama City.
4. According to the interview survey with then-members of the vocational school establishment committee on March 13, 2021, and the conference minutes of the committee in 1989.
5. Information about TIGA was extracted from the official website, student recruitment guidelines, school pamphlets, school self-evaluation reports, *20th anniversary*, *Thirty Years of Toyama Institute of Glass Art Forms for the Future*, *Glass City Toyama Development*, and interviews survey with the Director, the Administrative Manager, the Chief Professor, other professors, graduates, and students (October 9, 2019; January 7, 2021; November 5&26, 2021; July 16, 2022), and other obtained materials.
6. Information about TGS was extracted from the official website, annual reports, and interviews survey with the Director and the Administrative Manager (November 26, 2021), the Deputy Director (July 16, 2022), and other obtained materials.
7. Major R&D includes the creation and sales of products in unique colors and designs from 1999, 2001, 2007, 2017, and 2021. Major projects include the glass wall installation at the newly renovated Toyama Station in 2015 and a collaboration with the US glass master Dale Chihuly and TGAM (Table 4.1). See note 2 for the production sales amount.

8. Annual visitors to TGS were 97,000 in FY 2019 and 73,000 in FY 2021. Attendees of the annual open workshop of blown-glass were 11,000 in FY 2021 and 12,000 in FY 2019. These figures include the closing periods during the COVID-19 pandemic.
9. Annual users were around 5,000.
10. Information about TGAM was extracted from the official website, annual reports, interviews survey with the Director, the Chief Curator, and the Administrative Manager (October 9, 2019), and other obtained materials.
11. Visitor numbers were provided by the Toyama Glass Art Museum (2021). *Thirty Years of Toyama Institute of Glass Art Forms for the Future*.
12. According to the official website of TIGA and various individuals.
13. University of Applied Art and Design.
14. Interview conducted with TIGA graduates who attended these overseas programs, were artists-in-residence, and/or participated workshops at TIGA.
15. See Maeda (2022). Data were obtained from TIGA.
16. Interview conducted with the Chief Professor at TIGA (January 7, 2021).
17. Interview conducted at TIGA (November 5 &26, 2021).
18. Annual users were 11 for 57 days in FY 2019.
19. Five or six young people have received subsidies for three years in recent years.
20. Refer to the official website of the artists, exhibition pamphlets and career surveys (Maeda 2021).
21. Interview conducted at his studio (November 6, 2021).
22. Interview conducted at TIGA (November 5, 2021; February 16, 2023). Refer to official website of the artist.
23. Refer to Matsuda (2016) and TGAM (2016).
24. Information about the museum was extracted from the official website and a presentation by the Senior Program Manager, the Corning Museum of Glass at TGAM (July 15, 2022).

REFERENCES

"Concept Of FutureCity Initiative" *FutureCity Eco-model City* available at future-city.go.jp as of January 31, 2023.

Florida, R. (2002). *The Rise of the Creative Class: and How It's Transforming Work, Leisure, Community, and Everyday Life*, Basic Books.

Ikegami, J., Fukuhara, Y., & Ueki, H. (Eds.) (1998). *Cultural Economics*, Yubinkaku.

Lazzeretti, L., Boix, R., & Capone, F. (2008). "Do Creative Industries Cluster? Mapping Creative Local Production Systems in Italy and Spain" *Industry and Innovation*, 15(5), 549–67.

Lazzeretti, L., Capone, F., Caloffi, A., & Sedita, S. (Eds.) (2021). *Rethinking Clusters: Towards a New Research Agenda for Cluster Research*, Routledge.

Maeda, A. (2021). "Formation Process of the Creative Environment Responsible for Innovation and Succession: Art University and Craft Artists in Kanazawa, Japan" *International Journal of Crafts and Folk Art*, 2, 27–50.

Maeda, A. (2022). "Policy and Human Resource Development for a Sustainable Creative Environment: Glass Art Hills Toyama and Ceramic Valley Mino, Japan" *Cultural and Economics*, 43–56.

Markusen, A. (2006). "Urban Development and the Politics of a Creative Class: Evidence from a Study of Artists" *Environment and Planning A*, 1921–1940.

Matsuda, A. (2016). "International Exchange: Visit to Academy of Art, Architecture, Design in Prague" Toyama University, Chapter 10, 22–23.

Nakajima, N., Takayanagi, Y., & S. Nagano (2020). *Urbanism of Compact City Toyama*, University of Tokyo Press.

OECD (2012). *Current Compact City Practices in OECD Countries*, OECD.

Petrova, S. (2005). "Captured Light and Space," *Czech Contemporary Glass*, Expo 2005 Aichi Japan, 19.

Piore, M., & Sable, C. (1984). *The Second Industrial Divide*, Basic Books.

Rockefeller Foundation, "100 Resilient Cities," available at d631b84b1e-fe41685a_3gm6b18ip1.pdf (rockefellerfoundation.org) as of August 31, 2022.

Sasaki, M. (2020). "The Creative Cities of 21st Century: From Japanese Cases" *International Journal of Crafts and Folk Art*, 13–29.

Saxenian, A. (1994). *Regional Advantage: Culture and Competition in Silicon Valley and Route 128*, Harvard University Press.

Throsby, D. (2001). *Economics and Culture*, Cambridge University Press.

Todate, K. (2016). *History of Modern Ceramics Art in Japan*, Abe Publishing.

Toshimitsu, I. (2019). *Bauhaus: History and Concept*, My Book Service.

Toyama City (2016). "Toyama City Cultural Creation City Vision" development policy available at https://www.city.toyama.lg.jp/bunka/bunka/1010545/1003006.html as of July 1, 2023.

Toyama Institute of Glass Art (TIGA) (2019–2022). Students Recruitment Guidelines; Annual School Pamphlets, School Self-Evaluation Reports available at https://www.toyamaglass.ac.jp/document as of July 1, 2023.

Toyama Institute of Glass Art (TIGA) (2011). *20th anniversary*.

Toyama Institute of Glass Art (TIGA) (2021). *30 years of Toyama Institute of Glass Art*.

Toyama Glass Art Museum (TGAM) (2021, 2018). *Toyama International Glass Exhibition*.

Toyama Glass Art Museum (TGAM) (2021). *Thirty Years of Toyama Institute of Glass Art Forms for the Future*.

Toyama Glass Art Museum (TGAM) (2019–2022). Annual Reports, Annual Plannings, Financial Statements released by Toyama City available at https:///www.city.toyama.lg.jp/bunka/bunka/1010544/1003027.html as of July 1, 2023.

Toyama Glass Craft Center (2018–2022). Staff Recruitment Guidelines of Toyama Glass Studio (obtained material), Annual Reports, Annual Planning, Studio Pamphlets available at https://www.toyama-garasukobo.jp/institution/finance.html as of July 1, 2023.

Yamada, K., & Ito, H. (2013). "The Restructuring of Regional Specialization in a Pottery Production Center and Entrepreneurship: A study of Shigaraki Pottery Production Center" *Organizational Science*, 4–15.

APPENDIX 4.1   THE POPULATION PYRAMID OF TOYAMA CITY AS OF SEPTEMBER, 2022

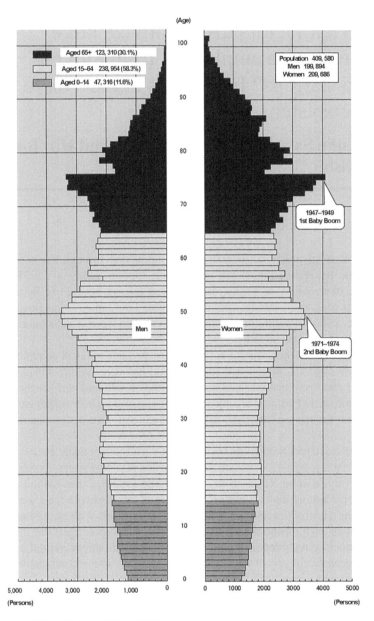

Source: Official Website of Toyama City.

5. What factors disincentivize large enterprise employees from moving to startups? Interviews in the Tokyo ecosystem

Yuho Sasamori, Moet Onodera, and Hirotoshi Kishi

5.1 INTRODUCTION

Japan's industrial policy actively promotes innovation through the support of startups, but delivering effective, efficient support poses a significant challenge. Particularly, in Tokyo, an ambitious plan is in place to increase the number of startups tenfold within a five-year timeframe (Japan Business Federation, 2022), instilling high expectations for the rapid expansion of the entrepreneurial ecosystem (EE).

However, one potential hurdle in this process pertains to talent acquisition. Previous research on human and social capital has revealed the substantial impacts of employee quantity and quality on the growth and performance of startup companies (Bosma et al., 2004; Koch et al., 2013). These earlier studies indicate that securing exceptional startup personnel is pivotal for expanding the EE.

Nonetheless, talent acquisition within Japan's EE faces two key challenges. The first relates to a passive attitude toward starting new businesses. According to a report by Mizuho Research & Technologies (2020), Japan exhibits the lowest scores among major advanced countries in terms of both the extent of entrepreneurial activities and the proportion of individuals with aspirations to establish their own businesses. Consistent survey findings suggest that Japan is internationally regarded as a country with a limited entrepreneurial spirit and a reduced likelihood of cultivating entrepreneurs. The second challenge revolves around a scarcity of entrepreneurs and startup employees. Despite a lack of comprehensive statistical data on this issue, practitioners involved in startup support have highlighted this concern. For instance, in a blog article by an advocate for startups at the University of Tokyo, Umada has presented the possibility, based on his own observations and investor perspectives, that the shortage of entrepreneurs might be a factor contributing to the limited investment in newly established startups in Japan:

> In my involvement with individuals in the early stages of entrepreneurship, I have come to believe that the decrease in the number of entrepreneurs is the primary reason. I often hear similar concerns from investors. There is an increasing trend of considering the establishment of venture capitalist-led programs and startup studios, with the mindset of "if entrepreneurs are not available, we will create them ourselves." Personally, I also have the impression that the number of entrepreneurs has not increased significantly. (Umada, 2022)

Tomoko Namba (founder of DeNA Co., Ltd., a provider of mobile online services, and a member of the Japanese government's Growth Strategy Council), has also drawn attention to the insufficient influx of entrepreneurs and employees into the startup sector:

> The current situation in Japan is such that there are fewer individuals aspiring to become entrepreneurs and there is a lack of people joining startups. This can be attributed to the fact that talented individuals tend to be locked into large corporations and also due to technical reasons that make it difficult to create attractive stock option incentives. (Namba, 2021)

One factor contributing to the uncertainties surrounding talent acquisition within the EE lies in Japan's distinctive employment practices. The Ministry of Economy, Trade and Industry (METI), responsible for overseeing Japan's economy and industry, identifies the "transition from the Japanese employment system" as a prominent challenge in economic and industrial policies. The term "Japanese employment system" encompasses Japan's unique employment systems and cultural norms. Since the post-war period of rapid economic growth, various systems and cultural practices, such as "bulk hiring of new graduates" (where large cohorts of university graduates are hired all at once), "seniority-based promotion" (where hierarchical positions within a company are determined by years of service), and "lifetime employment" (where individuals remain with a single company until retirement), have become prevalent, primarily within enterprises. These practices and cultural norms hinder the inflow of exceptional talent into startups and serve to inhibit Japan's EE (METI, 2021).

In conclusion, as talent acquisition assumes increasing significance within Japan's EE, concerns persist regarding the scarcity of entrepreneurs and startup employees, potentially influenced by traditional employment practices prevalent in the labor market. Therefore, this study aims to investigate the factors impeding the inflow of talent into Japan's EE. First, to identify significant pathways of talent movement, it undertakes a comprehensive review of previous studies on talent acquisition and mobility within the EE and the current state of talent mobility in Japan's labor market. Subsequently, it reports interviews with individuals who have undergone career transitions or possess expertise in facilitating such transitions and synthesizes their insights. Based on these findings, implications are discussed from the perspectives of research, enterprises, and policy development along with emerging trends that could contribute to future research agendas.

5.2   LITERATURE REVIEW

5.2.1   Human Resources (HR) in Startups and EE

Human capital has been acknowledged as an indispensable determinant of startups' initial viability and expansion. Theoretical investigations have revealed that investment in human capital substantially contributes to the perseverance and advancement of startups by surmounting the uncertainty associated with the latent potential of novel ideas and knowledge (Audretsch & Thurik, 2000, 2001) and by effectively addressing the unique challenges faced by nascent firms, such as the "liability of newness" (Cooper et al., 1994; Freeman et al., 1983; Stinchcombe, 1965).

While earlier studies have predominantly focused on the founders of start-ups, recent research has extended its scope to encompass analysis of entrepreneurial teams and employees, elucidating their impact on startup growth (e.g., Koch et al., 2013; Østergaard et al., 2011).

As a larger unit of analysis, companies as organizations have been focused on, especially in the human resources (HR) research. Empirical studies have shed light on the formation process of entrepreneurial teams (Held et al., 2018; Klada, 2018; Patzelt et al., 2020) and the patterns of recruiting initial employees and their interplay with founder attributes (Fairlie & Miranda, 2017). Furthermore, the distinctive behaviors exhibited by startups in their early stages, such as their utilization of more informal employment practices, suggest a differentiated concept of HR management compared to that in established corporations (Hornsby & Kuratko, 2003; Mayson & Barrett, 2006).

Moreover, the EE can be regarded as an even larger unit of analysis. Roundy and Burke-Smalley (2021) propose the concept of "Entrepreneurial Ecosystem – Human Resource Management," which entails collaborative efforts among organizations within the EE on HR management, including talent acquisition, even in the face of resource constraints encountered by early-stage startups.

To summarize, HR assumes a critical role in the survival and expansion of startups, and a wealth of research has accumulated across various units of analysis, encompassing entrepreneurial teams, employees, companies, and the EE as a whole.

5.2.2   Reality in Japan

5.2.2.1   Demand for HR in Tokyo's EE
This section examines the salient attributes of the human capital imperative within Japan's EE and considers strategies to procure such exceptional aptitude within the confines of said ecosystem. Among the entrepreneurial milieus making up Japan's entrepreneurial landscape, our research focuses on that of Tokyo. Tokyo, being the national capital and hub of political and economic affairs, has garnered an exalted stature, as elucidated by the Startup Genome's Global Startup Ecosystem Ranking 2022, in which it secured a coveted 12th position worldwide. This demonstrates its status as the most burgeoning ecosystem amid Japan's urban tapestry.

     Within Tokyo-centric ecosystem, the desired expertise predominantly resides in personnel whose contributions are pivotal in propelling business expansion from the nascent seed stage to the incipient phase. This claim rests on the cogent underpinnings delineated by the Startup Genome. First, governmental entities, including the Government of Japan and the Tokyo Metropolitan Government, have initiated fervent endeavors to furnish nascent enterprises with substantive economic assistance. Second, in terms of the median quantum of funding per funding round, the seed round typically approximates the global average, while the Series A round falls disappointingly at less than half of the global benchmark (Startup Genome, 2022).

     Moreover, survey-based research conducted by the Tokyo Chamber of Commerce and Industry (2022) has meticulously identified the stumbling blocks enfeebling the expansionary ambitions of small- and medium-sized enterprises within Tokyo's confines. The most salient predicaments encountered during the progression toward business expansion, ranked in descending order, are "pioneering novel sales channels," "procuring requisite funds," and "securing indomitable human resources." This shows that Tokyo's ecosystem exhibits a surging appetite for individuals possessing the acumen to navigate uncharted sales territories and orchestrate resourceful fundraising initiatives, thereby stimulating the growth of startups.

5.2.2.2   Structure of labor market
We now delve into the locations and methods of acquiring the highly sought-after talent mentioned earlier. First, we logically examine the sources of talent required for startups. In Japan, the labor market has traditionally been categorized based on the level of skill mastery. Its categories include the "new graduate market," which targets recent university graduates, and the

"mid-career market," which caters to individuals already employed in other companies or organizations. Generally, it is believed that mid-career professionals who are already working can contribute more actively to areas such as exploring new sales channels and securing funding, as discussed in the Section 5.2.2.1 on the Demand for HR in Tokyo's EE.

Next, we explore the structure of the mid-career job market. Despite a dearth of research examining the structure of the job market in the context of startups, we can draw upon a general overview of Japan's job market to conduct a logical analysis. The pool of mid-career professionals that startups can recruit can be divided into three categories: those within the EE, those outside the domestic EE but within Japan, and those located overseas. The first category encompasses individuals working in other startup companies, venture capital firms, and startup-related enterprises. second category includes individuals associated with non-startup sectors, including traditional enterprises. This third category consists of individuals affiliated with organizations located outside Japan (Figure 5.1).

Each of these three types of talent pools presents its own advantages and disadvantages in terms of talent acquisition for startups. As mentioned in the section on HR in startups and EE, hiring talent within the EE entails relatively lower adaptation costs to the unique working environment and culture of startups. However, the limited talent within the ecosystem hinders its expansion.

Therefore, talent from external sources is considered essential. However, it is considered challenging to attract external talent due to the low mobility of talent. This issue is associated with the concept of lifetime employment (the practice of individuals remaining with the same company from their initial employment until retirement, spanning approximately 40 years). This practice aims to recoup the educational investments made in new graduates by extending employee tenure. It is built on the premise of long-term continuous employment, with wage systems and retirement benefits designed to incentivize employees to remain with the company for an extended period, meeting the expectations of both employers and employees (Fujimoto, 2017). This practice persists, with the highest proportion of employees categorized by length of service being "20 years or more" (21.7%) as of 2020 (The Japan Institute for Labour Policy and Training, 2022). Japanese employers tend to have longer employee tenure than in other countries. Among 16 countries in Europe, the Americas, and Asia, Japan ranks second after Italy in terms of the proportion of employees with a tenure of over 10 years (Ministry of Health, Labour, and Welfare, 2022). Additionally, in Japan, larger companies tend to attract a greater number of prospective job seekers among new graduates compared to small- and medium-sized enterprises (The Small and Medium Enterprise Agency, 2022). Consequently, there is a perceived lack of mobility among employees of enterprises within Japan's labor market. However, as discussed later, there has been an increase in job transitions among employees of enterprises in recent years (Statistics Bureau of Japan, 2020). One factor contributing to this trend is the rise of employment agencies. According to the Ministry of Health, Labour, and Welfare (2021), there has been a growing number of agencies that connect companies with talent and receive rewards from companies. Although there is no readily available research specifically targeting agencies focused on the mid-career job market, it is assumed that such agencies play significant roles in that market.

Lastly, acquiring foreign talent has proven challenging due to the perception among individuals from abroad that Japan's working environment is unappealing (METI, 2022). For instance, according to the OECD's Talent Attractiveness 2023, Japan ranks 22nd out of 38 countries in terms of attractiveness to highly educated workers (OECD, 2023), and the International Institute for Management Development's World Talent Ranking 2022 places Japan 41st out of 63 countries (IMD, 2022). Reasons include Japan's distinctive employment system discussed earlier, the limited English proficiency among Japanese company employees, which hinders effective communication, and the perception of exclusivity toward foreigners (Morita, 2017, 2018; Oishi, 2012).

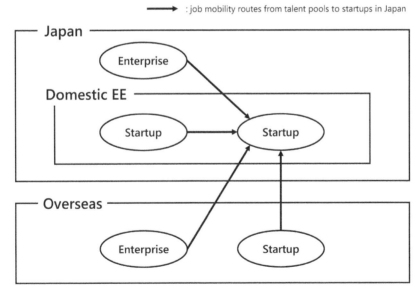

Source: Author's own work.

Figure 5.1   *HR pools and mobility routes around startups in Japan*

Given these current circumstances, the METI (2022) has identified two HR-related issues as economic policy focal points: the monopolization of talent by enterprises and the lack of highly skilled foreign individuals resulting from the homogeneity of the talent pool. In the startup context, one immediate challenge in improving talent acquisition is to attract talent from pools external to the EE, including enterprises, as well as from overseas, into the EE.

5.2.3   Labor Mobility and Job Shifts

Here, we provide a concise overview of research on labor mobility within the labor market. In the realm of academia, the movement of individuals within the market is termed labor mobility, encompassing the phenomenon of job shift (wherein individuals voluntarily depart or are terminated by their employers). With regard to voluntary job shift patterns, two prominent models have been posited. The reward–resource model posits that individuals possessing greater personal resources are less susceptible to dismissal and more inclined to relinquish their present employment (Tuma, 1976). Conversely, the segmented labor market model divides it into distinct classifications, concentrating on the ramifications of these typologies on employment mobility. For instance, within closed employment relations (where employees are less interchangeable) compared to open employment relations (characterized by heightened interchangeability), it is postulated that employees exhibit reduced proclivity for voluntary or involuntary job departure (Hachen, 1990).

Consequently, research investigating job shifts from the standpoint of individual employees and the labor market exists. Moreover, in relation to the challenges underscored in the section on the reality in Japan, namely the talent pool of enterprises and foreign talent pool, there are numerous empirical studies primarily centered on immigration policies and employment fluctuations. Nevertheless, to our current knowledge, there is a dearth of research specifically addressing job shifts from enterprises to startups.

5.3   RESEARCH METHODS

The preceding deliberations suggest that the challenges confronting Japan's EE pertain to the attraction of seasoned professionals from external origins, particularly non-startup sectors, such as prominent corporations and overseas sources. Furthermore, there is a dearth of research on entities that transcend the confines of the EE and transitions from enterprises to startups.

Consequently, we propose a study exclusively concentrating on job shifts from major corporations to startups within Japan. The research framework is portrayed in Figure 5.2. The framework postulates the existence of employees contemplating a transition from an enterprise to a startup, with an employment agency facilitating this job shift. However, note that the agency has entered into a contractual agreement with client companies seeking talent acquisition, entitling them to success-based remuneration for talent referrals. Additionally, job shifts from enterprises to other enterprises are far more frequent than to startups.

The research question to be addressed is as follows: What are the factors impeding job shifts from enterprises to startups?

To answer this question, the following investigations were conducted. The target population encompassed individuals in Japan who had undergone job shifts from enterprises to startups as well as the agencies who facilitated these transitions. The aim was to identify inhibitory factors that resonate with real-world circumstances. As previously mentioned, job shifts to startups are uncommon in Japan; hence, it is believed that there is a need for research on inhibiting factors from the perspective of individual job seekers. However, if the survey is targeted at individuals without any experience in job transitions, there may be significant variations in their intention, understanding, and seriousness regarding job shift, making it difficult to ensure the reliability and validity of their responses.

To gain an overview of job shifting experiences, a preliminary survey was conducted using a web-based questionnaire among 101 individuals who had moved from large corporations to startup companies. The respondents were selected from across Japan in collaboration with a web survey support company. The questionnaire included multiple-choice questions about their experiences during the job shift process and their perceptions of startups prior to the job shift. The results revealed that during the process of moving from large corporations to startups, a small number of individuals had gained informal work experience in startups, such as through pro bono work.

Considering this an innovative behavior pattern, interviews were conducted targeting individuals who had shifted jobs and acquired informal work experience in startup companies. From the initial pool of 101 respondents, six (five in their 30s and one in their 40s) with experience of informal employment in startups were chosen for interviews. Individuals with diverse pre- and post-transition industry backgrounds and career trajectories were selected to avoid undue bias in the responses. The interviews were conducted online between June 2021 and February 2022, each lasting approximately 60 minutes. Employing a semi-structured interview format, the questions predominantly focused on the anticipated drawbacks and inhibitory factors encountered during the job shift process, thereby eliciting insightful responses.

Lastly, interviews were also conducted with agencies. Companies within Japan that facilitate job shifts from enterprises to startups were identified, and interviews were conducted with seven such agencies to garner their perspectives on the challenges and inhibitory factors involved in facilitating the movement of enterprise employees to startups. Interview times and formats were consistent with those conducted with individuals who had experienced job shifts.

The collected data were subjected to thematic analysis (Braun & Clarke, 2006). Transcriptions of the interview recordings were employed to extract themes through an inductive coding process, with a minimum of two research-ers collaboratively ensuring the validity of the findings.

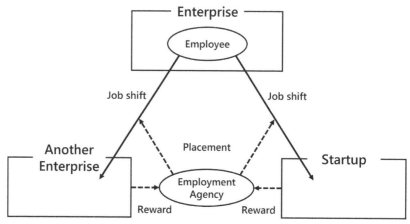

Source: Author's own work.

Figure 5.2   Research framework

5.4   RESULTS

A comprehensive analysis of the interviews revealed several noteworthy gaps within the organizational structure involving employees, startups, enterprises, and agencies (Table 5.1). These gaps emerged as factors that impede job shifts.

The first gap is the mismatch between the employees' preferences regarding employment forms and the rules set by enterprises. Some employees who express an initial interest in transitioning to startups prefer a partial engagement, such as undertaking side jobs or engaging in pro bono work. This preference originates from a keen interest in gaining a deeper comprehension of the intricacies involved in startup operations. Alternatively, it is driven by a desire to mitigate anxiety arising from the perception that the responsibilities of an individual employee within a startup surpass those within a larger enterprise, owing to the relatively smaller size of the workforce. However, it appears that enterprises frequently prohibit side jobs due to concerns about their potential impact on work obligations, thus creating challenges for employees seeking gradual involvement with startups. Consequently, this gap prevents employees from progressively familiarizing themselves with the intricacies of startup tasks.

The second gap is the difference in the costs for startups and employees during the hiring process. Employees need to acquire information about startups and explore new job prospects while simultaneously fulfilling their current job responsibilities. They aim to minimize the time and effort expended in the process. Conversely, startups tend to exercise caution during their hiring procedures. This cautious approach stems from their aspiration to attract high-caliber talent and mitigate the risk of new employees mishandling confidential information. Such startups often demand extensive document submissions and conduct multiple rounds of interviews, thereby prolonging and complicating the hiring process to mitigate risks. However, these pro-cedures increase the costs incurred by employees. The startup's recruitment process demands more from employees than initially anticipated, resulting in a discrepancy between expectations and reality.

The third gap relates to the disparity in job descriptions between the HR market and startups. A multitude of companies, including startups, actively seek talented individuals in the HR market. Typically, companies publicly disclose comprehensive job descriptions that delineate the nature of the work and associated responsibilities. Prospective employees utilize job descriptions as a foundation for exploring and comparing potential employers during the job search process. However, startups operate with relatively compact teams, engaging in diverse tasks and promptly responding to unforeseen circum-stances. Consequently, the job content and scope within startups are accompa-nied by higher levels of uncertainty. As a result, startups often face challenges in developing accurate job descriptions and fail to provide the information necessary for employees to compare them on an equal footing with other large corporations in the job market.

The fourth gap encompasses the discrepancy in rewards between enterprises and startups from the perspective of agencies. As elucidated above, agencies within the HR market facilitate the placement of employees in diverse compa-nies and receive compensation based on their success in matching candidates with employers. The compensation varies depending on the company, but startups often offer lower rewards than larger enterprises. This disparity can be attributed to the fact that startups operate with smaller overall budgets, including for research and development endeavors, due to the early stage of their business. Consequently, startups tend to have lower competitiveness in acquiring mid-career professionals in the HR market compared to enterprises.

Table 5.1   Gaps found through interviews

Types of gap	Differences between actors	Data from interviews
Work preferences	Employees want to gradually become involved with startups, but their current companies have rules prohibiting side jobs.	"Under my current employer's rules, I can't work at a startup while receiving compensation." (an employee) "Working on tasks unrelated to my current employer during weekdays is strictly prohibited, making it impossible to work at a startup that requires weekday availability." (an employee)
Recruitment process	Finding startup jobs costs employees little, but the recruitment process is time-consuming for startups.	"There is uneasiness about hiring C-class (e.g., CFO) CO candidates from large corporations who have no prior experience working at a startup." (an agency) "In contract arrangements such as pro bono work, it is common not to establish non-disclosure agreements (NDAs), which raises significant concerns about information leakage." (an agency)
Job descriptions	Startups have difficulties describing their jobs and the demand for employees in the HR market.	"The nature of startup work varies greatly depending on roles, business models, and phases, but it has not been effectively communicated to potential talent." (an agency)
Rewards to agencies	Agencies are incentivized to promote large enterprises (which offer higher rewards than startups).	"Supporting job recruitment for startups is less profitable compared to supporting job recruitment for large-scale enterprises. Additionally, the selection process for startups involves more rounds and longer durations, resulting in a higher workload for agents compared to supporting enterprise recruitment." (an agency)

Source: Author's own work.

5.5   DISCUSSION AND CONCLUSION

This study addresses the dearth of talent as a forthcoming challenge in the expansion of Japan's EE. Our research highlights that transitions from established enterprises to startups offer a promising avenue to attract highly sought-after professionals from external sources into the EE. While prior studies have acknowledged the potential difficulties of employee mobility within enterprises due to Japan's employment system, few have focused on this job shift trajectory and inhibitory factors.

Therefore, we conducted surveys and interviews with individuals who had undergone job shifts from enterprises to startups or facilitated such transitions.

We then categorized the factors that could impede job shifts into four distinct types.

Next, we address two limitations of this study. First, we acknowledge the need to enhance the validity of hypothesis construction. The objective data used to formulate the hypothesis partially align with the study's theme. More targeted investigations should be conducted to bolster the reliability of the hypothesis. For instance, while the demand for talent within Japan's EE is inferred from the recognition of challenges faced by startup companies, analyzing job postings data submitted by startups could provide a more accurate understanding of their actual needs. Second, we acknowledge the selection bias in our research subjects. Ideal study subjects would be individuals who attempted but ultimately abandoned job shifts from enterprises to startups. However, due to potential wide variations in their experiences, the challenge of judging the validity of each sample, and the limited willing participants who meet the criteria, we chose to focus on successful cases of job shifts and have the respondents reflect on their experiences. In this case, biases such as overlooking fundamental issues or discrepancies between respondents' recollections and actual events cannot be eliminated.

Furthermore, we discuss the present study's implications for academic research, management, and policymaking. In terms of academic research, the findings can be viewed as a starting point for forging connections between research on EEs and labor mobility from a fresh perspective. Previous studies on talent-related topics in startup research have often concentrated on entrepreneurial individuals and founding teams from the standpoint of company creation, with relatively few investigations delving into employee acquisition, which is deemed increasingly vital for company growth and EE expansion. Moreover, most have examined HR management within companies, paying scant attention to the inflow of talent from outside the EE. Conversely, previous studies on labor mobility have focused on the decision-making of individual workers, only partially exploring the distinctiveness of startups, such as studies on immigrant entrepreneurs. Given these shortcomings, the theme of talent influx from external enterprises into the EE holds significant potential for both EE and labor mobility research, and it can be regarded as meaningful for both fields. This theme is particularly pertinent for countries with low labor mobility, such as Japan, where its potential significance is considerable. In the future, we plan to develop this research by focusing on the content of the four identified gaps and studying their actual manifestations and the extent of their impact on job shifts.

From a management standpoint, we identified specific bottlenecks for both enterprises and startups. For enterprises, we suggest that talent mobility is impeded by rules hindering employees' involvement in startups, such as restrictions on participation in startups on a part-time or partial basis. Broader benefits could be achieved by means of (1) questioning and reevaluating assumptions surrounding side jobs and resignations, (2) perceiving engagement in startups as a positive means of acquiring cultural knowledge and expertise to enrich the company, and (3) recognizing former employees who have transitioned to startups as alumni rather than adversaries (viewing them as valuable contributors to expanding the company's network). On the other hand, for startups, we propose reevaluating the hiring process to reduce the demands placed on employees. It must be reaffirmed that proactive talent acquisition is crucial for startup growth, while striking a balance with risk mitigation.

We identified various potential focuses for policymakers. For instance, to address the hindrance to mobility stemming from internal systems within enterprises, support measures could include comprehensive guidelines to promote system reforms and financial assistance and certification for companies that implement mechanisms enabling employees to engage in startups without leaving. Additionally, the challenges related to crafting job descriptions for startups and the insufficient rewards provided to agencies can be attributed to the prevailing labor market logic shared by enterprises and startups. Consequently, by creating policies that reshape the market structure, such as establishing a favorable talent market for startups or subsidizing the disparity in rewards for agencies facilitating job shifts to startups compared to those in larger companies, the government can play a pivotal role.

5.6   FUTURE TRENDS

The focus so far has been on transition of employment from major corporations as we delved into the present condition of Japan's startup talent landscape. Here, we shed light on forthcoming trends regarding shifts within the domestic market.

Japan shows a growing inclination toward migrating from enterprises to mega-venture enterprises, expansive establishments that have flourished after their inception as startups, often exemplified by renowned companies like Yahoo! Japan and Mercari. Positioned between enterprises and startups, these mega-ventures exhibit work cultures and operational aspects akin to those of startups while resembling enterprises in terms of remuneration and the bestowed level of employee responsibilities. It is posited that these mega-venture enterprises possess the potential to serve as intermediaries in the progression from enterprises to smaller startups. By allowing employees to go from enterprises to mega-venture firms and subsequently gravitate toward smaller startups, these mega-ventures harbor the capacity to facilitate job transitions from enterprises to startups.

Moreover, the government has initiated supportive measures to expedite such transitions. For example, the METI has implemented subsidization programs that target the aforementioned employment agencies and enable employees to engage with startups on a partial basis while maintaining their employment within enterprises rather than wholly departing from the corporate environment to join startups. This is intended to bolster business initiatives wherein employees from enterprises can contribute to startups at relatively nominal costs. Through experiences of partial engagement at minimal expenses, employees affiliated with major corporations may develop an inclination toward shifting to startups, consequently fostering the overall job transition process. Given the inevitable challenges that will come with the transformation of the structure of Japan's talent market and job transitions, it is imperative to enact policies that can smoothly adapt to these evolving circumstances.

Conversely, factors capable of effectuating structural changes are also manifesting beyond Japan's borders. For instance, there exists a movement wherein foreign corporations are venturing into Japan's manufacturing sector, particularly in areas such as semiconductors, propelled by concerns pertaining to economic security. This development increases the likelihood of an influx of international talent into Japan. Additionally, layoffs within North American IT-centric major corporations may raise demand for job stability among the workforce. In this context, the limited mobility observed within Japan's labor market can be perceived as a manifestation of the heightened job stability it offers, thus serving as a potential impetus for the inflow of foreign talent. The evolving trends indicate the possibility of a stronger nexus between Japan's domestic talent market and foreign arenas, thereby underscoring the necessity for policies that foster connectivity between the two.

REFERENCES

Audretsch, D.B., & Thurik, A.R. (2000). Capitalism and democracy in the 21st century, from the managed to the entrepreneurial economy. *Journal of Evolutionary Economics*, 10, 17–34.

Audretsch, D.B., & Thurik, A.R. (2001). What is new about the new economy: Sources of growth in the managed and entrepreneurial economies. *Industrial and Corporate Change*, 10(1), 267–315.

Bosma, N., Van Praag, M., Thurik, R., & De Wit, G. (2004). The value of human and social capital investments for the business performance of startups. *Small Business Economics*, 23, 227–236.

Braun, V., & Clarke, V. (2006). Using thematic analysis in psychology. *Qualitative Research in Psychology*, 3(2), 77–101.

Cooper, A.C., Gimeno-Gascon, F.C., & Woo, C. (1994). Initial human and financial capital as predictors of new venture performance. *Journal of Business Venturing*, 9, 371–395.

Fairlie, R.W., & Miranda, J. (2017). Taking the leap: The determinants of entrepreneurs hiring their first employee. *Journal of Economics & Management Strategy*, 26(1), 3–34.

Freeman, J., Carrol, G.R., & Hannan, M.T. (1983). The liability of newness: Age dependence in organizational death rates. *American Sociological Review*, 48, 692–710.

Fujimoto, M. (2017). "What is Japanese long-term employment system? Has it vanished?" *Japan Labor Issues*,1(1), 22–25.

Hachen, D.S. (1990). Three models of job mobility in labor markets. *Work and Occupations*, 17, 320–354.

Held, L., Herrmann, A.M., & Mossel, A.V. (2018). Team formation processes in new ventures. *Small Business Economics*, 51, 441–464.

Hornsby, J.S., & Kuratko, D.F. (2003). Human resource management in US small businesses: A replication and extension. *Journal of Developmental Entrepreneurship*, 8, 73.

IMD (2022). World Talent Ranking 2022. https://www.imd.org/centers/wcc/world-competitiveness-center/rankings/world-talent-ranking/.

Japan Business Federation (2022). Startup Breakthrough Vision. https://www.keidanren.or.jp/policy/2022/024_honbun.html.

The Japan Institute for Labour Policy and Training (2022). *Databook of International Labour Statistics 2022*.

Klada, T. (2018). Unraveling entrepreneurial team formation: A qualitative study among funded ventures. *SAGE Open*, April–June, 1–15.

Koch, A., Späth, J., & Strotmann, H. (2013). The role of employees for post-entry firm growth. *Small Business Economics*, 41, 733–755.

Mayson, S., & Barrett, R. (2006). The 'science' and 'practice' of HRM in small firms. *Human Resource Management Review*, 16(4), 447–455.

Ministry of Economics, Trade and Industry (METI) (2021). Current Status of Talent Development in Response to Structural Changes in the Labor Market and Efforts by the Ministry of Economy, Trade, and Industry. https://www.jasso.go.jp/gakusei/career/event/guidance/__icsFiles/afieldfile/2021/07/09/keisan.pdf.

Ministry of Economics, Trade and Industry (METI) (2022). The Future Direction of Economic Industrial Policy. https://www.meti.go.jp/shingikai/sankoshin/sokai/pdf/031_01_00.pdf.

Ministry of Health, Labour, and Welfare (2021). Report of the Study Group on Employment Intermediation in the Labor Market. https://www.mhlw.go.jp/stf/newpage_19817.html.

Ministry of Health, Labour, and Welfare (2022). Analysis of the Labour Economy 2022. https://www.mhlw.go.jp/stf/wp/hakusyo/roudou/21/21-1.html.

Mizuho Research & Technologies (2020). Global Startup Ecosystem Enhancement Project (Survey on Entrepreneurship). https://www.meti.go.jp/policy/newbusiness/houkokusyo/GEM2020_report.pdf.

Morita, L. (2017). Why Japan isn't more attractive to highly-skilled migrants. *Cogent Social Sciences*, 3(1), 1306952.

Morita, L. (2018). Does doing things the Japanese way attract highly-skilled migrants? *Cogent Social Sciences*, 4(1), 1430725.

Namba, Tomoko (2021). Negative Cycle Surrounding Japanese Startups. https://www.cas.go.jp/jp/seisaku/seicho/seichosenryakukaigi/dai8/siryou4.pdf.

OECD (2023). Talent Attractiveness 2023. https://www.oecd.org/migration/talent-attractiveness/.

Oishi, N. (2012). The limits of immigration policies: The challenges of highly skilled migration in Japan. *American Behavioral Scientist*, 56(8), 1080–1100.

Østergaard, C.R., Timmermans, B., & Kristinsson, K. (2011). Does a different view create something new? The effect of employee diversity on innovation. *Research Policy*, 40, 500–509.

Patzelt, H., Preller, R., & Breugst, N. (2020). Understanding the life cycles of entrepreneurial teams and their ventures: An agenda for future research. *Entrepreneurship Theory and Practice*, 45, 1119–1153.

Roundy, P.T., & Burke-Smalley, L.A. (2021). Leveraging entrepreneurial ecosystems as human resource systems: A theory of meta-organizational human resource management. *Human Resource Management Review*, 32(8).

The Small and Medium Enterprise Agency (2022). White Paper on Small and Medium Enterprises in Japan.

Startup Genome (2022). Startup Ecosystems, Tokyo. https:// startupgenome .com/ ecosystems/tokyo.

Statistics Bureau of Japan (2020). The Number of People Who Change Jobs Continues to Increase: The Number of People Who Changed Jobs in 2019 is the Highest Ever. https://www.stat.go.jp/data/roudou/topics/topi1230.html.

Stinchcombe, A. (1965). Social structures and organizations. In *Handbook of Organizations*, ed. by J. March, pp. 142–193. Chicago: Rand McNally.

Tokyo Chamber of Commerce and Industry (2022). Report on Survey of Startups and Start-up Companies 2022. https://www.tokyo-cci.or.jp/page.jsp?id=1030023.

Tuma, N.B. (1976). Rewards, resources, and the rate of mobility: A nonstationary multivariate stochastic model. *American Sociological Review*, 41, 338.

Umada, Takaaki (2022). Shortage of Entrepreneurs: Challenges in Japan's Startup Ecosystem in 2022. https://blog.takaumada.com/entry/2022-lack-of-entrepreneurs.

PART II

European perspective on clusters in times of
uncertainty

6. Do clusters help companies to "go green"? Experience of Polish National Key Clusters

Anna Lis, Marta Mackiewicz, and Anna Wendt

6.1   INTRODUCTION

The process of green transformation including the green economy, decarbonization or circular models is becoming a key focus for the EU striving for climate neutrality. The aforementioned concepts are linked by a common concern for the environment through the pursuit of more efficient use of natural resources, reduction of carbon emissions and pollutants, and increased energy efficiency. The green economy, driven by public and private investment, is an example of a resource-efficient and low-carbon approach, based on the use of energy sources that generate low levels of greenhouse gases. The circular economy, in turn, is a new model of production and consumption that involves extending the life cycle of products by, among other things, sharing, renting, reusing, repairing and recycling or reclaiming. The European Commission (2020) explains that circularity is essential to a more comprehensive transformation of industry towards climate-neutrality and long-term competitiveness. It can deliver substantial material savings throughout value chains and production processes, generate extra value and unlock economic opportunities. Circular business models can lead to a green transformation by promoting sustainable practices, reducing waste and pollution, increasing resource efficiency, and creating new revenue streams. Circular business models promote the reuse, repair, and recycling of materials, which reduces the amount of waste generated and minimizes pollution. This reduces the environmental impact of business operations, making them more sustainable and green. By adopting circular business models, companies can optimize their resource use and reduce their reliance on virgin materials. This not only helps to conserve natural resources but also reduces the cost of production. Green transformation is not only happening at the macro level, but is also important at lower levels of aggregation. At the micro level, companies, as the last links, will have to adapt to changing climate regulations, on the other hand – looking especially from the meso level – they can be important precursors of change. The latter is especially true of the opportunities presented by cluster cooperation. The potential of clusters as agents of change in the processes of dissemination and implementation of green transformation practices has been recognized by the European Commission. This is reflected in the establishment of the Expert Group on Clusters, which has prepared recommendations on the use of formalized cluster structures to accelerate green and digital transformation (European Commission, 2021).

Unfortunately, research on the implementation of green transformation using clusters is still scarce. Very few works have been found in the literature referring to the concept of a cluster or related concepts, such as an innovation ecosystem (Del Vecchio et al., 2021; Konietzko et al., 2020; Korhonen, 2001; Spicka, 2022), eco-industrial park (Dong et al., 2018, Shi et al., 2010; Taddeo et al., 2012), or regional industrial system (Baas & Boons, 2004). Although the industrial cluster concept is very well established in the literature, there is little reference to the green economy or low-carbon economy. Slightly more papers have been published in relation to the circular economy (Baldassarre et al., 2019; Bressanelli et al., 2022; Ormazabal et al., 2018; Konietzko et al., 2020). The thread of cluster cooperation in the context of green transformation also appears in connection with industrial symbiosis (Wen & Meng, 2015; Bain et al., 2010; Baldassarre et al., 2019; Daddi et al., 2017) and industrial ecology (Baas & Boons, 2004; Deutz & Gibbs, 2008). The identified papers are primarily based on qualitative research (case studies) and are descriptive, conceptual or exploratory in nature, indicating the early stage of research in this area. Most studies focus on single countries, mainly European (due to well-developed cluster policies) and then Asian (especially with regard to China), with a single-industry approach dominating. Also notable is the omission of the aspect of formalized cluster cooperation in the form of a cluster initiative or cluster organization. And finally, no works were found that described a set of practices implemented by clusters in the field of green transformation, which, in addition to its cognitive value, would also carry application benefit.

Meanwhile, industrial clusters treated as geographic and industry concentrations, due to their attributes, can be extremely useful in implementing the idea of a green, low-carbon and circular economies. Particularly valuable in this regard can be formalized clusters, which additionally create coordination centers by providing an appropriate governance structure. For this reason, they can carry out some tasks related to green transformation, although this area has not yet been clearly identified in the cluster-based economic development policy framework. Our aim is to identify the fullest possible set of green practices used by cluster organizations, derived from their core attributes. The main research question we pose is what is the role of cluster organizations in supporting green transformation from the perspective of both cluster coordinators and members? In our research, we focused on Polish mature cluster structures, with a particular emphasis on National Key Clusters, which have both the characteristics of a cluster and a cluster organization. We considered that Poland, as a country with a well-developed cluster policy and at the same time an as yet underdeveloped area of green transformation, could provide a good background for research in this area.

Our chapter consists of four main parts. First, we discuss the concept of cluster and cluster organization, pointing out those attributes that can predestine cluster structures to be agents of change in the process of green transformation. Then, we present the research methodology. The fourth part contains the results of the research, with a focus on the perspective of cluster coordinators and members, while the last part includes a discussion, scientific and practical implications, as well as research limitations and directions for further research.

6.2 ATTRIBUTES OF THE CLUSTER AND CLUSTER ORGANIZATION AS A BASIS FOR GREEN TRANSFORMATION PROCESSES

6.2.1 Cluster Attributes

Consideration of the basic attributes of a cluster related to the green transformation process should begin by looking at the definition of a cluster as developed by Porter (2008). The cluster was described as "[...] geographic concentrations of interconnected companies, specialized suppliers, service providers, firms in related industries, and associated institutions (for example, universities, standards agencies, and trade associations) in particular fields that compete but also cooperate [...], linked by commonalities and complementarities" (Porter, 2008, pp. 213–215). The definition provided highlights five main attributes of a cluster, namely geographic and industry concentration, relationships, coopetition and complementarity. The attributes mentioned above are the most important, but not the only ones that describe the specifics of a cluster. To this list can also be added such characteristics as networking, specialization, proximity (in various dimensions) or a common development trajectory. In addition, the element that unites the entities in the cluster is also the range of benefits obtained from cooperation. Marshall (1890) was the first to recognize them in industrial districts, calling them externalities, which include the presence of a labor market with specialized skills, access to non-commercial industry-specific inputs, and the diffusion of knowledge, especially tacit knowledge shared within the industrial atmosphere. Porter

(2008), on the other hand, strongly emphasizes the effect of synergy as a result of interaction, which can be understood as the ability to create additional value by remaining in a relationship based on interaction with other entities, with this value being higher than the sum of the values that would be generated by each of these entities separately (Lis & Lis, 2021).

From the point of view of green transformation processes, the most important attributes of a cluster are geographical and industry concentration, for all other characteristics are basically derivatives of these. This applies primarily to geographical proximity, which can be the basis for the development of systemic cooperation, both in the implementation of the circular model and the creation of cluster structures focused on energy generation and distribution (e.g. in the form of energy clusters). In the context of industrial districts, Marshall has included "place" in the pool of the most important components of the industrial district concept, understood very broadly – as a "territorial community" formed from a network of relationships of actors grouped in a given territory. This is because geographical proximity can translate into the formation of social proximity, that is, relationships based on trust. The short distance separating the companies fosters frequent interactions, the establishment of further acts of exchange between the entities, and thus the development of informal relationships that, over time, can develop into permanent business ties (Lis & Lis, 2023). As this distance between partners shortens, the costs of exchange (including knowledge and information) and communication decrease (Hansen, 2015; Doloreux, 2002). The link between geographical proximity and social proximity and the positive impact of social proximity on cooperation results has already been well documented in the literature (Lis & Lis, 2023). It is only worth emphasizing, one of the effects of the entities remaining in geographical proximity, and the resulting social proximity, is to improve the processes of learning and knowledge exchange (especially tacit knowledge), which leads to an increase in innovation potential (Boschma, 2005, Boschma et al., 2014, Doloreux, 2002). Moreover, social proximity not only fosters the generation and flow of knowledge, but also reduces the risk of opportunistic behavior (Boschma, 2005) and lowers the likelihood of conflict between cooperating entities (Boschma et al., 2014). It can thus be a significant enhancer when building and developing links between partners in circular business models or energy clusters. An additional reinforcement of such localized interactions and repetitive acts of exchange in one area may be anchored in a single system of values and socio-cultural norms known to all actors (Simmie, 2003). This creates the ground for the formation of a sphere of common goals, values and a code of ethics (Balland et al., 2015). From the point of view of green transformation, this can mean a concerted effort by companies to ensure a favorable business environment not only in the economic pillar, but also in the social and environmental pillars. The latter mentioned is related to the implementation of green solutions, as part of a green, low-carbon or circular economies. Clusters are able to provide an effective institutional system for such activities, for they will ensure the coexistence of three key elements (Boschma, 2005): stability (they provide relatively stable conditions for interaction) while being open to emerging opportunities, and flexibility through rapid adaptation to changes in the surrounding environment.

The second attribute mentioned – industry concentration – provides good ground especially for the development of cooperation within circular models. This is because it enables the creation of a variety of relationships, based either on complementarity and diversity, which facilitates the development of vertical ties, along the value chain, or on similarity, which in turn strengthens the development of horizontal relationships, often based on coopetition. It should also be emphasized that cooperation within a cluster goes beyond cooperation within individual sectors, as Porter emphasizes: "[...] cluster boundaries rarely conform to standard industrial classification systems, which fail to capture many important actors in competition as well as linkages across industries. Clusters normally consist of a combination of end-product, machinery, materials, and service industries, usually classified in separate categories" (Porter, 2008, p. 220). The most important pillar of the cluster is enterprises producing final products and services, working with suppliers of specialized inputs, parts, machinery and services, enterprises in related sectors, manufacturers of complementary products and other enterprises located further down the value chain. In addition, as Porter points out, a cluster is made up of many other component entities. In addition to enterprises, the cluster structure includes R&D institutions, government agencies, specialized infrastructure consisting of financial institutions, bridging institutions, standards agencies, industry associations and other collective private institutions that support the development of the cluster. The necessity of the coexistence of different industries in a territory was already emphasized by Marshall (1890) in the context of the development of industrial districts. The presence of a particular variety of industry diversification was even a prerequisite for a specific area to be considered a district in the sense proposed by Marshall. It should be understood as differentiation based on related, cooperating and competing business entities that not only occupy different places in the value chain of the leading industry, but form additional chains, only indirectly related to the leading chain, however, affecting it. From the point of view of the implementation of the circular economy, a base of diverse enterprises, representing different links in the value chain, can guarantee the development of effective cooperation, based on the heterogeneity of partners that differ in the scope of competence, but at the same time represent similar perceptions and pursue common goals. On the other hand, from the point of view of implementing a green and low-carbon economy, a system of related institutions (especially those representing all the elements in the quadruple helix structure) can be a facilitator in introducing common green solutions that benefit the entire industry developing in a given region.

6.2.2   Cluster Organization Attributes

The cluster concept is treated not only as an analytical concept, but also as a tool for developing cluster policy, implemented at the intersection of regional, industrial and innovation policy, involving the stimulation of competition and simultaneous cooperation between enterprises, and looking more broadly: between sectors and regions (Porter, 2008). As a result of the launch of cluster-based policies in many EU countries, numerous cluster initiatives have been established to support cluster development (Sölvell et al., 2003). Cluster initiatives are defined as "[...] organized efforts to increase the growth and competitiveness of clusters within a region, involving cluster firms, government and/or the research community" (Sölvell et al. 2003, p. 15). They are also interchangeably referred to as cluster organizations, understood as formally established organizations which function at a higher level of aggregation and consists of institutional members who have intentionally and voluntarily joined it, engaging in collaboration to achieve common and/or individual goals (Lis, 2018; Lis & Lis, 2021). The members of a cluster organization are primarily businesses, but also include other entities, including R&D institutions, business support institutions and public authorities. The entity that manages the cluster organization is its coordinator, also called "facilitator" or "cluster manager." The cluster organization is therefore the organizational base of the cluster and performs representative functions. On the one hand, it is the disposer of funds allocated to support the development of a particular cluster, and on the other hand, it coordinates activities carried out in cooperation of its members.

Cluster organizations share the same attributes as clusters, while additional attributes can also be distinguished in them, which can provide organizational reinforcement for the cluster. This makes an excellent ground for carrying out changes as part of green transformation. Cluster organizations enhance the effects of geographical concentration, through social integration, by initiating repetitive contacts between members, and by providing access to information and knowledge through the organization of various events and training. They also strengthen the effects of industry concentration by fostering various forms of cooperation, both in the context of process integration (group purchasing, launching joint sales platforms, setting quality standards), in the context of organizational integration (e.g. joint project implementation, value chain cooperation), as well as in regard to integration of the entire industry (cooperation with public authorities and with external entities to implement common green transformation activities for the industry). They can also initiate innovative activities by collaborating on the development of green technologies or eco-friendly products and services. In addition, the effects of activities undertaken by cluster organizations are not limited to their members; they also affect external stakeholders, which primarily include companies in the same industry (not affiliated with a cluster organization), public authorities or the local community. This is because the idea behind the functioning of the cluster organization is to develop (in cooperation between the private and public sectors) solutions that are beneficial from the point of view of the industry and the region, which is the basis for the implementation of a green, low-carbon and circular economies. In addition, functioning in cluster organizations can promote access to information about issues common to the industry and region and help spread green practices. The aforementioned joint activities were also distinguished by Sölvell et al. (2003). Among the areas identified as priorities for cluster initiatives, they listed education and training (provide technical training, provide management training), innovation and technology (facilitate higher innovation, promote innovation, new technologies, analyze technical trends, diffuse technology within the cluster, enhance production processes, establish technical standards), and policy action (lobby government for infrastructure, improve regulatory policy, lobby for subsidies, conduct private infrastructure projects).

However, most relevant to building effective systems of cooperation within the green transformation is the organizational environment provided by cluster organizations, as opposed to a cluster, which is devoid of this. This is because cluster organizations offer a complex governance structure, facilitating the implementation of a variety of activities leading to the implementation of green transformation changes. They create an integrated management system for inter-organizational cooperation that can include thinking about the entire product life cycle and interactions with internal and external stakeholders. This is particularly important for the implementation of circular economy-based models, which require appropriate governance structures. The problems associated with implementing the circular economy, but also looking more broadly: green transformation processes, are complex and require more governance structures that facilitate the pooling of resources and capabilities that are beyond the boundaries of companies (Niesten et al., 2017).

6.3   METHODOLOGY

In our chapter, we refer to the results of the exploratory study aimed at addressing the following research question: In view of the accounts of both cluster coordinators' and members' accounts, what is the role of cluster organizations in supporting green transformation? Our intention is to identify the main green practices used by cluster organizations, which stem from the attributes of both the cluster and the cluster organization. In doing so, we focus on activities aimed at implementing the objectives of a green, circular, and low-carbon economies.

In order to answer the research question posed, we conducted a two-stage quantitative study, taking into account both the perspective of coordinators (first stage) and members (second stage). The selection of the sample was based on critical cases. We decided to include in the sample primarily Polish National Key Clusters, which, due to their organizational maturity, are undertaking numerous activities in the field of green transformation. National Key Clusters are cluster organizations that are accredited by the Ministry of Development and Technology. Competitions, based on which accreditation is granted, have been held since 2015. Accreditation is granted for three years. To receive it, a cluster must undergo a three-stage competition procedure, during which the following characteristics are evaluated: (i) Human, organizational, infrastructural, financial resources of the cluster, (ii) Economic potential of the cluster, (iii) Innovation of activities in the cluster, (iv) Sustainability of the cluster, and (v) Customer orientation. Moreover, these clusters must prove to have a critical mass expressed by a number of cluster members, including universities and research institutes and a number of joint research projects and so on. These clusters are considered particularly relevant to the economy, as they bring together companies and science sector institutions in areas of smart specialization. They are expected to provide directions for businesses, inspire change and set trends. There are currently 20 National Key Clusters, at the time of the survey there were 18.

The selection of clusters was based, on the one hand, on the similarity resulting from their maturity (which was determined, among others, by the age and the scope of activities), on the other hand, on the differences resulting from industry affiliation and location (surveyed clusters represent different industries and are located in different parts of Poland).

The first phase of the study was conducted in the first half of 2022. The survey included 18 Polish Key National Clusters, that is, all those that had been granted this status at the time of the survey. Questions were addressed to the coordinators of the surveyed clusters, that is, the institutions that formally managed them. The questionnaire was sent directly to cluster managers, that is, those involved in coordination and facilitation activities, which translated into a high (100%) response rate. Eighteen clusters participated in the first phase of the study. These are mature clusters – the oldest was established in 2003 and the youngest in 2018, with the median year of cluster establishment being 2007, and only two clusters in the sample operating for less than 10 years. The average number of members is 133, and the largest of the clusters in the study has 331 members. The surveyed clusters are spread across the country, or more precisely in 12 of the 16 regions (technically there are 17 regions in Poland, but one covering the capital was singled out for statistical reasons). The sample included clusters with diverse activities, with two representing Aviation and space, two representing Construction, two in Health and medical science, two in Mobility: Vehicles, rail, traffic systems, and two in Production and engineering. The others represent Manufacture of food products, Advanced packaging, New materials and chemistry, Transportation and mobility and other professional, scientific and technical activities, digital industries. Only one is classified under Energy and environment.

The second-phase study was conducted in late 2022 and early 2023. The survey was conducted with representatives of cluster companies that are members of Polish National Key Clusters and with members of other clusters with a similar level of maturity. The survey was sent to members of 20 clusters operating throughout Poland. The CAWI questionnaire was distributed to companies by clusters management and directly by the authors. Lastly, the survey sample included 54 cluster members from 11 clusters. The respondents are enterprises from various industries. These are two ICT clusters, two metalworking clusters, two aviation and space clusters, two recycling and environment clusters, one production and engineering cluster, one digital industry cluster. One cluster is related to food and biomedical industry.

The same survey questionnaire was used in both phases of the study. The measurement instrument used was based on the concept of the trajectory of development of cooperative relationships in cluster organizations (Lis, 2018; Lis & Lis, 2021), which was adapted to assess the maturity level of clusters in terms of green transformation. According to this concept, four levels of cluster cooperation maturity can be recognized, starting with level I "Integration at the unit level," through level II "Allocation and integration at the process level" and level III "Impact on the environment," and ending with level IV "Creation and integration at the organizational level." Moreover, at each level, clusters can play three main roles, namely that of integrator, direct resource provider and broker. Specific activities were abductively identified and assigned to each of the distinguished levels and roles, which were then tailored to the area of green transformation. Regarding the maturity level of clusters in terms of green transformation, it was decided that the proposed four-level life cycle would be preserved, with only a slight change to the roles of COs to emphasize their green focus, distinguishing three groups of their activities: integration, enabling access to and co-creation of resources, and education and awareness building. Besides, in order to identify additional cluster activities in the analyzed area, a literature review and in-depth interviews with coordinators of Polish National Key Clusters were additionally conducted (Lis & Mackiewicz, 2023). In this way, a structured set of green practices was created, forming the core of a validated measurement tool. The questionnaire consisted of a total of

27 questions, of which 24 questions corresponded to identified green practices, while three questions related to the strategy and organization of the cluster and company. In the case of cluster managers there were 26 questions (of which two related to the strategy). The questions were formulated in the same way – the only difference was that the cluster manager was asked about the activities undertaken by the cluster and the company about the activities undertaken by the company with relation to the membership in the cluster.

The adopted categorization of practices made it possible to assess the level of maturity of clusters in green transformation efforts. Cluster coordinators were asked to assess the importance of the practices to the green transformation process and the level of sophistication of the cluster in implementing these practices. Cluster members, in turn, evaluated opportunities to engage in particular green practices through participation in a particular cluster. All questions were based on a five-point Likert scale. In both phases, the questionnaire was pilot-tested to verify that all questions were worded in a sufficiently clear and understandable manner.

First, the distributions of cluster members' responses to the survey questions were analyzed. The survey included a set of questions previously answered by cluster managers, so it was possible to compare whether actions taken by the manager at the cluster level translate into actions by companies. The comparative analysis was conducted in the three areas described (integration, resources and education). The analysis was then carried out according to the levels of integration described above. For this purpose, the averages for each level in the two groups of respondents were compared with each other to see if there were differences between the groups of respondents, and whether activities at lower levels were more popular than more advanced activities. The final step was a correlation analysis to indicate relationships between the responses of managers and members within each cluster. Since the survey used a Likert scale, the Spearman test was used in the analyses. The empirical study was complemented by the analysis of secondary data (including internal documents of the studied clusters, Internet resources, etc.).

6.4   RESULTS

The survey, which was completed by managers and cluster members, consisted of four blocks of questions corresponding to the three roles (i.e. Integration in various dimensions, Resource access and resource co-creation, Education and awareness building) and a block of three questions about the company's strategy in relation to green transformation. The survey results are presented according to these blocks.

6.4.1   Strategy

The survey shows that there is a relatively high awareness of the need to switch to green technologies, as the majority of respondents declared that this issue is addressed in their development strategy. The relatively high propensity to implement green technologies indicates that this issue is becoming increasingly important for companies, and the activities undertaken by the cluster have a favorable ground. This is evidenced by the results obtained (Table 6.1).

Table 6.1   *Responses of cluster member companies concerning "strategy"*

Green practices in cluster strategy	I strongly disagree	I disagree	Hard to say	I agree	I strongly agree
The strategy of our company includes goals and activities related to green economy, circular economy and low-carbon economy	3.7%	5.6%	20.4%	33.3%	37.0%
The strategy of the cluster includes the goals and activities related to a green economy, circular economy and low-carbon economy	0.0%	1.9%	27.8%	27.8%	42.6%
Within the cluster, we belong to smaller subgroups (e.g. task groups) related to green economy, circular economy and low-carbon economy	18.5%	27.8%	11.1%	11.1%	31.5%

Source: Authors' own elaboration.

In a survey of cluster managers, we found that seven out of 18 National Key Clusters form working groups dedicated to green transformation. The companies surveyed only partially participate in such groups: 31.5% strongly affirmed, while 11% rather participate. Eight out of 18 of the National Key Clusters include green transformation goals in their development strategy, and seven refer to the green economy but to a limited extent. Cluster member companies are mostly aware that the cluster includes green transformation in its development strategy, but also 28% declare lack of knowledge on the subject. The number of responses saying that the cluster's strategy does not include these goals is marginal. The inclusion of green transformation goals in the cluster's strategy translates into the inclusion of these goals in companies, as 70% of respondents declare that the company's strategy includes goals and activities corresponding with these goals related to the green economy.

6.4.2   Integration

Most cluster managers declared that they initiate contacts between cluster members in the field of green economy, low-carbon economy or circular economy. One might intuitively assume that cluster activities in this area play an important role, since integration is in the DNA of clusters, and companies join clusters to reap the benefits of networking. This assumption has turned out to be questionable, as activities undertaken at the cluster level are only partially reflected in the companies' responses (Table 6.2).

The majority (63%) of surveyed cluster members declare establishing contacts with other cluster members willing to cooperate in the area of the green economy. In the remaining activities, where at the level of the whole cluster the answers gave a very positive picture, it can be doubted whether this translates into actions of cluster member companies. This applies in particular to obtaining support in improving processes related to green economy, low carbon economy or circular economy, or implementation of common standards affecting the environment, cooperation with other clusters or other entities external to the cluster, in the area of green transformation, or cooperation with public authorities in consulting new regulations or helping in lawmaking. This mainly refers to involvement in legislative work, consultations, lobbying and so on, in the area of green transformation.

Slightly worse results can be observed in companies' participation in the creation of joint product or service offered in the area of green economy, low carbon economy or circular economy, building local value chains or involvement in launching new ventures (e.g. start-ups, special purpose vehicles, energy clusters) related to the green economy.

6.4.3   Resource Access and Resource Co-creation

Clusters create a favorable environment for knowledge exchange. This is especially true for knowledge about the green economy. Knowledge flows between entities in the cluster are more efficient than outside the cluster, thanks to the fact that there are common goals in the cluster, mutual trust, and thanks to the involvement of the cluster manager, barriers that limit knowledge exchange are eliminated. This is also reflected in the results of the survey (Table 6.3).

The largest share of cluster member companies (61%) declare that through participation in the cluster they gain access to information on green economy through organized meetings and thematic events (e.g. conferences, seminars). A relatively large number (56%) within the cluster participate in the develop-

Table 6.2 Responses of cluster member companies concerning "integration"

Green practices	Cluster members					Cluster members – average	Cluster managers – average
	I strongly disagree	I disagree	Hard to say	I agree	I strongly agree		
Contact initiation	9.3%	20.4%	7.4%	38.9%	24.1%	3.5	4.2
Joint procurement / joint sales	37.0%	16.7%	11.1%	18.5%	16.7%	2.6	3.1
Improving processes, common standards, green certificates	25.9%	14.8%	29.6%	13.0%	16.7%	2.8	3.9
Cooperation with public authorities in the field of lawmaking	24.1%	22.2%	14.8%	22.2%	16.7%	2.9	3.8
Cooperation with external entities (e.g. other clusters)	22.2%	20.4%	11.1%	20.4%	25.9%	3.1	4.2
Creating a joint offer	24.1%	18.5%	16.7%	16.7%	24.1%	3.0	3.1
Building local value chains / raw material base	22.2%	24.1%	20.4%	18.5%	14.8%	2.8	3.4
Launching new ventures	27.8%	20.4%	13.0%	16.7%	22.2%	2.9	3.3

Source: Authors' own elaboration.

Table 6.3   Responses of cluster member companies concerning "resource access and resource co-creation"

Green practices	Cluster members					Cluster members – average	Cluster managers – average
	I strongly disagree	I disagree	Hard to say	I agree	I strongly agree		
Access to information	5.6%	16.7%	16.7%	14.8%	46.3%	3.8	4.7
Platform for inventory and exchanging resources	20.4%	9.3%	24.1%	27.8%	18.5%	3.1	3.2
Access to resources and infrastructure	16.7%	22.2%	20.4%	18.5%	22.2%	3.1	3.3
Environmental monitoring and information sharing with key external actors	13.0%	18.5%	24.1%	22.2%	22.2%	3.2	3.2
Access to up-to-date knowledge on changes in legislation	14.8%	11.1%	22.2%	27.8%	24.1%	3.4	4.1
Implementing R&D / innovative projects	16.7%	20.4%	13.0%	14.8%	35.2%	3.3	4.2
Developing green technologies	13.0%	22.2%	9.3%	20.4%	35.2%	3.4	4.1
Creating infrastructure for energy production and distribution	29.6%	20.4%	13.0%	9.3%	27.8%	2.9	2.9

Source: Authors' own elaboration.

ment of green technologies (e.g. in cooperation with the R&D sector). Half of the respondents confirmed that within the cluster the company participates in the implementation of joint R&D or innovation projects in the field of green economy. More than half acknowledged they gain access to up-to-date knowledge on how to prepare for changes in legislation. The smallest share of surveyed cluster members participates in the creation and development of infrastructure for energy generation and distribution.

6.4.4   Education and Awareness Building

Responses to questions about involvement in various education and awareness-building activities also show that it is knowledge sharing with other cluster members that is the activity for green transformation (Table 6.4). This is particularly valuable, as combining knowledge from different fields leads to solutions that could not be created by a single company.

In response to questions related to education, more than half of the respondents confirmed that they participate in open trainings and workshops aimed at all cluster members on general principles, as well as in trainings and workshops on green economy, low carbon economy or circular economy aimed at selected cluster members dedicated to specific industries. They also participate in knowledge exchange with other members in the field of green economy (through mutual trainings, study visits, etc.). Activities aimed at education and awareness-building in the field of green economy, low carbon economy or circular economy through cooperation with educational institutions, regional authorities or other regional partners are far less popular.

6.4.5   Coordinators' Perspective vs Members' Perspective

No significant differences are apparent in evaluations of activities at different cluster cooperation maturity levels among cluster members. One would expect that activities at a fairly basic level of cluster cooperation maturity would be implemented far more often than those at higher levels, but this applies only to the first level of maturity – Integration at the unit level. At subsequent maturity levels, this relationship is not apparent.

A comparison of the average ratings from the survey of cluster managers and cluster members shows that in each area the ratings of cluster members are lower than those made by the cluster manager. The biggest differences between the ratings of the two groups of respondents are evident in the "Education and awareness building" area.

The area of "Integration" was rated rather modestly, both by cluster managers and member companies. The smallest discrepancies in evaluation are evident in the question concerning the creation of a joint product or service

Table 6.4   Responses of cluster member companies concerning "education and awareness building"

Green practices	Cluster members					Cluster members – average	Cluster managers – average
	I strongly disagree	I disagree	Hard to say	I agree	I strongly agree		
Open trainings and workshops	16.7%	13.0%	18.5%	25.9%	25.9%	3.3	4.1
Trainings and workshops dedicated to specific industries	14.8%	13.0%	18.5%	27.8%	25.9%	3.4	3.7
Knowledge sharing	11.1%	18.5%	18.5%	20.4%	31.5%	3.4	4.1
Information and education campaigns	16.7%	25.9%	20.4%	16.7%	20.4%	3.0	4.3
Promotion of pro-ecological products, services and initiatives	14.8%	29.6%	11.1%	14.8%	29.6%	3.1	4.2
Creating specialized knowledge within consortia / project groups	13.0%	27.8%	20.4%	13.0%	25.9%	3.1	3.9
Offering specialized consultancy tailored to the needs of a specific company	22.2%	16.7%	22.2%	18.5%	20.4%	3.0	3.4
Offering various forms of practical training tailored to the needs of a specific company	27.8%	13.0%	13.0%	25.9%	20.4%	3.0	4.0

Source: Authors' own elaboration.

in the area of the green economy. The largest differences in assessment are in support for streamlining processes related to green economy, low carbon economy or circular economy, or implementation of common standards affecting the environment, or in obtaining green certificates (Table 6.2).

The "Resource access and resource co-creation" area was rated higher. This area shows relatively the smallest differences between the ratings given by managers and those given by cluster members. There was the only case here where the ratings of cluster members were higher than those of the cluster manager. It relates to the exchange of information with key actors involved in designing and implementing green economy policies or legislation, and monitoring changes in the environment (Table 6.3).

The area of "Education and awareness building" was rated highest. There were also the greatest differences in the ratings given by managers and cluster members. The differences were revealed with regard to the involvement of the cluster and member companies in activities aimed at educating and building awareness of green economy (Table 6.4).

6.5   CONCLUSIONS

6.5.1   Discussion

The study shows that clusters are implementing various green practices that can facilitate the implementation of green transformation processes. Based on the survey, it is also possible to identify those activities in which the activity of clusters in this regard has become most evident. The most popular practices identified in the study can be divided into three sets. The first includes activities related to initiating contacts with other members willing to cooperate in the green transition. The second set includes those activities that obtain and exchange information and knowledge, such as access to information on the green transition and access to up-to-date knowledge on preparing for changes in legislation (through organized meetings and thematic events), participation in training and workshops on the green, low-carbon and circular economies, or participation in knowledge exchange with other members in the areas mentioned (through mutual training, study visits, etc.). Meanwhile, the third collection relates to innovation activities, that is, participation in the implementation of joint R&D and or innovation projects thematically related to green transformation and the development of green technologies (e.g. in cooperation with the R&D sector).

In contrast, the least involvement of clusters was revealed for those green practices that were associated with the most advanced forms of cooperation in process, organizational and industry integration. With regard to process integration, clusters are reluctant to engage in process improvement activities related to green, low-carbon and circular economies, implementing common standards with environmental impact, obtaining green certificates, or organizing joint procurement and joint sales for green solutions. They also show little interest in organizational integration: building local value chains or a raw material base, creating a joint product or service offering, or launching new ventures (e.g. start-ups, special purpose vehicles, energy clusters) related to the green areas under study. They are also quite passive in terms of industry integration around green transition issues. They engage poorly in cooperation with public authorities (at various levels) in lawmaking (legislative work, consultations, lobbying, etc.) or with other actors to implement green, low-carbon and circular economy activities. Finally, completely outside their interest is the activity of creating and developing infrastructure for energy generation and distribution.

The activities counted among the most popular stem from the basic attribute of a cluster – geographic concentration, emphasized in both the cluster concept and the concept of industrial districts. This is because it can be assumed that the green practices implemented by the clusters studied, related to both relationship development, knowledge exchange and innovation development, are facilitated by the common location of cluster members. In contrast, the practices identified in the least popular group are strongly related to the second cluster attribute – industry concentration. Low involvement in every dimension of integration (except social) may prove that common industry affiliation is not the glue that binds cluster members together in their joint efforts to implement green transformation processes. However, it should be emphasized that the above practices are at the same time those that are linked to the attributes of a cluster organization, so their low popularity may be due to the lack of an adequate organizational "envelope" provided by the studied clusters. Evidence of this may be the confirmed very low cooperation activity in smaller sub-groups associated with the analyzed "green" areas.

6.5.2   Theoretical and Practical Implications

Our study sheds new light on the functioning of industrial clusters, which we analyzed through the lens of cluster organizations, in the context of their role in implementing green transformation. Through our study, we were able to identify the green practices most often undertaken by clusters and further link them to the attributes of cluster structures. Our study confirmed previous findings on the relevance of geographical proximity to cluster collaboration, in our case limited to the implementation of green practices. Indeed, these practices are strongly linked to the development of social proximity, learning and knowledge-sharing processes, and the growth of innovation potential, which is combined with the advantages of geographical concentration. The link between geographic proximity and knowledge and innovation flows involving social capital is emphasized not only in the concept of cluster and industrial districts, but also in other concepts of regional development based on knowledge and innovation (such as regional innovation system, innovation ecosystem, learning region, growth poles, etc.).

The study also provides practical implications. The conclusions of the study may be relevant to cluster coordinators responsible for stimulating the cluster in specific areas and initiating joint activities. This is because it is important that clusters, building on their strengths derived from cluster attributes (i.e. co-location and sector integration) and cluster organization attributes (primarily governance structure), take a more active role in green transformation. This is especially true of creating favorable conditions for companies to implement green technologies, as well as raising knowledge and building awareness among its members. The formation of task groups can be helpful in this regard, as well as the initiation of joint projects and application for funding for the development of green technologies, and the dissemination of knowledge in this regard, both among internal (cluster members) and external stakeholders.

Our research can also be the basis for systemic solutions related to the use of cluster structures as change agents in implementing green transformation. It can be seen that clusters can play an important role in knowledge flow and awareness building. The knowledge generated in the cluster has a chance to reach other companies more effectively than outside the cluster. Therefore, a recommendation for policymakers is to give cluster members extra points when they apply for public funds for research and development in the green economy. Another recommendation is to identify the barriers that companies face in green transformation and start cooperation with clusters to remove these barriers within the instruments available under so called cluster-based development policy.

6.5.3 Research Limitations and Directions for Further Research

Our study is not free of limitations, primarily in terms of the research sample adopted. The study included a relatively small sample, additionally anchored in the Polish socio-economic conditions and cluster policy, which makes it impossible to generalize conclusions to the entire population of European clusters. Nevertheless, our survey shows some cluster inclinations in the selection of green practices initiated, as revealed from both coordinators' and members' perspectives. It is worth continuing this line of research focused on green transformation and the role of clusters in this process in a broader perspective, taking into account clusters from different countries, in order to emerge the most capacious set of cluster green practices on this basis, along with good practices that can inspire other clusters. This will simultaneously weaken the national context.

We perceive the second limitation in the research tool used. Although the tool has been validated in previous qualitative studies, we still treat it as an open set of practices. This is because we assume that our study is exploratory in nature and we need further rounds of research to finally validate the tool we are creating. Therefore, as a next step, we would like to conduct additional qualitative research based on focus groups involving two key parties, namely cluster members and coordinators. In the subsequent stages, after verifying a set of the most common green cluster practices, we intend to work on a measurement scale (using quantitative research).

REFERENCES

Baas, L. W., & Boons, F. A. (2004). An industrial ecology project in practice: Exploring the boundaries of decision-making levels in regional industrial systems. *Journal of Cleaner Production, 12*(8–10), 1073–1085. https:// doi .org/ 10 .1016/ j .jclepro.2004.02.005

Bain, A., Shenoy, M., Ashton, W., & Chertow, M. (2010). Industrial symbiosis and waste recovery in an Indian industrial area. *Resources, Conservation and Recycling, 54*(12), 1278–1287. https://doi.org/10.1016/j.resconrec.2010.04.007

Baldassarre, B., Schepers, M., Bocken, N., Cuppen, E., Korevaar, G., & Calabretta, G. (2019). Industrial symbiosis: Towards a design process for eco-industrial clusters by integrating Circular Economy and Industrial Ecology perspectives. *Journal of Cleaner Production, 216*, 446–460. https://doi.org/10.1016/j.jclepro.2019.01.091

Balland, P. A., Boschma, R., & Frenken, K. (2015). Proximity and innovation: From statics to dynamics. *Regional Studies, 49*(6), 907–920.

Boschma, R. (2005). Proximity and innovation: A critical assessment. *Regional Studies, 39*(1), 61–74.

Boschma, R., Balland, P.-A., & de Vaan, M. (2014). The formation of economic networks: A proximity approach. In A. Torre, & F. Wallet (Eds.) *Regional development and proximity relations* (pp. 243–267). Cheltenham, UK and Northampton, MA, USA: Edward Elgar Publishing.

Bressanelli, G., Visintin, F., & Saccani, N. (2022). Circular economy and the evolution of industrial districts: A supply chain perspective. *International Journal of Production Economics, 243*. https://doi.org/10.1016/j.ijpe.2021.108348

Daddi, T., Nucci, B., & Iraldo, F. (2017). Using Life Cycle Assessment (LCA) to measure the environmental benefits of industrial symbiosis in an industrial cluster of SMEs. *Journal of Cleaner Production, 147*, 157–164. https://doi.org/10.1016/j .jclepro.2017.01.090

Del Vecchio, P., Passiante, G., Barberio, G., & Innella, C. (2021). Digital innovation ecosystems for circular economy: The case of ICESP, the Italian Circular Economy Stakeholder Platform. *International Journal of Innovation and Technology Management, 18*(1). https://doi.org/10.1142/S0219877020500534

Deutz, P., & Gibbs, D. (2008). Industrial ecology and regional development: Eco-industrial development as cluster policy. *Regional Studies, 42*(10), 1313–1328. https://doi.org/10.1080/00343400802195121

Doloreux, D. (2002). What we should know about regional systems of innovation. *Technology in Society, 24*(3), 243–263.

Dong, H., Liu, Z., Geng, Y., Fujita, T., Fujii, M., Sun, L., & Zhang, L. (2018). Evaluating environmental performance of industrial park development: The case of Shenyang. *Journal of Industrial Ecology, 22*(6), 1402–1412. ProQuest Central. https://doi.org/10.1111/jiec.12724

European Commission (2020). A new circular economy action plan for a cleaner and more competitive Europe, Communication from the Commission to the European Parliament, the Council, the European Economic and Social Committee and the Committee of the Regions (COM/2020/98 final). https:// eur -lex .europa .eu/ legal -content/EN/TXT/?uri=CELEX:52020DC0098

European Commission, Expert Group on Clusters (2021). Recommendation report. Publications Office of the European Union. https://doi.org/10.2873/025534

Hansen, T. (2015). Substitution or overlap? The relations between geographical and non-spatial proximity dimensions in collaborative innovation projects. *Regional Studies, 49*(10), 1672–1684.

Konietzko, J., Bocken, N., & Hultink, E. J. (2020). Circular ecosystem innovation: An initial set of principles. *Journal of Cleaner Production,* 253. https://doi.org/10.1016/j.jclepro.2019.119942

Korhonen, J. (2001). Co-production of heat and power: An anchor tenant of a regional industrial ecosystem. *Journal of Cleaner Production, 9*(6), 509–517. https://doi.org/10.1016/S0959-6526(01)00009-9

Lis, A. M. (2018). *Współpraca w inicjatywach klastrowych. Rola bliskości w rozwoju powiązań kooperacyjnych [Cooperation in cluster initiatives: The role of proximity in the development of cooperative relationships].* Gdansk: Wydawnictwo Politechniki Gdanskiej.

Lis, A. M., & Lis, A. (2021). *The Cluster Organization: Analyzing the Development of Cooperative Relationships.* London: Routledge.

Lis, A. M., & Lis, A. (2023). *Proximity and the Cluster Organization.* London: Taylor & Francis.

Lis, A. M., & Mackiewicz M. (2023). The implementation of green transformation through clusters. *Ecological Economics, 209.* https:// doi .org/ 10 .1016/ j .ecolecon .2023.107842

Marshall, A. (1890). *Principles of Economics.* London: Macmillan.

Niesten, E., Jolink, A., Lopes de Sousa Jabbour, A. B., Chappin, M., & Lozano, R. (2017). Sustainable collaboration: The impact of governance and institutions on sustainable performance. *Journal of Cleaner Production, 155*(2017), 1–6. https://doi.org/10.1016/j.jclepro.2016.12.085

Ormazabal, M., Prieto-Sandoval, V., Puga-Leal, R., & Jaca, C. (2018). Circular economy in Spanish SMEs: Challenges and opportunities. *Journal of Cleaner Production, 185,* 157–167. https://doi.org/10.1016/j.jclepro.2018.03.031

Porter, M. E. (2008). *On competition.* Boston: Harvard Business School Publishing.

Shi, H., Chertow, M., & Song, Y. (2010). Developing country experience with eco-industrial parks: A case study of the Tianjin Economic-Technological Development Area in China. *Journal of Cleaner Production, 18*(3), 191–199. https://doi.org/10.1016/j.jclepro.2009.10.002

Simmie, J. (2003). Innovation and urban regions as national and international nodes for the transfer and sharing of knowledge. *Regional Studies, 37*(6–7), 607–620.

Sölvell, Ö., Lindqvist, G., & Ketels, C. (2003). *The Cluster Initiative Greenbook.* Stockholm: Ivory Tower.

Spicka, J. (2022). Cooperation in a minimum-waste innovation ecosystem: A case study of the Czech Hemp Cluster. *International Journal of Emerging Markets.* https://doi.org/10.1108/IJOEM-08-2021-1189

Taddeo, R., Simboli, A., & Morgante, A. (2012). Implementing eco-industrial parks in existing clusters. Findings from a historical Italian chemical site. *Journal of Cleaner Production, 33*, 22–29. https://doi.org/10.1016/j.jclepro.2012.05.011

Wen, Z., & Meng, X. (2015). Quantitative assessment of industrial symbiosis for the promotion of circular economy: A case study of the printed circuit boards industry in China's Suzhou New District. *Journal of Cleaner Production, 90*, 211–219. https://doi.org/10.1016/j.jclepro.2014.03.041

7. Green innovation and B Corps: an exploration of the technological space

Silvia Blasi, Mattia Buggio, and Silvia Rita Sedita

7.1 INTRODUCTION

The global challenge of climate change has led to increased restrictions on carbon dioxide (CO_2) emissions (Bataille et al., 2016). The negative impact of CO_2 emissions on human well-being is well-documented, and reducing these emissions is essential to preserve the living conditions of current and future generations and to build a sustainable future with high standards of living. The Paris Agreement, which came into effect in 2016, marked a significant milestone in acknowledging this challenge on a global scale. However, the journey towards decarbonization is complex and requires the participation of companies as well as the influence of national, social, and political factors (Kanie et al., 2019).

B Corps are for-profit organizations that seek to integrate social and environmental goals into their business model (Demir, 2020; Serafeim & Cao, 2013; Blasi & Sedita, 2022). These companies are legally bound to consider the impact of their decisions on all stakeholders, including employees, customers, suppliers, the community, and the environment, and not just their shareholders. The B Corp certification is awarded by the non-profit organization B Lab and indicates that a company has met rigorous standards of social and environmental performance, accountability, and transparency. B Corps are a growing movement of companies that believe in using business as a force for good and are leading the way in creating a more sustainable and equitable future. As such, they might play a key role in promoting sustainable capitalism (Chen, 2008; Tang et al., 2018).

This chapter focuses on B Corps that are involved in the development of green technology innovation. Green technologies refer to a range of knowledge, procedures, products, services, and management practices that consume fewer resources, emit less pollution, and rely on renewable energy sources. These technologies are aimed at reducing the negative impact of human activities on the environment and can encompass a range of applications such as recycling, water and air purification, and the use of clean energy sources. Despite the growing body of literature on B Corps, the topic of green innovation has not yet been thoroughly explored. This chapter aims to shed light on the technological space of B Corps and their role in green innovation through an analysis of green patents.

This chapter will address three research questions: (1) What is the prevalence and diversity of B Corps that are actively involved in technological innovation? (2) How significant is the contribution of B Corps to the advancement of green innovation? and (3) Do B Corps with a focus on innovation tend to cluster in certain geographic locations?

Our analysis of 17,933 patents showed that European countries hold the largest number of patents (over 50% of the total), followed by the United States (with 40.9%). However, patents related to environmental issues make up a relatively small portion of the total, numbering 696. Managers interested in the development of green technologies should take note that one in four innovative B Corps is also focused on green innovation, making it a potentially fertile environment for advancing green technology.

7.2   LITERATURE REVIEW

7.2.1   Hybrid Organizations and B Corps

The emergence of social entrepreneurship and dissatisfaction with the limitations of both non-profit and for-profit structures prompted jurisdictions to explore new hybrid organizational forms as a response (Kim et al., 2018; Kim et al., 2016; Kramer & Porter, 2011; Sen, 2009). The United Kingdom was one of the first countries that introduced in 2005 the Community Interest Companies (CICs), through the Companies Act 2004, as a new type of company that could be established for the benefit of the community, and since then they have become increasingly popular in the UK and other countries. They are a flexible form of organization that can take the form of a company limited by guarantee, a company limited by shares, or a community benefit society. CICs are legally required to operate in the best interest of their designated community and to ensure that their assets and profits are used for the benefit of that community. They are also restricted from paying dividends to their shareholders beyond a reasonable rate of return. This structure allows CICs to access capital from private investors while ensuring that their social or environmental mission remains protected (Billis, 2010; Nicholls, 2010). Subsequently, new forms of organizations with a social or environmental mission at their core emerged, with the purpose to serve the wider community rather than solely benefiting their shareholders. Muhammad Yunus (2010) put forth the idea of a legal structure that could accommodate both for-profit and non-profit organizations. This structure allows non-profit entities to utilize business principles while retaining their primary social objective, while also enabling for-profit companies to achieve social impact while meeting the demands of profit-maximizing shareholders. The business models of these organizations typically frequently blend the characteristics of for-profit and non-profit models (Hoffman et al., 2012). The existing literature has referred to these organizations using various terms such as fourth sector, for-benefit, values-driven, mission-driven, benefit corporation, or more generally, hybrid organizations (Hoffman et al., 2012). The hybrid organization concept involves balancing both for-profit and non-profit objectives by incorporating social and environmental missions as a central component of their business strategy, while also generating income to sustain and fulfill these objectives, similar to traditional for-profit organizations. (Battilana et al., 2012; Battilana & Dorado, 2010; Doherty et al., 2014; Ebrahim et al., 2014). Sabeti (2011) believes that this type of for-benefit structures will support "the emergence of a fourth sector of the economy, interacting with, but separate from, governments, non-profits, and for profit businesses. The rise of that sector is likely to reshape the future of capitalism" (Sabeti, 2011, p. 99).

In the context of the fourth sector, B Lab, a US-based non-profit organization, plays a crucial role in establishing the necessary framework. The aim of B Lab is to harness the potential of business as a tool to address social and environmental challenges. B Lab pushes change via three initiatives (B Corporation, 2019): (1) developing a template that state legislators can use to draft the benefit corporation law, and it lobbies for the law in state legislatures; (2) building a community of Certified B Corporations (CBC) to highlight the difference between "good companies" and companies with good marketing strategies; (3) accelerating the growth of impact investing through use of B Lab's GIIRS Ratings and Analytics platform. B Lab's GIIRS Ratings was launched at the Clinton Global Initiative in 2011 and provides an external measurement framework for both benefit corporations and B Corps. But what exactly are CBCs? CBCs are organizations that voluntarily undergo third-party social and environmental audits by B Lab (Wilburn & Wilburn, 2014; Blasi & Sedita, 2022). CBCs do not possess a legal designation, however they are able to express their commitment to social objectives and submit an annual report documenting their progress towards those objectives. The certification began in 2006 and may be attained whether or not the state in which a company is incorporated has enacted a benefit corporation law. Through its certification process, B Lab helps entrepreneurs to measure, capture, and legitimize their "social" efforts while driving a movement for social change (Hiller, 2013; Woods, 2016). In order to be designated a CBC, an organization must undergo and successfully pass a B impact assessment with a minimum score of 80 out of 200. The assessment evaluates the organization against four key metrics: community, environment, governance, and workers. The score is typically self-reported and takes into account the organization's size, sector, and nationality (Wilburn & Wilburn, 2014; Rawhouser et al., 2015). The fees for obtaining certification are established using a sliding scale that is based on the organization's annual revenue.

The distinction between Benefit Corporations and B Corps is often unclear to those unfamiliar with the different configurations of social enterprises. This confusion between the two has been documented in the literature (Wilburn & Wilburn, 2014), however, the two concepts are distinct from one another. The concept of Benefit Corporations has gained recognition globally and is implemented through various corporate forms in different legislative systems. As of 2020, similar forms of Benefit Corporations, such as "Società Benefit" in Italy and "Société a Mission" in France, have been established in 36 states in the USA, Italy, British Columbia in Canada, France, Colombia, Ecuador, and Puerto Rico (Pellegrini and Caruso, 2023). In contrast, B Corps are companies that have received certification from B Lab, a non-profit organization based in the United States (Villela et al., 2019). B Corps are also perceived by entrepreneurship scholars as new forms of organizations (Blasi & Sedita, 2022), Muñoz et al. (2018 p. 150) describe B Corps as a new category of purposeful organizations: "B Corps represent a new form of prosocial enterprising that requires to incorporate the purpose of serving the common good into the legal fabric of the business."

7.2.2   Green Innovation

Recently, a proliferation of studies has emerged that address a range of environmental challenges, likely due to the heightened interest among policymakers in implementing the Green Deal (Liu et al., 2020; van den Bergh et al., 2011). Despite this, the notion that environmental technology advancements can enhance environmental quality and foster sustainable economic growth has not yet been widely acknowledged and scientifically proved. Therefore, much has still to be analysed and reported (Castellacci, 2022). Environmental Innovation can be defined as "new or modified processes, techniques, systems and products to avoid or reduce environmental damage" (Kemp & Arundel, 1998, p. 1). Empirical and theoretical studies explored the topic of environmental innovation from a variety of angles. Arranz et al. (2021) analyse the determinants that influence the development of environmental innovation. Other authors like Chen and Ma (2021); and D'Angelo et al. (2022) show a positive effect of green investments on firm growth and productivity. Lastly, Marin and Mazzanti (2013) pinpoint the environmental effects of the adoption of environmental technologies.

Despite their potential to contribute to the development of an innovative and sustainable ecosystem, the role of socially responsible enterprises in promoting green innovation has received limited attention in the literature. Hao and He (2022) provided evidence that companies engaging in CSR practices are more likely to develop green innovation. This is because "CSR engagement requires firms to consider the interests of stakeholders such as the environment, society and consumers during their operations" (Hao and He, 2022, p. 1). Amore and Bennedsen (2016) investigated the relationship between corporate governance and green innovation, confirming a positive effect of "good governance." Moreover, they stated that the green innovation performance is positively influenced by the pressure of the context, that is areas with higher pollution abatement measures and energy sources dependence show higher number of companies engaged in green innovation. We expect to observe a similar effect when counting the role of a corporate governance certification, such as the B Corp.

Green technologies play a critical role in promoting long-term sustainability transitions. Given that environmental considerations are a significant aspect of the evaluation criteria for B Corps, this study aims to examine the connection between B Corp certification and green innovation, specifically in terms of the number of green patents applied.

There are several ways in which B Corps and green innovation are linked: (1) One of the key goals of B Corp is to promote sustainability. Green innovation can help companies achieve this goal by developing new products and services that reduce the environmental impact of their operations (Tseng et al., 2013); (2) Green innovation can provide companies with a competitive advantage by improving their environmental performance and reducing costs through increased efficiency (Porter & Linde, 1995); (3) Social and environmental responsible practices of B Corps can enhance their reputation by demonstrating their commitment to sustainability (Gehman & Grimes, 2017). Green innovation can further enhance this reputation by developing products and services that meet the needs of environmentally conscious consumers; (4) B Corp certification often requires compliance with environmental regulations (Hao & He, 2022). Green innovation can help companies meet these requirements by developing products and services that are compliant with environmental laws and regulations; (5) B Corps need to establish a fruitful collaboration with stakeholders, including customers, suppliers, and communities (Strambach, 2017). Green innovation can facilitate such collaboration by providing a platform for stakeholders to participate in the development of environmentally sustainable products and services.

7.3   METHOD

We conducted a quantitative analysis of patent data using the list of B Corps available on data.world.com, which is a cloud-based data collaboration and management platform that provides access to a vast array of publicly available data sets and allows users to discover, clean, analyze, and share data. It is designed to make it easier for individuals and organizations to work with data and collaborate with others to solve complex data problems. The platform provides tools for data preparation, analysis, and visualization, and it supports integration with other tools such as R, Python, and SQL. Data.world.com also includes features for managing data quality, privacy, and security, making it a powerful and flexible platform for working with data. The B Corp data that was retrieved from data.world.com refers to information about companies that have been certified as Benefit Corporations (B Corps) by B Lab, and include details such as the company's name, location, sector, and impact on the community, environment, governance, and workers.

We matched the list of B Corps retrieved from data.world.com with information coming from Orbis. Orbis is a database used for company information and business analysis. It provides access to comprehensive and up-to-date company information, including company profiles, ownership structures, financial data, and key personnel. The information can be used for a variety of purposes, including market research, due diligence, and credit risk assessment. The database is maintained by Bureau van Dijk, a leading provider of business information and market intelligence. From the matching, we were able to integrate data available in data.world.com with the following information:

- company name;
- country;
- city (Latin characters);
- main web site;
- company headquarters's longitude coordinates;
- company headquarters's latitude coordinates;
- NACE Rev.2 code;
- BvD ID number.

A total of 1,928 results were confirmed after matching checks. Subsequently, we cross-referenced the obtained data with the Orbis Intellectual Property (Orbis IP) database, which is a database that provides information on global patent data and the companies and groups that hold the patents. It links patent data to the companies and groups that have filed for them, providing a comprehensive view of the patent landscape. Orbis IP helps to match patents filed with the companies and organizations in question, allowing users to understand the relationships between patents, companies, and the industries they operate in. This allowed us to associate the patents filed by each B Corp in our sample. For each patent we selected the following information:

- Publication number
- Publication date
- International Patent Classification (IPC) main
- International Patent Classification (IPC) others
- Cooperative Patent Classification (CPC) main
- Cooperative Patent Classification (CPC) others
- Applicant(s) name(s)
- Applicant(s) BvD ID Number(s).

To identify which patents were considered green and to associate them with their respective applicants (i.e. innovative green B Corps), we used the list of environment-related technologies (ENV-TECH) released by the OECD. This classification divides green patents into nine main categories and 36 sub-categories using specific IPC and CPC codes. To be considered an ENV-TECH patent, it must contain at least one of the listed technological classes, either in the main categories or in the others. If a patent has multiple ENV-TECH technological classes, it is associated with the first class identified, following this order: (1) IPC main, (2) CPC main, (3) IPC others, (4) CPC others.

We first provided descriptive statistics on the innovation intensity of B Corps, disentangling the innovation effort by technological classes of patents. By doing so we were able to identify the overall innovation intensity and the green innovation intensity of B Corps, calculated as the percentage of green technology patents. We further provided a picture of the industries where the innovative B Corps operate by looking at the NACE code classification of industries declared by the companies. Finally, we mapped the geographical distribution of B Corps engaged in green innovation, by geo-localizing the companies and focusing on the differences between the distribution of innovative B Corps in US and in Italy.

7.4   RESULTS

Overall, our analysis identified 17,933 patents filed by 231 B Corps. The majority of these patents (50%) were filed by companies in European countries, followed by companies in the United States (40.9%). Out of these patents, 696 were classified as "green patents" based on the OECD's environment-related technologies (ENV-TECH) list.

When looking at the main technological classes of these patents, we found that the largest proportion (50%) was classified under class A, which encompasses human necessities. The second largest proportion (26.6%) was classified under class C, which covers chemistry and metallurgy. In the case of green patents, the largest proportion (46%) was classified under class C, followed by class B (30%) which covers performing operations and transporting (see Table 7.1).

Table 7.1   Number of patents grouped per IPC classification

IPC Classification	n. patents	%	n. green patents	%
#ND	606	3.4%	1	0.1%
HUMAN NECESSITIES	8847	49.3%	66	9.5%
PERFORMING OPERATIONS; TRANSPORTING	1436	8.0%	211	30.3%
CHEMISTRY; METALLURGY	4776	26.6%	321	46.1%
TEXTILE; PAPER	47	0.3%	1	0.1%
FIXED CONSTRUCTION	54	0.3%	12	1.7%
MECHANICAL ENGINEERING; LIGHTING; HEATING; WEAPONS; BLASTING	143	0.8%	56	8.0%
PHYSICS	1175	6.6%	16	2.3%
ELECTRICITY	849	4.7%	12	1.7%
Tot.	**17933**	**100%**	**696**	**100%**

Source: Authors' elaboration.

The largest number of green patents among the ENV-TECH categories belongs to Class 1, "Environmental Management," with 305 patents, and Class 9, "Climate Change Mitigation Technologies in the Production or Processing of Goods," with 234 patents. The geographical distribution of these identified green patents can be seen in Figure 7.1.

In terms of temporal distribution, the number of patents was grouped in seven-year intervals from 1990 to 2017. The trend shows growth for both the total number of patents and the number of green patents. Out of the 231 B Corps that applied for at least one patent, 5.4% were considered innovative. Out of those innovative B Corps, 24.7% were also considered innovative green companies because they had applied for at least one green patent. These findings are presented in Table 7.2.

The majority of B Corps operate in the manufacturing sector (23.9%), followed by the information and communication (15.7%) and financial and insurance activities (15.8%) industries. Among the innovative B Corps, manufacturing remains the leading sector (40.7%), followed by wholesale, retail

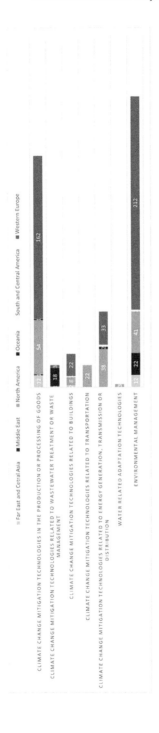

Source: Authors' elaboration.

Figure 7.1   *Geographical distribution of green patents*

Table 7.2   *Number of total B Corps, innovative B Corps and green*
                 innovative B Corps (at 30/07/2021)

n. B Corps	4248
n. Innovative B Corps	231
n. green innovative B Corps	57
Innovative B Corps/tot. B Corps	5.4%
Innovative green B Corps/innovative B Corps	24.7%

Source: Authors' elaboration.

trade and repair of motor vehicles and motorcycles (16.9%) and professional, scientific, and technical activities (13.9%). For innovative green B Corps, the manufacturing sector dominates (40.4%), with professional, scientific, and technical activities (21.1%) and wholesale, retail trade, and repair of motor vehicles and motorcycles (10.5%) also being significant contributors.

The geographical distribution of innovative and green innovative B Corps was analyzed, with Europe leading the way with 44% of the total, followed by the United States with 36.8% and 38.6% respectively. To further understand the distribution within these regions, maps were created for the top two countries by number of innovative B Corps and green innovative B Corps: the United States and Italy. On these maps, innovative B Corps are represented by dark grey dots while green innovative B Corps are represented by light grey dots.

As seen in Figure 7.2, which depicts a map of Italy, most of the companies are located in Northern Italy, with some presence in Central Italy and only one company located in Southern Italy. It was noted that two companies, Novamont S.p.a. and Aboca S.p.a., stand out for having a higher number of patent applications compared to the average of other companies.

The map of the United States in Figure 7.3 reveals a more widespread distribution of innovative B Corps compared to Italy. However, three areas stand out for their concentration of companies: the San Francisco Bay Area, the Los Angeles area, and the New York area. Companies such as Avon Products Inc. (Natura & Co. group), New England Biolabs Inc., and Brewer Science Inc. are among those with the highest number of patents.

7.5   DISCUSSION AND CONCLUSIONS

The role of innovation in driving the green transition is evident, as the Green Deal aims to achieve decarbonization by 2050. With this in mind, responsible innovation is becoming increasingly crucial in providing innovative solutions to pressing social challenges amidst converging climate, economic, pandemic,

Table 7.3   Main economic activity distribution between B Corps, innovative B Corps and green innovative B Corps

Nace Rev. 2, main sector	n. B Corps	%	n. innovative B Corps	%	n. green innovative B Corps	%
#N/D	36	0.8%	16	6.9%	2	3.5%
A - Agriculture, forestry and fishing	126	3.0%	4	1.7%	2	3.5%
B - Mining and quarrying	1	0.0%	1	0.4%	1	1.8%
C - Manufacturing	1016	23.9%	94	40.7%	23	40.4%
D - Electricity, gas, steam and air conditioning supply	111	2.6%	1	0.4%	0	0.0%
E - Water supply; sewerage, waste management and remediation activities	210	4.9%	4	1.7%	3	5.3%
F - Construction	42	1.0%	3	1.3%	2	3.5%
G - Wholesale and retail trade; repair of motor vehicles and motorcycles	70	1.6%	39	16.9%	6	10.5%
I - Accommodation and food service activities	41	1.0%	1	0.4%	0	0.0%
J - Information and communication	669	15.7%	20	8.7%	3	5.3%
K - Financial and insurance activities	671	15.8%	7	3.0%	0	0,00%
L - Real estate activities	45	1.1%	1	0.4%	0	0.0%
M - Professional, scientific and technical activities	286	6.7%	32	13.9%	12	21.1%
N - Administrative and support service activities	48	1.1%	6	2.6%	2	3.5%
P - Education	158	3.7%	1	0.4%	1	1.8%
Q - Human health and social work activities	362	8.5%	1	0.4%	0	0.0%
S - Other service activities	356	8.4%	0	0.0%	0	0.0%
Total	**4248**	**100%**	**231**	**100%**	**57**	**100%**

Source: Authors' elaboration.

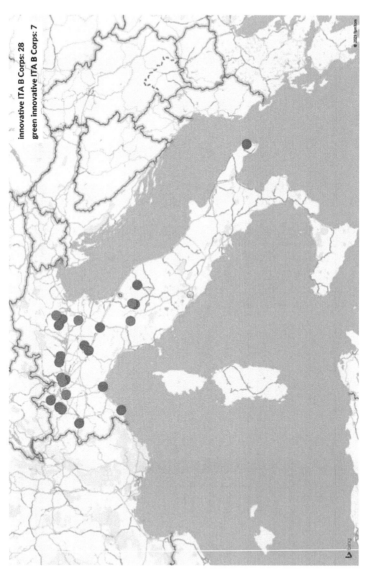

Source: Authors' elaboration.

Figure 7.2   Mapping of innovative B Corps (dark grey dot) and green innovative B Corps in Italy (light grey dot)

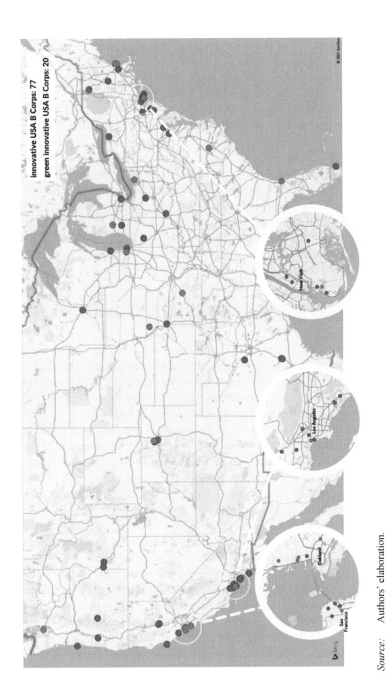

Source: Authors' elaboration.

Figure 7.3   Mapping of innovative B Corps (dark grey dot) and green innovative B Corps (light grey dot)

and geopolitical crises (Castellacci, 2022). In this study, out of the 4,248 B Corps analyzed, 231 were found to be innovative companies (having at least one patent) and 57 of these were further identified as green innovative (having at least one green patent) using ENV-TECH technology classes. The majority of these innovative and green innovative B Corps are located in Northern Italy. However, in the United States, there is a more widespread distribution with areas of higher concentration in the cities of San Francisco, Oakland, Los Angeles, and New York. The creation of "innovative districts" has emerged, where clusters of innovative enterprises, both large and small- or medium-sized, drive economic and social performance and prosperity in a particular territory. Despite this, our patent analysis reveals that patents related to green innovation remain a marginal aspect. Therefore, it is imperative to escalate efforts and investments in innovative and environmentally friendly technologies to create a meaningful change that prioritizes the economic and social well-being while adhering to the principle of "do no harm" outlined in the European Taxonomy. This is crucial in the coming years to rebuild the world's economies with more sustainable, inclusive, and resilient models by 2030.

7.5.1   Theoretical and Practical Implications

Despite the growth in literature on B Corps over the years, their relationship to the topic of green innovation has not yet been fully examined. This chapter aims to shed light on the technological advancements made by B Corps that have developed green patents. Social and environmentally sustainable practices and green innovation are closely related and complementary concepts (Amore & Bennedsen, 2016). B Corps are companies that operate in an ethical and sustainable manner that benefits society and the environment (Blasi & Sedita, 2022). On the other hand, green innovation involves the development of new products, services, and processes that are environmentally friendly and sustainable. One of the key ways in which B Corps demonstrate their commitment to environmental sustainability is through the support of green innovation. This involves investing research and development of sustainable products and services that aim to reduce the environmental impact of businesses on planet (D'Angelo et al., 2022). B Corps recognize that they have a responsibility towards the environment and society, and they take seriously. By supporting green innovation, B Corps are not only fulfilling their responsibility towards the environment, but are also creating a competitive advantage for themselves. Moreover, B Corps have a rigorous certification process ensures that they meet high standards of environmental and social performance (Gehman & Grimes, 2017). These standards include transparency, accountability and legal responsibility, which are all important elements for fostering sustainable business practices.

The research found that the number of innovative green B Corps identified is still limited, however, they show growth in the number of green patents over the years. In conclusion, the B Corps that are at the forefront of supporting green innovation might become exemplar cases for other traditional for-profit companies. By prioritizing the environment along with profits, B Corps are changing the way businesses operate and demonstrating that sustainable business practices are crucial for a healthier and a brighter future, also in terms of technological progress (Demir, 2020).

Green technologies, also known as clean technologies, are essential for decarbonization, which is the process of reducing our carbon footprint and transitioning to a more sustainable, low-carbon, and it is much supported by national and international industrial policies (Bataille et al., 2016). The use of fossil fuels and other carbon-intensive industries are responsible for the majority of greenhouse gas, and green technologies offer a range of alternatives to traditional energy sources coal, oil, and gas. These technologies rely on renewable energy sources like solar, hydropower, geothermal, and bioenergy. Additionally, these technologies are becoming more affordable and cost-competitive making them a viable option for large-scale commercial use (Liu et al., 2020).

Thus, green technologies play a crucial role in the decarbonization of economy by reducing emissions, promoting sustainable growth, and creating new job opportunities (Østergaard et al., 2021). B Corps involved in green innovation can play a crucial role in paving the way towards a green economy. The process presents challenges and opportunities, and it is affected by internal and external factors. Internal factors, such as company size, require a long-term approach from management that involves multiple business functions and promotes employee awareness and training. Corporate strategies should align with international standards and gradually expand to include the entire value chain, including suppliers and partners. To achieve real transformation in the industry, it is important for managers to involve suppliers, supply chains, and districts in their efforts to create sustainable and competitive areas on a national and global level. From the external perspective, policy makers must consider ways to encourage the development of green technologies, particularly for environmentally conscious companies like B Corps. One solution could be to streamline the patent granting process for technologies that play a significant role in combating climate change. Additionally, it is essential to involve all stakeholders, such as trade associations, civil society, and relevant parties, in the transition through partnerships and discussion forums. Finally, access to finance and new capital has become increasingly important for current decarbonization and sustainability initiatives.

Clusters in times of uncertainty

7.5.2   Limitations and Future Studies

This study is not without limitations. First, it should be noted that only 1,928 B Corps were identified in the Orbis database out of the total 4,248 B Corps. Additionally, there are limitations regarding the time frame of the study, as it is difficult to find academic research that uses the same methodology for quantifying the level of green innovation and identifying ENV-TECH technology classes. To obtain more comprehensive geographical information and specific data, it is suggested that future research utilize professional software, such as QGIS, in conjunction with statistical techniques for defining technological clusters of green innovative B Corps.

Moreover, by collecting more data at the company level (such as R&D investments, human capital, collaboration networks), it would be possible to improve the present understanding of the determinants of green innovation in B Corps compared to other sustainable entrepreneurship forms and other companies in general. In conclusion, future research could focus on conducting case studies on individual companies with the highest number of green patents to gain a deeper understanding of their green innovative nature and the role of agglomeration in the green innovation performance.

REFERENCES

Amore, M. D., & Bennedsen, M. (2016). Corporate governance and green innovation. *Journal of Environmental Economics and Management, 75*, 54–72.

Arranz, N., Arguello, N. L., & Fernández de Arroyabe, J. C. (2021). How do internal, market and institutional factors affect the development of eco-innovation in firms? *Journal of Cleaner Production, 297*, 126692. https://doi.org/10.1016/j.jclepro.2021.126692

B Corporation. (2019). *They're a B Corp?* https://1pdf.net/ben-jerrys-b-corporation_59eef716f6065deb71b2b48c

Bataille, C., Waisman, H., Colombier, M., Segafredo, L., Williams, J., & Jotzo, F. (2016). The need for national deep decarbonization pathways for effective climate policy. *Climate Policy, 16*(sup1), S7–S26. https://doi.org/10.1080/14693062.2016.1173005

Battilana, J., & Dorado, S. (2010). Building sustainable hybrid organizations: The case of commercial microfinance organizations. *Academy of Management Journal, 53*(6), 1419–1440.

Battilana, J., Lee, M., Walker, J., & Dorsey, C. (2012). In search of the hybrid ideal. *Stanford Social Innovation Review, 10*(3), 50–55.

Billis, D. (2010). *Hybrid Organizations and the Third Sector: Challenges for Practice, Theory and Policy*. Macmillan International Higher Education.

Blasi, S., & Sedita, S. R. (2022). Mapping the emergence of a new organisational form: An exploration of the intellectual structure of the B Corp research. *Corporate Social Responsibility and Environmental Management, 29*(1), 107–123. https://doi.org/10.1002/csr.2187

Castellacci, F. (2022). Innovation and social welfare: A new research agenda. *Journal of Economic Surveys*. https://doi.org/10.1111/joes.12537

Chen, Y.-S. (2008). The driver of green innovation and green image–green core competence. *Journal of Business Ethics, 81*(3), 531–543.

Chen, Y., & Ma, Y. (2021). Does green investment improve energy firm performance? *Energy Policy, 153*, 112252. https://doi.org/10.1016/j.enpol.2021.112252

D'Angelo, V., Cappa, F., & Peruffo, E. (2022). Green manufacturing for sustainable development: The positive effects of green activities, green investments, and non-green products on economic performance. *Business Strategy and the Environment*. https://doi.org/10.1002/bse.3226

Demir, I. (2020). The B Corporation movement: From a legal to a social innovation. *Sustainability, 12*(6), 2172. https://doi.org/10.3390/su12062172

Doherty, B., Haugh, H., & Lyon, F. (2014). Social enterprises as hybrid organizations: A review and research agenda. *International Journal of Management Reviews, 16*(4), 417–436.

Ebrahim, A., Battilana, J., & Mair, J. (2014). The governance of social enterprises: Mission drift and accountability challenges in hybrid organizations. *Research in Organizational Behavior, 34*, 81–100.

Gehman, J., & Grimes, M. (2017). Hidden badge of honor: How contextual distinctiveness affects category promotion among certified B corporations. *Academy of Management Journal, 60*(6), 2294–2320.

Hao, J., & He, F. (2022). Corporate social responsibility (CSR) performance and green innovation: Evidence from China. *Finance Research Letters, 48*, 102889.

Hiller, J. S. (2013). The benefit corporation and corporate social responsibility. *Journal of Business Ethics, 118*(2), 287–301.

Hoffman, A. J., Badiane, K. K., & Haigh, N. (2012). Hybrid organizations as agents of positive social change: Bridging the for-profit & non-profit divide. In Golden-Biddle, K., & Dutton, J. (eds.) *Using a Positive Lens to Explore Social Change and Organizations: Building a Theoretical and Research Foundation* (pp. 131–153). Taylor & Francis.

Kanie, N., Griggs, D., Young, O., Waddell, S., Shrivastava, P., Haas, P. M., Broadgate, W., Gaffney, O., & Kőrösi, C. (2019). Rules to goals: Emergence of new governance strategies for sustainable development. *Sustainability Science, 14*(6), 1745–1749. https://doi.org/10.1007/s11625-019-00729-1

Kemp, R., & Arundel, A. (1998). *Survey indicators for environmental innovation*. The IDEA Working Paper No. 8, Indicators and Data for European Analysis.

Kim, Seongtae, Colicchia, C., & Menachof, D. (2018). Ethical sourcing: An analysis of the literature and implications for future research. *Journal of Business Ethics, 152*(4), 1033–1052.

Kim, Suntae, Karlesky, M. J., Myers, C. G., & Schifeling, T. (2016). Why companies are becoming B corporations. *Harvard Business Review, 17*.

Kramer, M. R., & Porter, M. (2011). Creating shared value. *Harvard Business Review, 89*(1/2), 62–77.

Liu, Y., Zhu, J., Li, E. Y., Meng, Z., & Song, Y. (2020). Environmental regulation, green technological innovation, and eco-efficiency: The case of Yangtze river economic belt in China. *Technological Forecasting and Social Change, 155*, 119993. https://doi.org/10.1016/j.techfore.2020.119993

Marin, G., & Mazzanti, M. (2013). The evolution of environmental and labor productivity dynamics. *Journal of Evolutionary Economics, 23*(2), 357–399. https://doi.org/10.1007/s00191-010-0199-8

Muñoz, P., Cacciotti, G., & Cohen, B. (2018). The double-edged sword of purpose-driven behavior in sustainable venturing. *Journal of Business Venturing, 33*(2), 149–178.

Nicholls, A. (2010). Institutionalizing social entrepreneurship in regulatory space: Reporting and disclosure by community interest companies. *Accounting, Organizations and Society, 35*(4), 394–415.

Østergaard, C. R., Holm, J. R., Iversen, E., Schubert, T., Skålholt, A., & Sotarauta, M. (2021). Environmental innovations and green skills in the Nordic countries. In Sedita S.R., & Blasi S. (eds.) *Rethinking Clusters: Place-based Value Creation in Sustainability Transitions* (pp. 195–211). Springer International Publishing.

Pellegrini, C. B., & Caruso, R. (2023). *Società benefit: Profili giuridici ed economico aziendali*. EGEA spa.

Porter, M. E., & Linde, C. V. D. (1995). Toward a new conception of the environment-competitiveness relationship. *Journal of Economic Perspectives, 9*(4), 97-118.

Rawhouser, H., Cummings, M., & Crane, A. (2015). Benefit corporation legislation and the emergence of a social hybrid category. *California Management Review, 57*(3), 13–35.

Sabeti, H. (2011). The for-benefit enterprise. *Harvard Business Review, 89*(11), 98–104.

Sen, A. K. (2009). *The Idea of Justice*. Harvard University Press.

Serafeim, G., & Kao, J. (2013). The performance frontier: Innovating for a sustainable strategy. *Harvard Business Review, 91*(9), 56–65. ttps://doi.org/10.5465/amr.2011.0094

Strambach, S. (2017). Combining knowledge bases in transnational sustainability innovation: Microdynamics and institutional change. *Economic Geography, 93*(5), 500–526.

Tang, M., Walsh, G., Lerner, D., Fitza, M. A., & Li, Q. (2018). Green innovation, managerial concern and firm performance: An empirical study. *Business Strategy and the Environment, 27*(1), 39–51.

Tseng, M. L., Wang, R., Chiu, A. S., Geng, Y., & Lin, Y. H. (2013). Improving performance of green innovation practices under uncertainty. *Journal of Cleaner Production, 40*, 71–82.

van den Bergh, J. C. J. M., Truffer, B., & Kallis, G. (2011). Environmental innovation and societal transitions: Introduction and overview. *Environmental Innovation and Societal Transitions, 1*(1), 1–23. https://doi.org/10.1016/j.eist.2011.04.010

Villela, M., Bulgacov, S., & Morgan, G. (2019). B Corp certification and its impact on organizations over time. *Journal of Business Ethics*, 1–15.

Wilburn, K., & Wilburn, R. (2014). The double bottom line: Profit and social benefit. *Business Horizons, 57*(1), 11–20.

Woods, C. S. (2016). The implications of the B Corp movements in the business and human rights context. *Notre Dame Journal of International and Comparative Law, 6*, 77.

Yunus, M. (2010). *Building Social Business: The New Kind of Capitalism that Serves Humanity's Most Pressing Needs*. PublicAffairs.

8. Exploring the role of museums in the digital era: the successful case of the Uffizi Galleries[1]

Luciana Lazzeretti, Paola Beccherle, and Stefania Oliva

8.1 INTRODUCTION

Over the last decades, museums have transformed their functions, raising importance and legitimacy in society and increasing their role as a "social engine" for urban renewal and regional development (Lazzeretti and Capone, 2015). Recently, with the advent of information and communication technologies (ICTs), the museum sector has experienced a paradigm shift where online communication has assumed increased importance. The growing use of online platforms and social media has enhanced community participation, fostering dialogic communication with audiences (Arnaboldi et al., 2021). The museums in the digital era have become a hybrid space where online and on-life interactions overlap. They have become facilitators for access to cultural heritage by creating a participatory context typical of an online platform, activating processes of co-creation of meaning with the online public and accentuating the proactive role of the audience (Simon, 2010; 2016; Solima et al., 2021).

In addition, online communication and social media in museums have fostered the conveyance of places' values and identities. They also contribute to cities' attractiveness, competitiveness and transformation (Beccherle et al., 2023). Thanks to digital technologies, museums may be crucial in increasing places' consensus and legitimacy (Lazzeretti, 2023). These aspects underline the importance of "value" creation related to concepts such as reputation, trust, visibility and a sense of community, which are increasingly lacking in the society of digitalisation (Suchman, 1995).

Based on such considerations, relevant importance assumes for scholars to understand the role played by museums in the digital era and how technology may help them develop new forms of engagement and city promotion. Moreover, although this positive vision of the future role of museums in society, literature recognises that data-driven arts and cultural organisations are still in an open debate, and it is not clear if digital transformation is an "opportunity" or a "chimaera" for the cultural sector (Nuccio and Bertacchini, 2022).

To contribute to this debate, the chapter analyses the case of the Uffizi Galleries in Florence, Italy, following the qualitative methodology of the case study. The analysis is a preliminary exploration to understand how new technologies changed the museum's business model focusing on online communication and engagement and the relationship between the museum and the city of Florence.

The Uffizi Galleries represent a noteworthy case in the field of museum digital communication and management. They are one of the world's oldest and most important Italian museums. During the closure due to the COVID-19 pandemic, they experimented with new technologies for audience engagement and accelerated the adoption of digital tools, becoming increasingly "pop" through social media. In 2021, the Uffizi Galleries were the most visited Italian state museum. They have the largest number of followers among Italian museums, with more than one million followers on Facebook, Instagram, X (Twitter) and TikTok accounts. Furthermore, they have developed a strategy for engaging with young online audiences, being one of the first museums in Europe to have opened a profile on TikTok.[2]

In order to analyse the Uffizi Galleries case, fourteen semi-structured face-to-face interviews were conducted between December 2021 and March 2023 with the museum director and the managers of several departments. Moreover, a period of participant observation has been undertaken in the institution. Finally, institutional reports, documents, social media, website, and press releases have been analysed to triangulate information.

The first results show the increasing role of digital channels in the museum's communication strategy, underlining the narrative and informal style assumed by the institution in its communication, devoted to engaging the new public. Finally, with the advent of the digital age, the museum plays an increasingly central role in the public debate about the cultural development of Florence city of art and its surroundings.

8.2   THE MUSEUMS BETWEEN ENHANCEMENT AND TECHNOLOGICAL PRESERVATION OF CULTURE

Contemporary society is experiencing a period of radical change due to the transformations brought by technological progress and new technologies' pervasiveness in the economy, cultural institutions, and organisations. Recent studies on the relationship between economy, culture and society have highlighted the crucial role assumed by technology, also in changing the practices for the enhancement and conservation of culture, not only in the technological dimensions but also in socio-economic and cultural ones.

Some scholars have called this new relationship between culture and technology "Culture 3.0" regime (Sacco et al., 2018). In this context, Lazzeretti (2022) discusses the rise of a new phase of "Enhancement and technological preservation of culture." This phase requires paying greater attention to both conservation and technological enhancement of culture, where culture can be considered a "digital resource and capacity" able to generate economic and social value, preserve heritage, develop new products, services and sectors or renew existing ones. At the same time, it represents a tool for overcoming the risks of the digital revolution.

Museums are important actors in this transformation. Exploring the effects of ICT's adoption on the organisation and management of museums, Taormina and Bonini Baraldi (2022) observe that changes in the museums' business models, new digital professionals and digital strategy are promising research topics. New technologies, in fact, offer opportunities to transform museums' business models towards a participatory configuration that positions the visitor at the centre of the value creation process, exploiting the online environment alongside their traditional physical sites (Simone et al., 2021). This change requires investments in new digital professions as well as planning a museum's digital strategy.

A business model is a tool for representing the organisation's relevant activities in a simplified and aggregated way in order to analyse the value created (Amit and Zott, 2012; Wirtz et al., 2016). Osterwalder and Pigneur (2010) proposed a business model framework that identifies the key categories of the organisation's value creation. These categories are represented by nine basic building blocks grouped into four main areas: customers, offer, infrastructure, and financial viability (Table 8.1).

Investments in new technologies have several effects on museums' business models. Lazzeretti and Sartori (2016) recognise that digitalisation significantly increases museums' external partnerships. Analysing the case of the Louvre Museum, Coblence and Sabatier (2014) highlight the emergence of a "global and innovative" business model focused on ICT technologies to foster national and international partnerships and increase museum visibility. Alshawaaf and Lee (2021) show that digital technologies might promote the adoption of business model innovation and enhance audience engagement. However, they evidence differences in digital adoption depending on the institutional environment and stakeholders' demands.

Social media have become crucial tools for developing museum business model innovations in this scenario. They allow museums to engage with digital audiences, increasing attractiveness and cities' tourist flow (Smith Bautista,

Table 8.1   *Business model's nine building blocks*

Building Blocks	Description
Customer Segments	An organisation serves one or several customer segments.
Value Propositions	Value propositions focus on the benefits that the organisation offer to the customer. They are represented by the product or service of the organisation.
Channels	Communication, distribution and sales channels for reaching the customer.
Customer Relationships	They represent the relationships established and maintained with the customer.
Revenue Streams	They are the revenue generated from value propositions successfully offered to customers.
Key Resources	Key resources are the assets required to offer and deliver the value proposition.
Key Activities	Key activities are the actions taken by the organisation to operate successfully.
Key Partnerships	They represent the network of partners that optimise the organisation's business model.
Cost Structure	They are the costs sustained by the organisation for operating under the specific business model.

Source: Authors' elaboration from Osterwalder and Pigneur (2010).

2014). Museums' online and offline visitors can share their opinions, experiences, values and identities in the digital space. Furthermore, social media facilitate access to cultural heritage by creating a participatory context that can foster online audience engagement and dialogic communication, reshaping their value creation (Simone et al., 2021).

In terms of new relationships and partnerships, the literature suggests that new technologies allow differentiation strategies to increase museums' attractiveness and foster their reputation (Izzo et al., 2023). In particular, the strategic use of social media attracts more visitors by influencing the museum's notoriety and recognition, that is, the reputational capital. Visitors can be encouraged to share their experiences on social media, contributing to building and maintaining the museums' online reputation (Fernández-Hernández et al., 2020). The latter, supported by social media management, facilitates the museum's relational capacity by attracting public and private investments, gaining importance on the local and international scene and developing new relationships.

By promoting themselves through social media, museums have a significant role in fostering the appeal of places and increasing their consensus and legitimacy (Lazzeretti, 2023). Cities can use the reputation of the museum brand to improve and enhance their reputation as a place to live, do business, and visit, sustaining the online city diplomacy strategy and narrative (Grincheva, 2020; 2022). With their online and offline participatory character and function, museums are configured as crucial partners to be involved in city branding, as they are the keepers of the peculiar local identity reflected in their collections. This element can lead to proposing a non-stereotyped image of the city's uniqueness based on its historical memory and local identity capable of generating a competitive advantage in the medium-long term. Consequently, museums can lead to cultural, social and economic development for all city stakeholders (Ulldemolins, 2014).

8.3   THE UFFIZI GALLERIES CASE STUDY

8.3.1   Methodology and Data Collection

In order to explore the role of museums in the digital era, the chapter analyses the case of the Uffizi Galleries through the qualitative methodology of the case study (Eisenhardt, 1989; Yin, 2009). The analysis is a preliminary exploration to understand how new technologies changed the museum's business model focusing on online communication and engagement and the relationship between the museum and the city of Florence.

The case study methodology has been extensively applied to study museums' strategies and activities (Plaza and Haarich, 2015; Solima et al., 2021) as well as their business model (Coblence and Sabatier, 2014; Alshawaaf and Lee, 2021). In addition, the Uffizi Galleries have been the focus of recent studies aimed at analysing the digitisation of the collection (Lazzeretti and Sartori, 2016) and the impact of the COVID-19 pandemic on the museum (Giusti, 2023). However, the digital revolution's implications for the museum's business model are still under-researched (Taormina and Bonini Baraldi, 2022).

Data were collected from several sources during a period going from December 2021 and March 2023 to enable data triangulation and allow a comprehensive understanding of the museum's strategy. Multiple sources of evidence can contribute to tracing the evolution of the phenomenon under research and help to corroborate the results from a single source (Yin, 2009). The primary sources involved in the data collection are fourteen semi-structured face-to-face interviews with seven actors in managerial or leadership roles within the museum departments (Table 8.2). The choice to interview the museum's management allows for collecting information from who is in a leadership role concerning the strategies adopted by the museum. Moreover, the departments involved were the most informants in the activities developed concerning using new technologies and social media. The interviews were structured to collect information on (1) the role of the interviewee within the organisation; (2) the evolution of management strategies; (3) the role of digital technologies and social media on the organisation's strategies; (4) the digital strategy and its impact on museum's business model.

Table 8.2   List of interviewees with role and number of interviews

Interviewee Id	Role	N° of interviews
1	Director	2
2	Contact person for the curatorial division and archaeology and art history structures	7
3	Director's spokesperson and press officer	1
4	Digital strategies area representative	1
5	Cultural mediation and accessibility area coordinator, department of education	1
6	Head of the education department and coordinator of the school and youth area	1
7	Representative of the legal department, department of enhancement and economic strategies	1
Total		**14**

Source: Authors' elaboration.

In addition, a period of participant observation at the institution was carried out, attending conferences, exhibitions and events. Participant observation is a method through which research is carried out with the direct participation of the researcher in the situation of interest. It is beneficial for obtaining deeper information and knowledge, especially if public information is unavailable (Vinten, 1994). Finally, data were collected from secondary sources. These sources involved collecting data from institutional reports, social media and website analysis, and press releases. As the case study theory suggests (Yin, 2009), data triangulation through several sources can be crucial to limit bias and strengthen the findings' validity.

8.3.2   The Context of the Analysis

The Uffizi Galleries are located in Florence, Italy, an international art city with an endowment of artistic and cultural heritage and a museum cluster that involves several activities and institutions (Lazzeretti, 2004; Lazzeretti and Oliva, 2018). They are a national museum complex that includes the Uffizi Gallery museum, the Palazzo Pitti's museums, the Vasari Corridor and the Boboli Gardens. This new configuration results from a Ministerial Decree that in 2014 gave special autonomy – scientific, financial, accounting and organi-sational – to several major Italian museums (MiBACT, 2014; Curioni, 2018).

Before this reform, the museums of the Uffizi Galleries were part of the Florentine Museum Hub (Polo Museale Fiorentino), managed by the

Special Superintendence for the Historical, Artistic and Ethno-anthropological Heritage, as it was for other Museum Hubs in major Italian cultural cities (Zan et al., 2018). The Museum Hub counted twenty-five cultural places and institutions (SSPSAE and PMCF, 2014). Each museum had a director that dealt with the ordinary administration by proposing scientific projects (Interviewee 2). After the 2014 reform, the institutions under the Florentine Museum Hub were disaggregated, and the Uffizi Galleries gained scientific, administrative, financial and accounting autonomy with a unique director – Eike Schmidt – nominated in 2015. In 2017, the museum adopted a statute expressing the fundamental principles concerning its organisation. As declared in the statute, the organisation's mission concerns the conservation, management and enhancement of the collection through research, accessibility and fruition, considering the identity value of art and its history at local, regional, national and international levels and promoting the exchange between visitors of different cultures (Gallerie degli Uffizi, 2017).

Already under the direction of the Florentine Museum Hub, new technologies were adopted to increase accessibility and fruition of collections. In collaboration with a technology company, the Hub developed "Uffizi Touch", a multimedia product for exploring high-resolution works of art images. The museums had partnered with Google for the Google Art Project to increase virtual accessibility, although the project was later discontinued. In addition, an application for iPhone, iPad and iPad Touch was developed to allow visitors to organise the tour and explore the collections. The Superintendency also started the adoption of social media and outsourced the online communication activities of the Hub. In April 2001, the YouTube channel was opened, while between 2012 and 2014, Facebook, Twitter and Google+ profiles were created (SSPSAE and PMCF, 2009, 2011, 2014).

Although these pioneering tentatives, as Lazzeretti and Sartori (2016) have pointed out, the Florentine Museum Hub stood out for its use of new technologies, mainly in the digitisation of collections. According to the literature (Agostino and Arnaboldi, 2021), the period before the 2014 state museum reform overlapped with a period of the highest interest of museums in conservation activities. However, in those years, a need to introduce professional figures specialised in web communication emerged to exploit new technology opportunities.

With the new direction, the role of new technologies has gained increasing importance. The management strategy, along with the conservation and protection of museum collections and historical buildings, increasingly focused on the accessibility to the museum through new technologies. The communication function has become strategic to increase the visibility of the Galleries, especially through social media, developing a museum's digital strategy. As the digital strategy department head states, "the director considers the digital strategy a fundamental strategic axis for the growth and enhancement of the museums" (Interviewee 4). The Uffizi Galleries' digital strategy deals with several objectives: attracting young generations, increasing the international dimension of the museum, connecting the global and local dimensions, and developing new forms of enhancement.

8.4   THE ROLE OF NEW TECHNOLOGIES IN THE UFFIZI GALLERIES' BUSINESS MODEL

The adoption of new technologies in the Uffizi Galleries has several effects on different dimensions of the organisation. In terms of *customer segments and relationships*, the use of new technologies involves mainly three typologies of audience. First, young visitors represent a crucial segment. The attraction of young audiences through new technologies is strictly related to the museum's physical visits and educational activities. As stated by the director, it is important to "make the museum as a space of experience and learning through the visit, a place for the reactivation of thinking" (Interviewee 1). This aspect is in line with the literature on museums studies that highlight the digital empowerment of museums through new technologies as instrumental in attracting younger generations and promoting tailored digital narratives (Izzo et al., 2023).

Second, according to the interviews, new technologies should increase the share of international visitors involved with content communication in English and from English – using technology – to other languages. The museum's relationship with China, the USA, France and Germany, among international visitors, is particularly important. The director pointed out that "the USA and China, economically, are the biggest players" (Interviewee 1). This statement is in line with the data on global tourism. According to the OECD Tourism Statistics, France, Germany, the USA and China represented Italy's most important markets for international tourism arrivals in 2019.

Third, the involvement of local communities through new technologies is crucial for the museum. This aspect is mentioned in the organisation statute highlighting the strict relationship with the territory, especially local schools and universities (Gallerie degli Uffizi, 2017).

Another relevant effect is the use of social media and website as new *channels* to communicate with the museum's audience. Online communication's centrality also required introducing new resources and capabilities in the organisation. Since 2016, the Uffizi Galleries have opened an IT and Digital Strategies Department. The same year, they launched the website and the official Twitter, Instagram, and YouTube accounts. During the COVID-19 lockdowns in March 2020, the museum opened Facebook and TikTok accounts to connect with wider audiences and diversify online communities.

Moreover, in the last three years, the museum collaborated with local, national, and international influencers (Interviewee 4). In 2020, according to data from the Italian Cultural Ministry, the Uffizi Galleries was the most visited public museum institute in Italy, with an increase of 24.9% of young visitors under the age of 25 and an increase of 134.4% of young visitors aged between 19 and 25 compared to 2019 (Gallerie degli Uffizi, 2021). Figure 8.1 shows the trend in the number of followers among the different social media of the museum.

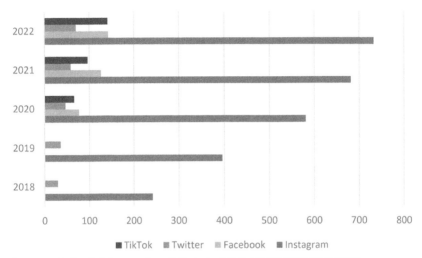

Source: Authors' elaboration from Gallerie degli Uffizi (2018, 2019, 2022, 2023).

Figure 8.1   Followers of the Uffizi Galleries' social media 2018–2022, thousands of persons

According to the director, online communication is differentiated by the typologies of visitors. While Facebook is mainly used to engage with a broad, adult, Italian, or Italian-speaking public, Instagram and TikTok are dedicated to the younger, national, and international public. Social media followers' age data confirm this segmentation (Gallerie degli Uffizi, 2023). In 2022, Facebook engaged 24.7% of people from 45 to 54 years old, Instagram had a public of 29.3% from 25 to 34 years old, and TikTok counted an audience of 51% between 18 and 25 years old. In terms of geographical distribution, the national public was the most engaged. However, also a share of the international public interacted with the museum online, especially from the USA (TikTok: 89% from Italy and 5% from the USA; Twitter: 42.5% from Italy and

10.2% from the USA; Facebook: 70.3% from Italy and 3.9% from the USA. Instagram: 33.1% from Italy and 8.5% from the USA).

The main aim of online museum communication is to recount the museum's everyday life and enter the city and the international social and political debate (Interviewee 3). As regards the first modality, the Uffizi's communication aims to tell the story behind the scenes, the perspectives, and the dynamics that accompany the organisation of large exhibitions or events. This type of narration seeks to tell the museum as a living entity inserted in the city of Florence's and international context. This online communication form helps museums communicate daily with followers and create an integrated audience (Simone et al., 2021). As regards the second modality, the Uffizi Galleries aims to position itself as a museum institute hinged on local social and political dynamics. Concerning this aspect, social media and new technologies increase museums' role in city diplomacy (Grincheva, 2020). The museum participates in the public debate, offering new reflections. This approach leads it to be recognised as an active reality in the city, leading to greater visibility in both the local and international press. During the pandemic, the Uffizi Galleries recorded an increase of around 250% in published articles in national and international newspapers, with a reduction of -32% in 2022 (Gallerie degli Uffizi, 2020, 2022, 2023).

Moreover, the purpose of using social media by the Uffizi Galleries is to transform the online dialogue into an actual visit and offer to ones who already visited the museum additional tools for exploring content, producing new value for the visitors. The museum's digital offer is conceived not to replace the physical experience (Interviewee 3). This aspect is in line with the literature on museum studies that recognise that technological tools might increase the strategic value of visitors and play a crucial role in the visitors' decisions to attend museums (Fernández-Hernández et al., 2020).

A relevant effect of the adoption of new technologies on the Uffizi Galleries relates to the new *key activities* developed by the museum. Regarding the educational activities, the museum confirms that education has moved to the forefront of institutional activities and the success of their social media depends on primarily using online channels for education, not promotion (Schmidt, 2018). The Education Department of the Galleries consists of the School and Youth Area and the Cultural Mediation and Accessibility Area. The first involves activities with schools and families. It takes up the legacy of the historic "Educational Section", in existence since 1970, one of the first structured offices dedicated to museum education in Italy. The Cultural Mediation and Accessibility Area was established in 2016 to facilitate heritage enjoyment and participation. Education Department has a specific Facebook page to enhance communication with schools (Interviewees 5 and 6). The data on educational activities shows that digital tools have been particularly important in maintaining education activities during the pandemic. In 2021, the museum counted 989 online classes and 10,648 online and in-presence students (Gallerie degli Uffizi, 2022). In 2018, the activities organised in presence by the Education Department were 881, with 19,669 participants (Gallerie degli Uffizi, 2019). In 2021, digital activities involved schools of different levels in 989 online lessons. The same year, the Uffizi Education Department organised 42 online events for children and families, while in 2022, they increased to 60 (Gallerie degli Uffizi, 2022; 2023). To engage high school students online, the "Digital Ambassadors of Art" project involved teenagers in making creative videos reinterpreting the Uffizi collection in light of contemporary societal challenges (Gallerie degli Uffizi, 2021).

The new key activities also involve the digitisation of the Galleries collections. The museum has three main digital archives: the photo archives and inventories with more than 600.000 items, the Uffizi catalogue dedicated to the Uffizi Gallery museum, the Pitti Palace and the Boboli garden containing more than 24,000 items, and the Cabinet of Drawings and Prints, with 180,000 catalogue cards (Interviewee 2). The literature highlights that the process of digitising collections, already started at the time of the Florentine Museum Hub, fosters local exchanges and collaborations as well as social, cultural and economic relationships fuelled by a common sense of belonging and trust (Lazzeretti and Sartori, 2016).

Finally, another significant effect regards the strength of *partnerships* with the city of Florence and other local institutions. According to the interviews, the need to create a new relationship between the municipality and local museums emerged. As stressed by the director, a new form should be found to bring local museums together, involving state museums, municipal museums, and public and private foundations. Even in this case, new technologies can represent a tool to establish a new relationship with local institutions and museums.

In 2021 the Galleries launched a project for the enhancement of the cultural and artistic heritage of Florence and its surrounding territories with the label "Uffizi Diffusi" (Diffuse Uffizi) and "Terre degli Uffizi" (Uffizi Lands). The project is conducted in partnership with a local banking foundation to regenerate lesser-known centres in the surrounding area by focusing on local art and history to encourage more sustainable tourism. Already in 2008, with the project "The City of the Uffizi", the past director intended to develop exhibitions in museums or other venues located in the surroundings of Florence to present works of art from the Uffizi Galleries' storerooms (SSPSAE and PMCF, 2009). However, the "Uffizi Diffusi" project emphasises communication and new technologies, especially through the museum website, showcasing the organised activities. As clarified on the museum's website, an extensive communication and promotional campaign will be activated on the Uffizi website and social media to ensure the maximum exploitation of the activity. As discussed by the director, "the strategy behind the 'Uffizi Diffusi' project is to enhance works of art that are not exposed in the museum by temporarily loaning them to another exhibition venue that has a connection to the artwork, to develop a narrative chapter for the painting" (Interviewee 1). In 2021, nine exhibitions were organised, with 26 works of art and eight agreements with municipalities. As a result of physical and digital enhancement initiatives in the territories included in the "Uffizi Diffusi" project, in 2021, an average increase of 16% in the number of visitors to the surrounding locations compared to 2020 was recorded. 83% of those interviewed at the local museum venues said they were visiting the museum for the first time, attracted by the exhibition (Gallerie degli Uffizi, 2022). In 2022, the number of exhibitions increased to 13, with 52 artworks exhibited (Gallerie degli Uffizi, 2023).

In summary, the analysis reveals that new technologies have been a crucial factor in driving changes in the Uffizi's business model. In particular, social media have become one of the main instruments of this transformation, fostering a new model of informal communication and audience engagement and strengthening the relationship with other cultural institutions and surrounding places. The business model's elements mostly involved in this process are the *communication channels*, *key activities, partnership* and *value proposition*. Figure 8.2 shows the actual configuration of the Uffizi Galleries' business model.

8.5   CONCLUSIONS

The analysis is a preliminary exploration to understand how new technologies changed the museum's business model focusing on online communication and engagement and the relationship between the museum and the city of Florence.

According to a cultural and creative approach named "Enhancement and technological preservation of culture" (Lazzeretti, 2022), the success of the Uffizi Galleries case has been discussed following three main arguments. First, the new management of the Uffizi Galleries aligns with the current trends in the technological enhancement and conservation of culture that characterise the new so-called "documedia revolution" (Ferraris, 2020). Second, Uffizi's strategies and policies are based on a digital strategy aimed at communicating with new audiences through social media, which is very successful among new generations, renewing the relationship between traditional art and new artistic and cultural forms. Finally, the focus on the territory and dialogue with the community and local institutions, for example with the "Uffizi Diffusi" project, and the continuous participation in the life of the city contribute to revitalising the relationship between the museum and the territory.

Key Partners	Key Activities	Value Proposition	Customer Relationship	Customer Segments
• Ministries of Culture, of Foreign Affairs and International Cooperation, and of Economy and Finance • Municipality of Florence • Concessionaires for additional services • Tourist operators • Restoration institutions • Foundations of bank origin • Friends of the museums • Schools • Universities and research centers • Healthcare structures • Cultural and creative enterprises • Cultural institutions • Civil protection • Insurance agencies • Transport companies • Publishing houses • Content providers • Influencers • Donors and Sponsors	• Conservation and enhancement of the collection • Audience development and engagement • Event organization • Research • Content production • Management of safety • Buildings maintenance • Editorial and merchandising production • Fundraising and marketing	• Make available and accessible a unique cultural offer • Scientific research • Education activity • Organization of exhibitions, conferences, events and other public initiatives • Welfare, health and well-being activities	• Differentiated entrances • Newsletter • Director's private meetings with potential donors	• Tourists • Tourist operators • Residents • Young people • Families • Schools • Researchers • Elderly people • People with disabilities • Institutions
	Key Resources		**Channels**	
	• Museum spaces and collections • Uffizi brand • Human resources • Intellectual capital • Financial capital • Community • Software for online ticketing		• Website • E-commerce • Social media • Press and TV	

Cost Structure	Revenue Streams
• Restoration • Content production • Acquisition of artworks • Insurance Security/maintenance • Marketing and communication • Research and development	• Ticketing • Public Funds • Private donations • Concessions for additional services • Concessions for the use of cultural assets for exhibitions and displays • Licensing for filming and use of images of the Uffizi collection • Sale of merchandise online and on-site • Publishing revenues • Museum spaces rentals for events

Source: Authors' elaboration based on business model canvas.

Figure 8.2   The Uffizi Galleries' business model

In terms of managerial implications and according to the literature on the value creation of museums in the digital era (Simone et al., 2021), it is possible to observe a transformation in the Uffizi Galleries' business model. This change is particularly relevant in terms of communication *channels*, new *key activities* and *value proposition* increasingly focused on audience development and engagement.

Regarding the theoretical contribution, the chapter answers the call to develop research on the digital tools and digital strategy adopted by museums (Taormina and Bonini Baraldi, 2022). The analysis reveals that the Uffizi Galleries are experiencing the *Digital Period* of Italian state museums after the 2014 reform, which gives centrality to digital technologies in further stimulating the transformation of museums into participatory bodies (Agostino and Arnaboldi, 2021). Moreover, the results align with previous research on business models, which underlines the need to create new digital technology skills and capabilities (Lazzeretti and Sartori, 2016). This challenge has been taken up by the Uffizi Galleries, which has been transforming and increasing skills and capabilities among employees since 2016. Finally, results confirm that through digital technologies, Uffizi is seizing the opportunities offered by the new "Culture 3.0" regime (Sacco et al., 2018) by promoting activities for producing a new cultural offer based not only on the physical visit to the museum. Through virtual classes, online conferences and events, the museum becomes a producer of content which, through new technologies, can reach an ever-wider audience, making the museum more competitive internationally. The museum can be considered a *social-oriented* museum (Simone et al., 2021) that mostly invests in social media and web services to communicate with followers, while the potential of new technologies applied to the visitor experience should still be explored, as well as dialogic communication.

Concerning the relationship between the museum and the territory, the numerous activities recently promoted, such as the "Uffizi Diffusi" project, confirm the museum's willingness to interact with local actors and neighbouring institutions and confirm that digital technologies through the channels of great cultural attractors as the Uffizi Galleries, can develop synergies to promote alternative tourist itineraries (Pasquinelli et al., 2022), enhancing the cultural heritage of smaller institutions through co-reputation. The Uffizi Galleries case shows that new technologies can be a tool to connect the local to the global dimensions of both the museum and the city of Florence and increase the role of cultural organisations as interlocutors for city diplomacy (Grincheva, 2022). These considerations are echoed in the recent literature on cultural and creative organisations, which highlights the risk for Europe and Italy of falling behind in the global market for cultural content creation and emphasises the need to enliven local cultural production and more constructive use of new technologies (Sacco et al., 2018). However, it remains to be evaluated whether its online communication can actually influence the city's soft power. This theme, as well as those of revitalisation of surrounding areas, could be the subject of future research aimed at understanding the impact of museum strategies on sustainable tourism and studying the museum's online reputation.

NOTES

1.   We sincerely thank the Director and the staff of the Uffizi Galleries for the data and information provided. This work was supported by CHANGES, PNRR, Mission 4, PE5, NextGenEU (CUP B53C22004010006).
2.   See https://www.morningfuture.com/en/2021/12/27/what-are-museums-doing -on-tik-tok/.

REFERENCES

Agostino, D., & Arnaboldi, M. (2021). From preservation to entertainment: Accounting for the transformation of participation in Italian state museums. *Accounting History*, 26(1), 102–122. DOI: 10.1177/1032373220934893.

Alshawaaf, N., & Lee, S. H. (2021). Business model innovation through digitisation in social purpose organisations: A comparative analysis of Tate Modern and Pompidou Centre. *Journal of Business Research*, 125, 597–608. DOI: 10.1016/j. jbusres.2020.02.045.

Amit, R., & Zott, C. (2012). Creating value through business model innovation. *MIT Sloan Management Review*, 53(3), 41–49.

Arnaboldi, M., & Diaz Lema, M. L. (2021). The participatory turn in museums: The online facet. *Poetics*, 89, 101536, 1–13. DOI: 10.1016/j.poetic.2021.101536.

Beccherle, P., Lazzeretti, L., & Oliva, S. (2023). Brescia as a cultural city: the role of museums and digital technologies. *Scienze regionali*. DOI: 10.14650/107315.

Coblence, E., & Sabatier, V. (2014). Articulating growth and cultural innovation in art museums: The Louvre's business model revision. *International Studies of Management & Organization*, 44(4), 9–25. DOI: 10.2753/IMO0020-8825440401.

Curioni, S. B. (2018). 'I've seen fire and I've seen rain'. Notes on the state museum reform in Italy. *Museum Management and Curatorship*, 33(6), 555–569. DOI: 10.1080/09647775.2018.1537617.

Eisenhardt, K. M. (1989). Building theories from case study research. *Academy of Management Review*, 14(4), 532–550. DOI: 10.2307/258557.

Fernández-Hernández, R., Vacas-Guerrero, T., & García-Muiña, F.E. (2020). Online reputation and user engagement as strategic resources of museums. *Museum Management and Curatorship*, 36(6), 553–568. DOI: 10.1080/09647775.2020.1803114.

Ferraris, M. (2020). From capital to documediality. In Andina T. & Bojanić P. (eds) *Institutions in Action: The Nature and the Role of Institutions in the Real World.* Cham: Springer, 107–121. DOI: 10.1007/978-3-030-32618-0_8.

Gallerie degli Uffizi (2017). *Statuto delle Gallerie degli Uffizi*.

Gallerie degli Uffizi (2019). *Uffizi: tutti i numeri del 2018.*

Gallerie degli Uffizi (2020). *I numeri del 2019.*

Gallerie degli Uffizi (2021). *I numeri del 2020.*

Gallerie degli Uffizi (2022). *I numeri del 2021.*

Gallerie degli Uffizi (2023). *I numeri del 2022*.

Giusti, S. (2023). Museums after the pandemic, from resilience to innovation: The case of the Uffizi. *International Journal of Cultural Policy*, 1–14. DOI: 10.1080/10286632.2023.2167986.

Grincheva, N. (2020). Museums as actors of city diplomacy: From "hard" assets to "soft" power. In Amiri, S. & Sevin, E. (eds) *City Diplomacy*. London: Palgrave Macmillan Series in Global Public Diplomacy, 111–136. DOI: 10.1007/978-3-030-45615-3_6.

Grincheva, N. (2022). Cultural diplomacy under the "digital lockdown": Pandemic challenges and opportunities in museum diplomacy. *Place Branding and Public Diplomacy*, 18, 8–11. DOI: 10.1057/s41254-021-00237-z.

Izzo, F., Camminatiello, I., Sasso, P., Solima, L., & Lombardo, R. (2023). Creating customer, museum and social value through digital technologies: Evidence from the MANN Assiri project. *Socio-Economic Planning Sciences*, 86, 101502, 11–12. DOI: 10.1016/j.seps.2022.101502.

Lazzeretti, L. (2004). *Art Cities, Cultural Districts and Museums*. Firenze: Firenze University Press. DOI: 10.26530/OAPEN_356366.

Lazzeretti, L. (2022). What is the role of culture facing the digital revolution challenge? Some reflections for a research agenda. *European Planning Studies*, 30(9), 1617–1637. DOI: 10.1080/09654313.2020.1836133.

Lazzeretti, L. (2023). *The Rise of Algorithmic Society and the Strategic Role of Arts and Culture*. Cheltenham, UK and Northampton, MA, USA: Edward Elgar Publishing.

Lazzeretti, L., & Capone, F. (2015). Museums as societal engines for urban renewal. The event strategy of the museum of natural history in Florence. *European Planning Studies*, 23(8), 1548–1567. DOI: 10.1080/09654313.2013.819073.

Lazzeretti, L., & Oliva, S. (2018). Rethinking city transformation: Florence from art city to creative fashion city. *European Planning Studies*, 26(9), 1856–1873. DOI: 10.1080/09654313.2018.1478951.

Lazzeretti, L., & Sartori, A. (2016). Digitisation of cultural heritage and business model innovation: The case of the Uffizi gallery in Florence. *Il Capitale Culturale. Studies on the Value of Cultural Heritage*, 14, 945–970. DOI: 10.13138/2039-2362/1436.

MiBACT (2014). "Organizzazione e funzionamento dei musei statali", G.U. 10 marzo 2015, n. 57. https://www.gazzettaufficiale.it/eli/id/2015/03/10/15A01707/sg (Ministerial Decree published 30 March 2023).

Nuccio, M., Bertacchini, E. (2022). Data-driven arts and cultural organisations: Opportunity or chimera?. *European Planning Studies*, 30(9), 1638–1655. DOI: 10.1080/09654313.2021.1916443.

Osterwalder, A., & Pigneur, Y. (2010). *Business Model Generation: A Handbook for Visionaries, Game Changers, and Challengers*. London: John Wiley & Sons.

Pasquinelli, C., Trunfio, M., Bellini, N., & Rossi, S. (2022). Reimagining urban destinations: Adaptive and transformative city brand attributes and values in the pandemic crisis. *Cities*, 124, 103621.

Plaza, B., & Haarich, S. N. (2015). The Guggenheim Museum Bilbao: Between regional embeddedness and global networking. *European Planning Studies*, 23(8), 1456–1475. DOI: 10.1080/09654313.2013.817543.

Sacco, P. L., Ferilli, G., & Tavano Blessi, G. (2018). From culture 1.0 to culture 3.0: Three socio-technical regimes of social and economic value creation through culture, and their impact on European Cohesion Policies. *Sustainability*, 10(11), 3923, 1–23. DOI: 10.3390/su10113923.

Schmidt, E. (2018). Eike Schmidt, Director, Uffizi Galleries, Florence. *Museum Management and Curatorship*, 33(6), 611–613. DOI: 10.1080/09647775.2019.1537626.

Simon, N. (2010). *The Participatory Museum*. Santa Cruz, CA: Museum 2.0.

Simon, N. (2016). *The Art of Relevance*. Santa Cruz, CA: Museum 2.0.

Simone, C., Cerquetti, M., & La Sala, A. (2021). Museums in the infosphere: Reshaping value creation. *Museum Management and Curatorship*, 36(4), 322–341. DOI: 10.1080/09647775.2021.1914140.

Smith Bautista, S. (2014). *Museums in the Digital Age. Changing Meanings of Place, Community, and Culture*. Maryland: Altamira Press.

Solima, L., Tani, M., & Sasso, P. (2021). Social innovation and accessibility in museum: The case of "SoStare al MANN" social inclusion project. *Il capitale culturale. Studies on the Value of Cultural Heritage*, (23), 23–56. DOI: 10.13138/2039-2362/2518.

SSPSAE & PMCF (2009). *Rapporto di attività 2007–2008. Soprintendenza speciale per il patrimonio storico, artistico ed etnoantropologico e per il polo museale della città di Firenze*. Firenze: Giunti.

SSPSAE & PMCF (2011). *Rapporto di attività 2009–2010. Soprintendenza speciale per il patrimonio storico, artistico ed etnoantropologico e per il polo museale della città di Firenze*. Firenze: Giunti.

SSPSAE & PMCF (2014). *Rapporto di attività 2011–2012. Soprintendenza speciale per il patrimonio storico, artistico ed etnoantropologico e per il polo museale della città di Firenze*. Firenze: Giunti.

Suchman, M. C. (1995). Managing legitimacy: Strategic and institutional approaches. *Academy of Management Review*, 20(3), 571–610. DOI: 10.2307/258788.

Taormina, F., & Bonini Baraldi, S. (2022). Museums and digital technology: A literature review on organisational issues. *European Planning Studies*, 30(9), 1676–1694. DOI: 10.1080/09654313.2021.2023110.

Ulldemolins, R. J. (2014). Culture and authenticity in urban regeneration processes: Place branding in central Barcelona. *Urban Studies*, 51(14), 3026–3045. DOI: 10.1177/0042098013515762.

Vinten, G. (1994). Participant observation: a model for organisational investigation?. *Journal of Managerial Psychology*, 9(2), 30–38. DOI: 10.1108/02683949410059299.

Wirtz, B. W., Pistoia, A., Ullrich, S., & Göttel, V. (2016). Business models: Origin, development and future research perspectives. *Long Range Planning*, 49(1), 36–54. DOI: 10.1016/j.lrp.2015.04.001.

Yin, R. K. (2009). *Case Study Research: Design and Methods* (Vol. 5). Thousand Oaks, CA: Sage.

Zan, L., Bonini Baraldi, S., & Santagati, M. E. (2018). Missing HRM: The original sin of museum reforms in Italy. *Museum Management and Curatorship*, 33(6), 530–545. DOI: 10.1080/09647775.2018.1537608.

9. Industry 4.0 in clusters: how openness boosts innovation in Industry 4.0 technologies

Francesco Capone, Filippo Baldetti, Niccolò Innocenti, and Vincenzo Zampi

9.1 INTRODUCTION

Industry 4.0 represents a new paradigm in automation technologies and supported by the progress of Information and Communication Technologies (ICT) and data storage, is considered the Fourth Industrial Revolution (Schwab, 2017; Park, 2018). It consists of a new industrial scenario in which the convergence of various emerging technologies, strengthened by the Internet of Things (IoT), results in physical-digital systems capable of facing the complexity of production and creating greater value for companies.

Given the importance that I4.0 has assumed, there has been growing academic research on I4.0 intending to provide insights into issues, challenges and solutions related to the design, implementation and management of I4.0 (Piccarozzi et al., 2018; Capone & Innocenti, 2023). However, few studies focused their attention on the innovation process in this area and in particular investigating the role of collaboration and openness in I4.0, leading to the question: *how do firms adopt Open Innovation (OI) dynamics for innovation in I4.0?*

To answer this question, the present chapter is based on the concept of Open Innovation, developed by Chesbrough (2003), regarding the firms' opening of the innovative process to external sources of knowledge. It is the overcoming of the closed innovation model, according to which the entire innovation process is carried out by the R&D department, without the influence of external actors.

By adopting an OI model, companies can draw on knowledge not present internally and seize new technological opportunities, increasing their innovative capacity. Research on the theme of openness expanded after the Chesbrough study (Dahlander & Gann, 2010; Chesbrough et al., 2014).

Several studies have shown a curvilinear relationship between the level of openness of the innovation process and innovative performance (Laursen & Salter, 2006; Leiponen & Helfat, 2010; Lazzarotti et al., 2014).

This chapter aims to investigate the relevance of the characteristics of companies on innovative performance in I4.0, with particular reference to the concepts of breadth and depth of openness (Laursen & Salter, 2006; Leiponen & Helfat, 2010; Capone & Innocenti, 2020).

The relationship between these two elements (breadth and depth) of openness and innovation in I4.0 is thus studied through an empirical study on a sample of 54 Italian companies located in clusters of I4.0 in Italy. The firms operating in I4.0 have been identified through a search on LinkedIn Sales Navigator. The identified companies then filled out a questionnaire to investigate the role of opening the innovative process in the context of I4.0.

To answer the previous research question, the study also presents an analysis of the geography of I4.0 innovation to map the I4.0 clusters in Italy (Hervas-Oliver et al., 2021; Burlina & Montresor, 2021).

The results highlight the relationship between the level of openness and innovative performance in I4.0. In particular, an inverse U-shaped curvilinear relationship is also confirmed in I4.0 innovation and the opening of the innovative process, underlining how collaborations are also important in I4.0, but these also hide dangers and costs.

The chapter is structured as follows. After this introduction, the next section will analyse the literature on openness and innovation in the I4.0 context. Section 9.3 describes the research design and the source of the data. Section 9.4 presents the empirical analysis. The final section concludes by indicating some managerial implications.

9.2   INDUSTRY 4.0 AND THE OPENNESS OF THE INNOVATION PROCESS

9.2.1   Industry 4.0

The term *Industry 4.0* derives from its German equivalent "Industrie 4.0", introduced in 2011 at the Hanover fair and indicated as an integral part of the German High-Tech Strategy 2020 (Kagermann et al., 2011). Since then, it is considered the Fourth Industrial Revolution (Schwab, 2017; Ghobakhloo, 2018).

It consists of a new industrial scenario in which the convergence of different emerging technologies translates into physical-digital systems capable of addressing the complexity of production and creating greater value for businesses (Zhou et al., 2015). Thus, intelligent factories are emerging, where machines, devices and products are interconnected to adapt to market changes in real-time. It is therefore well known that I4.0 can have an important long-term strategic impact on global industrial development (European Parliament, 2015).

Although there is no real definition of I4.0, it was initially developed around four main technologies: *Cyber-Physical Systems*, *the Internet of Things* and *Services* and *Smart Factories*. However, later a wide range of interdisciplinary technologies identify I4.0 such as *Cloud Computing* and *Big Data and analytics*. Some additional technologies are also examined, often treated by some authors, as useful for the improvement and versatility of *Smart Manufacturing* such as *additive manufacturing*, *visual technology* and *cyber security* (Capone & Innocenti, 2023).

I4.0 represents a huge opportunity for companies increasingly aware of the advantages they can offer. According to European Commission (2018), almost 9 out of 10 European companies consider these new technologies an opportunity.

There is, however, a high heterogeneity between the various economies in the world which determines a different ability to cope with the I4.0. The differences between States concern, the flexibility of the labour market, the level of skills of human capital, the adequacy of the digital infrastructure and the level of legal protection. Park (2018) has compiled a ranking on the readiness of the various economies to face I4.0. The countries of western Europe and particularly those of northern Europe (Finland, Sweden, Denmark and Norway), are at the top of the ranking. In addition, the United States and the United Kingdom play a leading role among Anglo-Saxon countries.

Deloitte (2018) shows how Italy holds a solid position in Europe and the world as regards the state of adoption and application of the technologies that enable I4.0. Italy is in fact among the first states in Europe for high-tech companies, both manufacturing and services. Italy is also above the European average for the production and application of industrial robots and the use of technologies such as IoT and Machine to Machine communication. However, according to the report prepared by the Ministry of Economic Development (2018) concerning the spread of I4.0, in 2017 only 8.4% of companies use at least one enabling technology.

Also at a geographical level, there is a heterogeneous diffusion of these technologies with a prevalence in the regions of central-northern Italy. At the regional level, Lombardy and Emilia-Romagna are the regions with the largest number of I4.0 companies operating in automation and smart systems.

In this context, it is important to note that some of the literature has investigated the role of I4.0 in different specific locations such as clusters and industrial districts (Hervas-Oliver et al., 2021; De Propris & Bailey, 2021; Bellandi et al., 2020). Some works deal with the link between I4.0 and clusters on a theoretical level, but mainly cluster studies analyse case studies of specific clusters investigating issues such as the adoption, implementation, and impact of I4.0 in different places (e.g., Poland–Germany (Götz & Jankowska, 2017)).

Works on industrial clusters are less numerous and focused mainly on countries such as Italy and Spain (Pagano et al., 2020; Hervas-Oliver et al., 2021; Hervas-Oliver, 2022; Burlina & Montresor, 2021) underlining the importance impact the I4.0 can have in Italy (Bellandi et al., 2020).

9.2.2 Openness in Industry 4.0

Several authors underline that the openness of the innovation process is particularly crucial in complex technological industries such as I4.0 (Capone & Innocenti, 2023). According to Reischauer (2018), I4.0 mobilises actors to innovate more collaboratively than in innovation in traditional sectors. I4.0 offers opportunities to allow more flexible management, with an open and collaborative culture for the development and use of digital innovations, and to build and strengthen collaborative networks with a wide variety of partners.

Rocha, Mamedio and Quandt (2019) demonstrate the importance of obtaining external sources of knowledge and technology for I4.0 innovations, with particular reference to collaborations with startups, strengthening the theoretical approach of OI contextualised to I4.0.

Considering also the increasingly important role of end users, the innovation ecosystem concept is investigated by Rocha et al. (2019) as an important enabling factor for I4.0. In the same context, WIPO (2015) described the innovation ecosystems of some revolutionary innovations focusing on I4.0 technologies (robotics and 3D printing). Urbinati et al. (2017) also highlight the role of digital technologies to manage an open innovation process, with particular reference to Big Data, the Internet of Things and Cloud Computing. In fact, several studies have shown the impact of digital technologies on how to innovate openly and collaboratively (Brunswicker et al., 2015).

However, despite this growing interest in I4.0 and the importance of collaboration, few studies have investigated the role of opening up the innovative process in this evolving context. Several authors have focused on the process of opening up the innovation process, but outside the I4.0 context (Henkel, 2009; Herzog & Leker, 2010; Chiaroni et al., 2011; Enkel & Bader, 2013; Capone & Innocenti, 2020).

Chesbrough (2003) originally underlined that adopting OI practices can boost the innovation productivity of firms, and firms adopting OI are generally more innovative than closed innovation organisations. Recent studies have proposed several potential benefits of opening up the innovation process (Huizingh, 2011; Greco et al., 2015).

Laursen and Salter (2006) have made a great contribution to the effect of strategies for researching external ideas on innovation, introducing two concepts that represent the opening of firms' innovative processes. The first term, the *breadth* of collaboration, is defined as the number of external sources or research channels on which companies rely in their innovative activities. It ranges from close to extensive collaboration with an increasing number of external partners. The second concept refers to the *depth* of the collaboration, defined instead in terms of the intensity with which companies draw ideas from different external sources. It ranges from superficial to deep collaborations with the intensification of collaborative interactions.

The reduction of uncertainty, the variety of resources and the greater technological opportunities are among the advantages that the literature on *the breadth* and *depth* of the opening has highlighted (Bernal et al., 2019). The approach used in the Laursen and Salter study (2006) focuses on research channels, such as customers, suppliers, competitors and universities, which companies use to identify innovative opportunities. The two authors, exploring the innovation process on a sample of 2707 manufacturing companies in the United Kingdom, found that *breadth* and *depth* are positively correlated with innovative performances, allowing companies to take advantage of new ideas and resources, and seize innovative opportunities.

Summarizing, several studies suggest that collaborations carried out in a wider and more intense way allow for obtaining a higher level of innovative performance (Parida et al., 2012; Laursen & Salter, 2014), implying that *breadth* and *depth* may favour the innovative performances also in I4.0.

However, the opening of the innovative process does not only entail benefits but also costs, both monetary and non-monetary (Laursen & Salter, 2014; Knudsen & Mortensen, 2011). They tend to grow as the opening increases. The latter in fact implies, according to Salge et al. (2013), the use of financial and human resources, necessary to absorb or identify, assimilate and use, external knowledge (Ferreras-Méndez et al., 2015).

There are two other reasons why excessive openness can have a negative influence on innovative performance (Laursen & Salter, 2006). The first is given by the problem of timing, according to which innovative ideas do not always arrive at the right time to be exploited. The second reason refers to the so-called attention allocation problem, which arises if there are numerous ideas. In fact, in such cases, companies fail to pay the necessary attention to some ideas, even though they are relevant. These problems suggest that businesses may incur higher marginal costs due to the greater complexity of managing a wider variety of knowledge (Leiponen & Helfat, 2010).

Summarising, the literature suggests that there is a point where the costs of *breadth* and *depth* of the opening outweigh the benefits, becoming disadvantageous (Laursen & Salter, 2006; Leiponen & Helfat, 2010; Capone & Innocenti, 2020). The researchers thus found a non-linear relationship, with an inverse

U-shape, between these two components of the opening and the innovative performances and in our view, this may hold also for the I4.0 case.

9.3   METHODOLOGY

The following paragraph describes the questionnaire administrated to approximately 600 Italian firms based in I4.0 clusters and specialised in I4.0 technologies, to investigate the role of openness of the innovative process in I4.0.

In particular, the questionnaire was constructed starting from the "Statistical survey of innovation in enterprises" carried out by ISTAT and the Report on Industry 4.0 realised by Federmeccanica[1] (2016). The first questionnaire is coordinated at the European level with the Community Innovation Survey (CIS) as the main statistical tool of the European Union to measure innovation activities on a business level and compare them internationally.

Federmeccanica's research (2016) instead investigates the evolution of I4.0 among metal-working companies in Italy. It presents questions related to the adoption of I4.0 technologies. In our questionnaire, specific questions have also been added on the collaborations and open innovation in I4.0 that would allow the construction of some variables, with particular reference to the *breadth* and *depth* (Laursen & Salter, 2006).

LinkedIn Sales Navigator was therefore used to identify, with target companies, those with a likely focus on I4.0. To do this, firms were searched using keywords related to the phenomenon under examination, such as "Industry 4.0", "Internet of Things", "Cloud Computing", "Robotics", and so on[2] and localised in "clusters" of the I4.0 specialisation (see next section).

The questionnaire was administered by sending an invitation to approximately 600 companies through LinkedIn. All selected employees had managerial roles (CTO, CEO, I4.0 managers, etc.), and 54 valid replies were thus received. The overall response rate was 8.7%. Given that almost all the responses came from qualified people within the companies, the data can be considered of good quality.[3]

9.3.1   Characteristics of the Interviewed Firms

The 54 companies are located throughout Italy in 12 different regions, mainly concentrating in the northeast-centre industrial triangle. Seventy per cent of the sample focuses on Information and Communication Technologies (ICT), while 9% belongs to the industrial automation sector. The remaining part of the sample (21%) concerns manufacturing sectors with a focus on activities not directly related to 4.0 technologies, such as the energy, mechanical, automotive sector, and so on.

As far as company size, those with less than 50 employees (micro and small enterprises) prevail, with a percentage equal to 65%. Medium-sized enterprises (50–249 employees) represent 15% of the sample and large enterprises 20% (with over 250 employees).

Seventy-one per cent of the companies in the sample declared to innovate in I4.0. All companies in the industrial automation sector have innovated in this area. The percentage is 70% for companies in the ICT sector, while it drops to 60% for those in other sectors.

The main technologies in which the firms are specialised are the Internet of Things, with 84%, Big Data (68%), augmented and virtual reality and Artificial Intelligence (both at 57%). 3D printing is the technology on which companies focus less. Finally, all companies state to develop open innovation processes to innovate and establish collaboration with external innovation firms and research centres.

9.4   EMPIRICAL ANALYSIS

9.4.1   The Geography of I4.0 in Italy

This section analyses the production of inventions in technologies related to I4.0 in Italy. To identify clusters specialised in I4.0 technologies, we departed from a database of about 70,000 patents developed by at least one Italian inventor in the period 2000–2016 retrieved from PATSTAT.

To identify the I4.0 patents, a database was built containing all the IPC codes relating to these technologies, following the EPO study (2017). Other studies have used the IPCs identified in EPO (2017) for the identification of innovations in I4.0 technologies (Corradini et al., 2021; Benassi et al. 2020).

Using the IPC codes, it was possible to identify 2,585 patents related to I4.0 with at least one Italian inventor. The patents were then georeferenced, based on the inventor's residence and fractions of patents-inventors have been calculated as usual.

Figure 9.1 presents the evolution of patents in I4.0 technologies in Europe (Figure 9.1a) and Italy (Figure 9.1b). The two figures show a similar evolution of patent production in Italy and Europe. Similar results were also registered in other works at the European level (EPO, 2017; Benassi et al. 2020, 2022).

Figure 9.2 presents the geography of I4.0 patents production in Italy. Patenting in I4.0 technologies has been mainly concentrated in the Central-Northern provinces. Looking at the top Italian cities by the number of patents, it is not surprising that Milan has the highest value, almost twice as many as Bologna, second in this ranking. It is important to note, however, that the largest number of provinces in this ranking belongs to Emilia-Romagna, demonstrating a more uniform spread of patenting activity than Lombardy. Patenting in I4.0

Fig 9.1a

Fig 9.1b

Figure 9.1   Patents in I4.0 technologies in Italy

is also branched out in Veneto and Tuscany, also following the pattern of the Industrial District in Italy (Pagano et al., 2020).

Figure 9.2   The geography of I4.0 patents production in Italy

9.4.2   Open Innovation and I4.0

This section analyses the relationship between the level of openness of the firm's innovation process (measured in terms of *depth* and *breadth*) and their innovative performances in the I4.0. Figure 9.3 illustrates this relationship through a scatter plot. The horizontal axis indicates the openness of the firms, with values between 0 and 10, indicating how many sources of knowledge a firm usually uses to realise innovations (Laursen & Salter, 2006), while the vertical axis represents the innovative performances in I4.0 (with a number of innovations between 0 and 9) (the number of technologies in I4.0). The various companies, for privacy reasons, are represented through a numeric code assigned to the firm. The chart is also divided into four quadrants, to indicate different attitudes towards high or low levels of openness and innovation in I4.0.

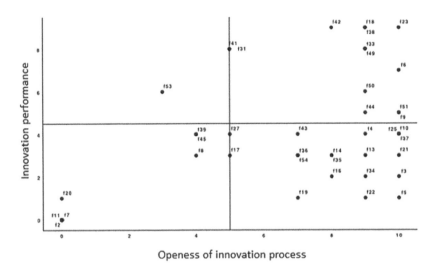

Figure 9.3   *The paradox of innovation in I4.0 and openness*

The quadrants on the left represent the companies that develop innovations mainly following the *closed innovation* paradigm, while the quadrants on the right are those that innovate most through the *Open Innovation* paradigm, where collaborations prevail on self-organised activities. In particular, the lower left quadrant (*Low closed innovators*) identifies those companies with a low level of openness and a low level of innovation in I4.0. The upper left quadrant (*Closed innovators*) shows high levels of innovation in Industry 4.0, despite the small number of knowledge sources used. There are only a few firms in this quadrant, indicating that most firms, with high innovation performances, adopt an open innovation approach.

As for the quadrants to the right of the graph, with high levels of openness, it is possible to notice a substantial difference in the innovative performances between the different companies. In particular, in the lower right quadrant (*Low open innovators*), 19 companies have low levels of innovation in I4.0, despite a high number of collaborations. Other 13 companies, on the other hand, demonstrate high innovative performances associated with high levels of openness (*Open innovators*). As a result, their OI strategies seem more effective than other companies that collaborate with a large number of partners.

Since the same levels of openness lead to different levels of innovation performances, the following analysis aims to assess the impact that different opening strategies have on innovation. In particular, it focuses on breaking down the opening up of companies in terms of *breadth* and *depth* of openness (Laursen & Salter, 2006). Collaboration can be focused or wide depending on the number of external partners and can be superficial or deep based on the intensity of relations with the various sources of knowledge. Open innovation strategies may depend on these two dimensions. It is therefore interesting to investigate the contribution that the openness of the innovation process could have to innovative performance in the context of I4.0.

9.4.3   Empirical Analysis on I4.0 and Openness

The dependent variable (*Inno*) is given by the number of innovations relating to I4.0 technologies, a proxy of the innovative performance of companies in this area. This is determined by the number of different technologies to which innovation is connected and is a number between 0 and 9.

The variables of interest that are included in the analysis are represented by breadth (*Breadt_I40*) and depth (*Depth_I40*). The concept of *breadth* is defined as the number of external sources or research channels on which companies rely in their innovative activities (Laursen & Salter, 2006). The *depth* is defined instead in terms of the intensity with which companies draw ideas from different external sources or research channels (Laursen & Salter, 2006). In this research, the two variables relate exclusively to innovation in I4.0 and, consequently, refer to the 10 different types of partners.[4]

For the construction of these two variables, we followed the methodology developed by Laursen and Salter (2006) using as a reference the question relating to the degree of importance of the partners for innovation in I4.0, which provided as answer "absence of partner" or the importance levels, measured according to a Likert scale from 1 to 5. Starting from the *breadth*, each of the 10 types of partners was considered as a binary variable, with a value of 0 if the respondent selected the option "absence of partner" or 1 if he had been assigned any level of importance on the Likert scale. Subsequently, the binary variables were added up. Consequently, each company shows a *breadth* of 0, in the case of no collaboration with any type of partner, and a value of 10, in the case of collaboration with all the different sources of knowledge. The higher this value, the greater the degree of openness of the company in terms of *breadth*.

Also, the *depth* was built by forming a binary variable for each type of partner. In this case, a value of 0 was assigned not only in the case of "absence of partners", but also when the company assigned a level of importance of 1, 2 and 3. In fact, the importance of the partners, as a measure of the intensity of the collaborations with the partners, was considered medium or low in these cases. If the respondent is assigned to a type of partner with a high level of importance, equal to 4 or 5, the binary variable instead has a value of 1. The *depth* of a company, therefore, assumes a value of 0 if there are no sources of knowledge with which it collaborates intensely, while a value of 10 if it collaborates deeply with all the different types of partners. The higher the value of this variable, the greater the level of openness of the company in terms of *depth*.

The model includes also control variables, the first one *large* is used to control for the size of the company in terms of employees as a binary variable, which assumes a value of 1 if the has over 250 employees or 0 otherwise. Since large companies have access to more financial and human resources, these may have a greater innovative capacity (Leiponen & Helfat, 2010).

Control variables for small and medium firms have been also tested, however both the variables showed to be not significant and thus they are omitted from the models.

The second control variable *inn_prod* is a binary variable that reflects the type of innovation it assumes a value of 1 if the company introduced product innovations or 0 otherwise.

Following the same logic *inn_proc* is a binary variable, which refers in this case to the process innovation. It assumes a value of 1 if the respondent company introduced a process innovation and 0 in the opposite case.

Finally, also the control variable *partner_cluster* is added to the model, which reflects the level of geographical proximity of the partners. This is largely acknowledged as an important factor that may facilitate knowledge flows and allows to decrease the costs related to collaborations. To construct this variable, we used the question regarding the location of the partners (Figure 9.2). The 10 different sources of knowledge were considered as binary variables, assigning a value of 1 if the company presented a partner within the same region or 0 in the other case. A company with a value of 0 for this variable indicates the total absence of regional partners, while a value of 10 indicates that it shows at least one partner within the same region for each source of knowledge.

9.4.4 Regression Analysis

The dependent variable of our analysis is represented by values that are limited (or censored). In fact, the number of innovations cannot take negative values. For this reason, we had to deal with models capable to estimate censored data. Among the possible options the Tobit model is commonly used when the dependent variable takes values within a limited range, for this reason, it is also called a censored regression model. Other researchers have used the Tobit analysis to analyse the effect on a dependent censored variable (Laursen & Salter, 2006; Leiponen & Helfat, 2010).

Four models have been tested, the first one includes only the control variables, namely *large*, *inn_prod*, *inn_proc* and *partner_cluster*. The second model instead analysed only the two variables of interest *breadth* and *depth* to test the relationship between them and innovation (*Breadth_I40, Depth_I40*). The third model was aimed to test the curvilinear relationship between the variables of interest and innovations, for this reason, it includes *breadth*, *depth* and also their squared values (*Breadth_I40, B2_I40, Depth_I40, D2_I40*). Finally, the fourth model is complete, presenting all the variables identified so far.

Table 9.1 shows the results of the regression analysis. Model 1 shows a significant and positive relationship between all the control variables considered and innovation in I4.0. It may be noticed that product innovations show a higher coefficient compared to process innovations. However, both are significant with the highest level of accuracy. Also, regarding the locations of the partners, the effect is positive and significant meaning that leads to an increase in innovative performance. As expected, the size of the company matters for innovation, the results show that large companies have higher performance than SMEs.

Model 2 highlights the positive relationship between the *breadth* and *depth* of the openness of the innovation process and I4.0 innovation. The first shows a positive and significant coefficient, meaning that as the number of sources of knowledge increases, also the innovative performance increases. Conversely, the depth does not show significant results in this case.

Model 3 provides evidence of the inverted U-shaped relationship between the breadth and depth of the openness of the innovation process and the innovation in I4.0. To investigate this trend, the model includes the squares of the variables *Breadth_I40* (B2_I40) and *Depth_I40* (D2_I40). To show this trend, the coefficients must be positive for the first-degree variables and negative for the second ones and this is exactly the case in this model. Regarding the Breadth, this means that the greater the number of different sources of knowledge to which companies draw, the greater the innovation in I4.0 assume a curvilinear shape, meaning that there is a tipping point where too many sources of knowledge negatively affect innovation. While regarding *depth* means that innovation initially increases as the sources with which companies collaborate intensively increase, also in this case, there is a maximum point after which a greater *depth* leads to a reduction in innovative performance.

Finally, Model 4 is the most complete and includes all the variables previously identified. The variables are all significant except for product innovation and all of them maintain the same sign. By focusing on the influence of *breadth* and *depth* on innovation in I4.0, the presence of an inverse U curvilinear relationship is confirmed.[5]

Table 9.1   *Estimations*

Variables	Model 1	Model 2	Model 3	Model 4
Constant	-2.929**	-2.176**	-3.447***	-4.794***
	(1.224)	(0.977)	(1.138)	(1.136)
Large firm	2.218*			2.160**
	(1.164)			(0.843)
Inno_prod	3.852***			0.568
	(1.093)			(0.909)
Inno_proc	2.461***			1.989***
	(0.939)			(0.690)
Partner_cluster	0.404**			0.205*
	(0.161)			(0.115)
Breadth_I4.0		0.754***	1.908***	2.289***
		(0.163)	(0.489)	(0.480)
Depth_I4.0		0.0955	1.544***	0.886*
		(0.252)	(0.554)	(0.486)
Breadth^2_I4.0			-0.135***	-0.182***
			(0.043)	(0.043)
Depth^2_I4.0			-0.205***	-0.128*
			(0.077)	(0.066)
Obs.	54	54	54	54
p-value residuals	0.309	0.973	0.003	0.009
Akaike	226.146	204.961	185.914	178.763
Avg. VIF	1.03	1.989	16.65	10.51

Notes: *: p>0.1; **: p<0.05; *** p<0.01.
Source: Our elaboration.

Akaike Information Criterion (AIC) allows the comparison between the different estimated models. The lower the AIC, the higher the quality of the estimated model and in our case the lowest AIC level is one of the fourth models, suggesting that the complete model is preferable to the previous ones.

As far as the residuals are concerned, they are normally distributed in the third and fourth models, as shown by the test with a p-value lower than 1%. As a result, the latter two models are also statistically robust. As regards the possible presence of multicollinearity in our models, we performed a Variance Inflation Factor (VIF) analysis, which shows results equal to or higher than the threshold of 10 only in the third model. These higher results are commonly due to the inclusion of the squared variables (breadth and depth in our case), as well as the number of observations of the sample that is not high.

As an additional robustness test, we also run the regression for the fourth model using robust standard errors. The results do not show relevant differences, the only one is represented by the higher significance of the *partner_ cluster* variable reaching a higher significance level.

9.5   CONCLUSIONS

The aim of this chapter is to investigate the innovation process in I4.0 and in particular the role of openness and collaboration in the fourth industrial revolution. This led us to the following research question: *how do firms adopt Open Innovation dynamics for innovation in I4.0?*

Companies show a growing openness to knowledge from external sources for innovation. This is even more important in a complex and multidisciplinary context such as that of I4.0, where different knowledge is needed and this technological variety is not always available within company boundaries. The importance of an open and collaborative culture for the development of digital innovations has been described by some authors (Reischauer, 2018; Rocha et al., 2019). It has been stated that the greater the breadth and depth, the greater the innovative performance of a company that invests in I4.0. Indeed, companies that draw on knowledge that is not present internally opening to new technological opportunities from a wide range of external sources tend to be more innovative than companies that focus exclusively on internal R&D (Laursen & Salter, 2006; Belderbos et al., 2014). The research results confirmed this, indicating that the breadth and depth are positively related to innovation in I4.0.

However, the search for external partners not only involves benefits but also costs. There are in fact costs due to the absorption of knowledge from the outside, in addition to those relating to the problem of timing of monitoring and control (Ferreras-Méndez et al., 2015). Establishing deep relationships with external partners also involves a company's dependence on them, generating a certain organisational rigidity. Consequently, excessive openness, both in terms of breadth and depth, can hinder innovation. In fact, the results of the regression analysis show an inverse U-shaped curvilinear relationship between the two components.

These results have clear managerial implications, this approach to Open Innovation applied in the context of I4.0 leads to confirm the previous studies that show how the opening of innovative processes allows seizing a greater number of innovation opportunities, allowing companies to obtain knowledge regarding new technologies that are not present internally. Consequently, the managers of companies that innovate in the context of I4.0 should consider openness as a strategic response to the need for knowledge that this context requires and to the risks associated with the innovation process.

The main results of the chapter however underline that companies need to adopt a mature, conscious and disciplined approach to Open Innovation. Firms should avoid indiscriminate openness, devoid of the method, but an efficient and effective management of a limited number of external sources of knowledge, so as not to dissipate the firm's innovative efforts. Given the different optimal levels of breadth and depth, managers should consider both components of openness to make appropriate decisions in terms of Open Innovation strategies.

Of course, the present work is not free of limitations. First, the proposed analysis does not allow to investigate the importance of breadth and depth for innovation within every single source of knowledge. Second, in this analysis, it was not possible to evaluate the effect of R&D spending, as the answers were inaccurate in this respect. It would be interesting to get information on this important factor, to insert into the model.

In conclusion, this chapter provides some interesting results in disentangling the opening innovation process dynamic in I4.0 that will be also more and more relevant in the future with the further development of ICT and new technologies.

NOTES

1. Trade union association of the Italian Mechanical Industry.
2. The keywords refer to the different technologies that can be included in the I40 evolution: "Industry 4.0", "Cyber-Physical Systems", "Internet of Things", "Artificial Intelligence", "Augmented Reality", "Cloud Computing", "Big Data", "Robotics", "Additive Manufacturing", "Cyber Security", "Smart Factory", etc.
3. Fifty-four per cent from innovation managers, 13% from CTO, 26% from CEO and 7% from others.
4. The analysis includes: (1) suppliers, (2) clients or customers, (3–4) competitors (in or outside the same industry), (5) consultants, (6) commercial laboratories/R&D enterprises, (7) universities or other higher education institutes, (8) government research organisations, or (9) private research institutes (10) startups.

5. We also tested some interactions between the variables: the interaction between Depth and Breath is significant and positive as expected, unfortunately the interaction between Depth^2 and Breath^2 is not significant. We prefer then to omit them from the models.

REFERENCES

Belderbos, R., Cassiman, B., Faems, D., Leten, B. & Looy, B. (2014). Co-ownership of intellectual property: Exploring the value-appropriation and value-creation implications of co-patenting with different partners. *Research Policy*, 43(5), 841–852.

Bellandi, M., Santini, E., Vecciolini, C. & De Propris, L. (2020). Industry 4.0: Transforming local productive systems in the Tuscany region, in De Propris L. & Bailey D. (eds), *Industry 4.0 and regional transformations*. Routledge, London, 84–96.

Benassi, M., Grinza, E. & Rentocchini, F. (2020). The rush for patents in the Fourth Industrial Revolution. *Journal of Industrial and Business Economics*, 47(4), 559–588.

Benassi, M., Grinza, E., Rentocchini, F. & Rondi, L. (2022). Patenting in 4IR technologies and firm performance. *Industrial and Corporate Change*, 31(1), 112–136.

Bernal, P., Salazar, I. & Montoya, P. (2019). Understanding the open innovation trends: An exploratory analysis of breadth and depth decisions. *Administrative Sciences*, 9(4), 1–15.

Brunswicker, S. & Bertino, E. & Matei, S. (2015). Big data for open digital innovation – a research roadmap. *Big Data Research*, 35(2), 53–58.

Burlina, C. & Montresor, S. (2021). On the territorial embeddedness of the fourth industrial revolution: A literature review about how Industry 4.0 meets industrial districts. *Scienze Regionali*, 21(1), 63–82.

Capone F. & Innocenti N. (2020). Open innovation and network dynamics. An analysis of openness of co-patenting collaborations in Florence, Italy. *Competitiveness Review*, 30(4), 379–396.

Capone, F. & Innocenti, N., (2023). *Innovazione, startup innovative e Industria 4.0. Aspetti teorici ed evidenze empiriche*. Franco Angeli, Milano.

Chesbrough, H. (2003). *Open Innovation: The New Imperative for Creating and Profiting from Technology*. Harvard University Press, Boston, MA.

Chesbrough, W., Vanhaverbeke, H. W. & West, J. (2014). (eds), *New Frontiers in Open Innovation*. Oxford University Press, Oxford.

Chiaroni, D., Chiesa, V. & Frattini, F. (2011). The open innovation journey: How firms dynamically implement the emerging innovation management paradigm. *Technovation*, 31(1), 34–43.

Corradini, C., Santini, E. & Vecciolini, C. (2021). The geography of Industry 4.0 technologies across European regions. *Regional Studies*, 55(10–11), 1667–1680.

Dahlander, L. & Gann, D. (2010). How open is innovation? *Research Policy*, 39(6), 699–709.

Deloitte. (2018). *Italia 4.0: siamo pronti? Il percepito degli executive in merito agli impatti economici, tecnologici e sociali delle nuove tecnologie*. Deloitte.

De Propris, L. & Bailey, D. (2021). Pathways of regional transformation and Industry 4.0. *Regional Studies*, 55(10–11), 1617–1629.

Enkel, E. & Bader, K. (2013). How to balance open and closed innovation: Strategy and culture as influencing factors. in Tidd, J. (ed.), *Open Innovation Research, Management and Practice.* Imperial College Press, London, 87–104.

European Commission. (2018). *Digital Transformation Scoreboard 2018 EU Businesses go Digital: Opportunities, Outcomes and Uptake.* Publications Office of the European Union, Luxembourg.

European Parliament. (2015). *Industry 4.0. Digitalisation for Productivity and Growth.* European Parliamentary Research Service.

European Patent Office (EPO). (2017). *Patents and the Fourth Industrial Revolution. The Inventions behind Digital Transformation.* Munich.

Federmeccanica. (2016). *Industry 4.0 – Un'indagine per costruire insieme il futuro.* Federmeccanica, Roma.

Ferreras-Méndez, J., Newell, S., Fernández-Mesa, A. & Vidal, J. (2015). Depth and breadth of external knowledge search and performance: The mediating role of absorptive capacity. *Industrial Marketing Management*, 47, 86–97.

Ghobakhloo, M. (2018). The future of manufacturing industry: A strategic roadmap toward Industry 4.0. *Journal of Manufacturing Technology Management*, 29(6), 910–936.

Götz, M. & Jankowska, B. (2017). Clusters and Industry 4.0 – do they fit together? *European Planning Studies*, 25(9), 1633–1653.

Greco, M., Grimaldi, M. & Cricelli, L. (2015). Open innovation actions and innovation performance: A literature review of European empirical evidence. *European Journal of Innovation Management*, 18(2), 150–171.

Henkel, J. (2009). Champions of revealing – the role of open source developers in commercial firms. *Industrial and Corporate Change*, 18(3), 435–471.

Hervas-Oliver, J. L. (2022). Industry 4.0 in industrial district SMEs: Understanding collective knowledge transfer by research and transfer institutes. *Competitiveness Review*, 32(5), 647–666.

Hervas-Oliver, J. L., Di Maria, E. & Bettiol, M. (2021). Industry 4.0 in firms, clusters and regions: The new digital imperative. *Competitiveness Review*, 31(1), 1–11.

Herzog, P. & Leker, J. (2010). Open and closed innovation: Different innovation cultures for different strategies. *International Journal of Technology Management*, 52(3–4), 322–343.

Huizingh, E. (2011). Open innovation: State of the art and future perspectives. *Technovation*, 31(1), 2–9.

Kagermann, H., Lukas, W. D. & Wahlster, W. (2011). Industrie 4.0: Mit dem Internet der Dinge auf dem Weg zur 4. industriellen Revolution. *VDI nachrichten*, 13(1), 2–3.

Knudsen, M. & Mortensen, T. (2011). Some immediate – but negative – effects of openness on product development performance. *Technovation*, 31(1), 54–64.

Laursen, K. & Salter, A. J. (2006). Open for innovation: The role of openness in explaining innovative performance among UK manufacturing firms. *Strategic Management Journal*, 27(2), 131–150.

Laursen, K. & Salter, A. J. (2014). The paradox of openness: Appropriability, external search and collaboration. *Research Policy*, 43(5), 867–878.

Lazzarotti, V., Garcia, M. & Manzini, R. (2014). Open innovation strategies in the food and drink industry: Determinants and impact on innovation performance. *International Journal of Technology Management*, 66, 212–242.

Leiponen, A. & Helfat, C. (2010). Innovation objectives, knowledge sources, and the benefits of breadth. *Strategic Management Journal*, 31(2), 224–236.

Ministry of Economic Deveopment. (2018). *La diffusione delle imprese 4.0 e le politiche: evidenze 2017*, MISE.

Pagano, A., Carloni, E., Galvani, S. & Bocconcelli, R. (2020). The dissemination mechanisms of Industry 4.0 knowledge in traditional industrial districts: Evidence from Italy. *Competitiveness Review*, 31(1), 27–53.

Parida, V., Westerberg, M. & Frishammar, J. (2012). Inbound open innovation activities in high-tech SMEs: The impact on innovation performance. *Journal of Small Business Management*, 50(2), 283–309.

Park, S. C. (2018). The Fourth Industrial Revolution and implications for innovative cluster policies. *AI & Society*, 33(3), 433–445.

Piccarozzi, M., Aquilani, B. & Gatti, C. (2018). Industry 4.0 in management studies: A systematic literature review. *Sustainability*, 10(10), 1–24.

Reischauer, G. (2018). Industry 4.0 as policy-driven discourse to institutionalize innovation systems in manufacturing. *Technological Forecasting and Social Change*, 132, 26–33.

Rocha, C. & Mamedio, D. & Quandt, C. (2019). Startups and the innovation ecosystem in Industry 4.0. *Technology Analysis & Strategic Management*, 31(12). 1474–1487.

Salge, O., Farchi, T., Barrett, M. & Dopson, S. (2013). When does search openness really matter? A contingency study of health-care innovation projects. *Journal of Product Innovation Management*, 30(4), 659–676.

Schwab, K. (2017). *The Fourth Industrial Revolution*. Currency, New York.

Urbinati, A., Chiaroni, D., Chiesa, V. & Frattini, F. (2017). The role of digital technologies in the innovation process. *R&D Management*, 50(1), 136–160.

World Intellectual Property Organization (WIPO). (2015). *Breakthrough Innovation and Economic Growth*. Economics & Statistics Series, Geneva.

Zhou, K., Liu, T. & Zhou, L. (2015). Industry 4.0: Towards future industrial opportunities and challenges. *2015 12th International Conference on Fuzzy Systems and Knowledge Discovery (FSKD)*, 2147–2152.

10. The evolution of the Italian industrial district: Arzignano's leather district from area monoculturale to area sistema integrata di innovazione

Italo Trevisan and Lucrezia Maria Mecenero

10.1 INTRODUCTION

More than a century ago, Alfred Marshall started to talk about "industrial districts", defining them as agglomerations of small and medium producers in a particular location, which in specific industrial sectors could represent an alternative to the big factory model.

The term "industrial districts" indicates the phenomenon that occurs when similar industrial businesses concentrate in the same territory, becoming the prevailing economic activity of the area. The significant flux of economic activity generated in this area of concentration, enhanced by the relations among the district's local community, creates advantages that the grouped firms can exploit. These advantages are available only to firms in a specific area of concentration, setting up a disparity between these companies and isolated enterprises.

Industrial districts are not static systems: during their existence, they evolve following different paths. The most successful ones became an "area sistema integrata" (integrated industrial system), the higher expression of complexity of an industrial district. These local productive systems work as a system of interrelations among firms and productive sectors, closely connected with the original specialization industry and directly stimulated from it. New sectors, "ancillary industries", are established next to the initial industry and in support of it. These industries are an extension of the types of prevailing industries. They become active in creating and exchanging know-how and qualified employees, thus becoming central factors of the district's success.

However, the area sistema integrata is not the last expression of the district. In the turbulent 21st-century's early decades, districts' evolution took different ways (De Marchi, Gereffi, and Grandinetti 2017).

The Arzignano leather district, which has its core in the territory of Arzignano and the Chiampo Valley, is an excellent example of how local dynamics can influence the growth and prosperity of a specific industrial sector both nationally and internationally. The area is Italy's most important hub for the tanning industry and one of the largest centers in Europe, and in 2019 its turnover exceeded 3 billion euros. The leather produced in this area, well known internationally for its quality, is exported to 125 countries and accounts for 1% of national exports.

Tanning was the first industry to grow in the Arzignano district. However, its development led to a corresponding rising establishment of suppliers of specialized inputs: in particular, producers of machinery for the tanning processes and companies that produce tanning-specific chemicals, but also services such as transportation, laboratories, and water recycling plants.

Industrial districts promote both competition and cooperation. Likewise, in the Arzignano district, rivals compete fiercely to maintain customers, and this rivalry pushes them towards constant innovation and improvement. At the same time, there is also cooperation, especially on a vertical level, involving companies in related industries and local institutions. When there is cooperation, related and supporting industries provide a real advantage in innovation and upgrading, thanks to the close working relationships that arise when suppliers and end-users are located nearby. The quick and constant flow of information and the exchange of ideas can become innovation accelerators.

This chapter aims to explain the factors behind Arzignano district's fortune and ability to meet never-ending challenges through the investigation of the innovation process in the area. In particular, the role of ancillary industries, tacit knowledge and face-to-face interactions and their contribution in R&D and innovation to the district competitiveness will be examined, pointing out how these processes created fertile ground for the evolution of the district into an *area sistema integrata d'innovazione* (integrated area of innovation).

10.2   METHODOLOGY

This research began with the need to investigate the sources of the Arzignano leather district's strength and resilience. The typical Area Sistema interconnections among firms from different sectors and their role in tacit knowledge creation are examined. In particular, this work analyses the contribution of innovation and synergies to the development of the industrial district.

First, bibliographical research was conducted on industrial districts and their development, with particular attention to the ones related to the Arzignano leather district. Primary data collected from trade associations such as "Camera di Commercio Industria Artigianato e Agricoltura di Vicenza", "Istat", "Unic", "Confindustria" and "Confartigianato" have been collected and analysed to give the quantitative dimension of the Arzignano district's recent evolutions. Moreover, informal interviews were conducted with sector experts (non-probability sampling – judgment sampling). The analysis results and the information gathered through the interviews had then been assessed in the light of the most recent literature on innovation.

10.3   THE ITALIANATE INDUSTRIAL DISTRICT

One of the most characterizing aspects of the Italian industrial structure is the clustering in industrial districts of SMEs belonging to the same industry. These districts are often located in parts of the country that are distant from the areas of early and more vigorous industrialization and have been the main drivers of economic development in those parts. Indeed, in many cases, districts were an unplanned response of peripheral areas that had a potential for growth but were largely ignored by an industrial policy oriented towards sectors of the state industry and towards the support of the large companies of the historical families of Italian capitalism.

The Italianate industrial districts[1] are socio-territorial entities characterized by active coexistence, in a geographically circumscribed and historically determined area, of a community of people and a population of industrial enterprises focused on one specific industry (Becattini 1989).

These productive systems show some peculiarities that distinguish them from Marshall's archetype. The "industrial atmosphere" of Marshallian memory is enhanced by the interaction between the local community (employers and workers feeling they belong to it), the system of values gluing this community and the institutions that spread those values in the area and assure their transmission through generations.

The interaction of disparate elements (SMEs, both specialized in a single phase of the production process and leading companies coordinating and guiding this hyper-specialization and selling the finished product, local authorities intervening in the development of joint initiatives) highlights the systemic nature of the Italianate industrial district. This complexity also indicates the evolution of the Italianate manufacturing districts from the traditional Marshallian industrial district to a more sophisticated entity called Area Sistema.[2]

The Italianate district and, later on, the Area Sistema, localized in small areas often peripheral to the main industrial centers, played a determinant role in the economic and social development of whole regions left behind in the early phases of the country's industrialization. Starting as areas where the productive structure is based on a single primary industry, they developed a higher degree of complexity, expanding their industrial focus to different, albeit related, industries.

The process towards increased complexity is the path many Italianate districts travelled, becoming more robust and thriving. This evolution, however, was not shared by all the districts; those that did not manage to evolve faltered, and even disappeared (Carminucci and Casucci 1997).[3]

The effect of this evolution is the building-up of differentiated capabilities owing to the solid functional links between the dominant (manufacturing) industry and the various activities that supply it with operational or strategic inputs. This arrangement gives greater resilience and more substantial competitive advantages both to the Area Sistema as a whole and to its firms. This integrated industrial system was and still is the distinguishing trait of the most successful among Italian industrial districts.

For a time, the Area Sistema was considered the last step in the evolution of Italianate industrial districts. Its characteristics allowed many Italian industrial districts to meet the momentous and disrupting changes in the competitive configuration of the world economy and maintain or regain their competitiveness in the face of the many challenges of the first decade of the 21st century.

However, these challenges, which intensified in the 2010s, require continuous adaptation of the firms' strategy. The combination of each firm's actions defines the district's collective evolution. Indeed, under the competitive pressure of a more globalized world economy and successive shocks ranging from sharper competition from emerging countries to the financial crisis and, more recently, to the pandemic, the Area Sistema continued to evolve.

De Marchi, Gereffi and Grandinetti (2017) developed a framework to explain the current configurations of industrial districts and growth opportunities, considering their ability to respond to global changes and to evolutionary directions. Three distinct directions seem to occur within the traditional configuration of Italian industrial districts: decline, hierarchy and resilience.

Recently, various authors (Bellandi, Plechero, and Santini 2022; Bettiol et al. 2022) have analysed the path of evolution of the districts, in many cases emphasizing the dematerialization of the district.[4]

In this view, fulfilling the requirements of global competitiveness required relinquishing the local dimension to integrate, more or less virtually, with other parts of the world. It would imply a process of either delocalization, outsourcing of production, or establishing international networks where all activities, from R&D to final touches to the product, can be carried out almost anywhere. In a sense, this evolution would mean the death of the district that would lose its defining characteristic of precise localization and the linked strength of the community feeling that only a circumscribed location can give. We maintain that this was a dead end,[5] and still is, even more so in consideration of the likely reconsideration of some practices of the globalization process as a consequence of the general evolution taking shape in the early 2020s.

Source: Authors' elaboration.

Figure 10.1   Arzignano's leather district area

The district's evolution continues, but the successful districts are those that, in their evolution, manage to keep a strong connection with the territory while fostering innovation and intersectoral collaboration. The next step in the district's evolution comes from building on the specialized knowledge of the area and the strong connections among its firms: they become an *area sistema integrata di innovazione* (integrated innovation-driven industrial system). The concentration on innovation and high-end segments of the market leads to a recovery of the production in the district, sometimes linked to partially reshoring some production activities (Fratocchi et al. 2014), with a consequent increase in local employment.

The evolution of the last few years points to the resilience of the district model. The districts that have weathered the storm have regained competitiveness by reinterpreting their traditional strength factor and integrating the Area Sistema's various components in an informal hub of innovation.

10.4   THE ARZIGNANO LEATHER DISTRICT

The Arzignano tanning district well typifies this resilient evolution that proves the capacity of the district model to resist and react to disruption. It was already an integrated Area Sistema, where the primary industry was well supported by the growing strength of ancillary industries (indeed, this integration caused the change of classification of the area from tanning district to leather district). Its performance in meeting the multiple challenges of the last two decades and overcoming the disruption of five long years of troubles was genuinely remarkable and placed it in an excellent position to face the more upsetting environment that emerged in the early 2020s.

10.4.1   The Tanning Sector

The initial core of the district was in the "triangle" Arzignano–Montebello Vicentino–Valle del Chiampo, known as the "Triangolo della pelle".[6] However, over the years, the area covered by the district extended to several other municipalities,[7] covering more than 132km in the provinces of Vicenza and Verona (see Figure 10.1). Even if the list of municipalities extended during the time, the most prominent are still Arzignano, Chiampo, and Montebello Vicentino, followed by Zermeghedo and Montorso Vicentino, which correspond to the initial core of the district. Together, these five municipalities account for 78% of local tanning units and 81% of employees.[8]

This local productive system is by far the most important hub for leather manufacture in Italy, and more than half of the total production value of the Italian leather sector in all years considered (2000–2019) was generated in the area. From 2014, in absolute terms, the turnover level remained relatively stable, around 2.7 billion euros; however, the relevance of the district in these years grew both at national and international levels. In 2019, the share of the Italian tanning sector turnover stemming from the Arzignano district was 58%, five percentage points more than in 2014. Furthermore, in the same years, the district's contribution to the global tanning turnover grew from 9.5% to 13.4% (data from UNIC).

The number of local units and employees the sector occupies further proves the district's resilience. Indeed, regardless of the disruptive times the Arzignano district underwent during the 2000s, at the end of the 2010s these numbers were not much different from what they were at the start. Despite a considerable decrease from 2003 to 2013, the number of people employed in the sector started rising again; in 2019, at 10,377 people employed, it was only down by 6.5% compared to the 11,101 in 2000. At the same time, the number of local units remained almost the same at the end of the period (-1%).

Local units were relatively stable during the whole period: at the highest peak in 2002, the local units were 799, only 78 units more than the lowest point in 2013 (-10%), connected with the 2008 international financial crisis (Balducci 2009).

Table 10.1   Leather sector production value and exports of Arzignano district. 2000–2019 (million €)

Year	Production value	% on Italian leather production	Exports*	% of export over production value
2000	3,295.6	53.40%	1,606.9	49%
2001	3,538.7	53.40%	1,773.2	50%
2002	3,303.4	53.40%	1,765.5	53%
2003	3,002.3	56.18%	1,537.7	51%
2004	2,859.7	57.03%	1,624.1	57%
2005	2,693.1	55.40%	1,464.1	54%
2006	2,896.1	54.44%	1,669.6	58%
2007	2,824.6	52.47%	1,700.7	60%
2008	2,339.9	51.26%	1,565.3	67%
2009	1,990.0	51.96%	1,229.1	62%
2010	2,309.4	51.06%	1,518.8	66%
2011	2,467.6	50.76%	1,734.9	70%
2012	2,484.5	51.54%	1,805.5	73%
2013	2,732.0	52.02%	2,022.4	74%
2014	2,815.0	52.80%	2,152.9	76%
2015	2,808.0	54.00%	2,313.0	82%
2016	2,750.0	55.00%	2,270.4	83%
2017	2,867.0	56.64%	2,378.0	83%
2018	2,825.5	57.68%	2,325.5	82%
2019	2,674.9	58.19%	2,452.6	91%
2020	2,179.0	62.25%	2,118.4	97%
2021	2,546.0	60.61%	2,286.6	89%

Note: * Data on exports are only available at province level. However, since 95% of tanning local units in Vicenza province are in the district area, we consider these figures as a good approximation.
Source: Own elaboration on data from ISTAT and UNIC – Concerie Italiane.

Table 10.1 shows that the district generated more than half of the total production value of the Italian leather sector in all years considered. The district's turnover decreased from 2000 to 2005, as did the Italian tanning sector. In these years, the Italian tanning industry lost ground and was forced to focus on quality to remain competitive. However, since the mid- and cheaper-product range remained prevalent, the industry was exposed to solid and aggressive foreign competition (mainly from China), causing the production values to drop (Mosconi 2005). The industry seemed to start to recover only in 2006; however, in 2007, the district was still not recording profits (it registered a loss of -75.6 million euros[9]). At the lowest point, in 2009, the district revenues fell by 30% compared to the pre-crisis value of 2007. This drop did not hit only the Arzignano district: the whole Italian leather sector turnover decreased by 29%. The district slowly started to recover in the following years, as shown in the table. It reached the pre-crisis production value level only in 2014. However, difficulties were not over. The turmoil, the international uncertainty and the lackluster trend in consumption that affected the whole business world did not help the tanning industry's slow recovery (Russo 2015). Furthermore, the introduction of alternative materials, such as the so-called "synthetic leather", posed even more pressure on the sector, forcing it to adapt and innovate to remain competitive. The table shows that the turnover level remained relatively stable after 2014 (with a dip in 2019); however, the relevance of the district in these years grew both at the national and international levels. Indeed, its weight in Italian leather production grew by five percentage points throughout this time and by more than three points on the international level, reaching 13.4% (author elaboration on data from UNIC – Concerie Italiane).

The stabilization of the situation was due mainly to the export performance. From 2000 to 2019, the district's export value grew by 53%. As Table 10.1 shows, exports value – after reaching a high point in 2001–2002 – oscillated at a slightly lower level until 2008 (the Chinese competition denting but not crippling the international capability of the district) to drop in 2009, when the Great Recession caused a 21% fall. However, in 2010 the exports were already similar to the pre-crisis values, and in 2011 they were 11% higher than in 2007. After that, they steadily grew year by year.

10.4.2 Ancillary Industries Evolution and Integration

The development of the tanning sector in the Arzignano district created fertile ground for the area's growth. The massive flow of wealth, employees and know-how brought to Arzignano by the tanning sector allowed the development of several different ancillary industries, among which the most prominent are the tanning-chemicals and the tanning-machinery sectors.

The tanning industry in the area boomed in the years of the post-war reconstruction between 1950 and 1960. In those years, in the light of increasing local demand for tanning machinery and chemicals, local ancillary industries started to develop. However, it was only in the new century that they became mature sectors in the area (see Table 10.2). The evolution of the tannery district into the leather Area Sistema resulted from the close integration of these ancillary industries with the tanneries. However, other activities, too, were involved in this transformation. For example, firms that process and recycle tanning wastes, such as water treatment plants, firms that process residues from leather, and firms that recover salt used for the preservation of raw hides. Also, in the area, multiple commercial enterprises buy and sell hides and leather for the local and international markets. Moreover, there are refrigerated warehouses, where rawhides can be stocked, and testing laboratories, which perform specific analyses on leather and chemicals.

The table shows an underlying growth trend in the period for the tanning-machinery sector (+11% for firms, +38% for local units), despite the drop of both these indicators after the 2008 financial crisis. This fall was connected to the difficulties suffered by the tanning sector because of the Great Recession. As tanning machinery is a high-value fixed asset, it is not surprising that tanneries chose to slow the investments in new machinery during the crisis. The tanning chemistry industry, on the other hand, appears barely affected by the crisis. These figures show an interesting detail. While the number of chemistry firms fluctuated within a narrow band and, in the end, increased by less than ten units (which is still around 75% increase), the number of local units shot up by 250% in the twenty years considered. The increasing number of non-district firms that invested and opened branches in the district explains this. These companies came to the area from other parts of Italy and abroad because the district had already become a hub of specialized innovation for tanning chemicals.

These sectors' production values increase in the last ten years highlight their growing importance: +117% for machinery and +86% for chemicals. In particular, the machinery sector's growing trend proves that the decrease in the number of firms in the sector is not linked to a weakening of the industry but rather the result of growth in the firms' dimensions.

In the Arzignano district, the close collaboration between the chemical firms, machinery manufacturers, and tanneries created synergies that led to increasingly more efficient production processes and highly technological products.

Product innovation is essential to follow, if not instigate, the changing trends of the market. In the Arzignano district, most firms kept making leather but managed to maintain and improve the high quality for which they were already well known. For this, they also had to improve the production process.

Process innovation not only offers a reduction of costs but also, more importantly, may allow the exploitation of new technology to make things in new ways, improving quality and reducing waste – a winning card for the Arzignano district. The role of firms in the ancillary industries, such as producers of chemicals or machinery specialized in the tanning process, was

Table 10.2   Ancillary industries 2000–2019 (2009–2019 for production values)

Year	Tanning-machinery				Tanning-chemistry			
	Firms	Local units	Employees	Production Million €	Firms	Local units	Employees	Production Million €
2000	35	43	n.a	n.a	12	16	n.a	n.a
2001	38	52	436	n.a	12	23	275	n.a
2002	38	59	443	n.a	12	22	273	n.a
2003	39	57	401	n.a	12	26	274	n.a
2004	42	61	407	n.a	12	30	273	n.a
2005	47	67	444	n.a	13	34	384	n.a
2006	46	65	444	n.a	15	40	395	n.a
2007	51	69	483	n.a	15	38	398	n.a
2008	50	67	n.a	n.a	14	36	n.a	n.a
2009	47	64	n.a	57.1	13	39	n.a	150.4
2010	44	57	n.a	73.1	13	39	n.a	200.1
2011	44	59	n.a	84.3	15	41	n.a	206.4
2012	40	53	n.a	79.0	15	42	n.a	210.5
2013	42	56	n.a	96.3	16	47	n.a	228.9
2014	39	54	486	107.5	17	48	622	246.6
2015	37	54	504	110.1	17	46	637	251.0
2016	38	58	530	120.0	17	48	632	260.8
2017	41	60	521	132.4	20	54	685	280.6

Year	Tanning-machinery				Tanning-chemistry			
	Firms	Local units	Employees	Production Million €	Firms	Local units	Employees	Production Million €
2018	41	59	528	137.1	20	54	705	272.7
2019	39	55	567	124.1	21	56	695	280.3

Source: Own elaboration on Vicenza's CCIAA data.

crucial. The introduction of new tanning processes and machinery allowed the district firms to exploit consumers' shift toward more environmentally friendly products and to become a leader in the "green" innovation of the industry. The net result is that by early 2020, this district has become a cluster of integrated firms and the world leader and innovator both in its core tanning industry and the ancillary ones of specialized chemicals and machinery.

The vital role of ancillary industries in the Arzignano district is further proven by data in Table 10.3, which reveals the evolution in the number of local units in the district from 2001 to 2018 by industry. The table shows that the total number of local units increased by 2% from 2001 to 2019 (from 864 units in 2001 to 879 in 2018). However, in the same period, the number of local tanning units decreased by 3%. The overall growth in the number of local units, thus, can be explained by the increased presence of local units of ancillary industries.

Table 10.3   *Local units' trend, by sector*

year	tanning	tanning – chemistry	tanning – machinery	total
2001	789	23	52	864
	↑ 1.41%	↑ 43.75%	↑ 20.93%	↑ 3.23%
2004	792	30	61	883
	= 0.38%	↑ 30.43%	↑ 17.31%	↑ 2.20%
2008	784	36	67	887
	↓ -1.01%	↑ 20.00%	↑ 9.84%	= 0.45%
2012	738	42	53	833
	↓ -5.87%	↑ 16.67%	↓ -20.90%	↓ -6.09%
2016	756	48	58	862
	↑ 2.44%	↑ 14.29%	↑ 9.43%	↑ 3.48%
2019	768	56	55	879
	↑ 1.59%	↑ 16.66%	↓ -5.17%	↑ 1.97%

Source: Own elaboration on Vicenza's CCIAA data.

When we consider shorter periods, the table proves that the increasing rate of ancillary industries was significantly higher than the tanning sector trend. In particular, the tanning-chemistry sector saw a local units increase even during the crisis years (+16,67% from 2008 to 2012, compared to -5,87% for the tanning sector and -20,90% for the tanning-machinery sector). Since the number of local units in the ancillary sectors is small, it is "easier" to have a higher increase rate. However, data are still very significant, as they prove the remarkable vitality of these sectors.

Table 10.4 further confirms this growing importance by showing how ancillary industries' weight on the total turnover of the district is over 10% in every year considered and seems to keep growing in the years (from 2009 to 2019, it gained more than three percentage points).

Table 10.4   *Incidence of ancillary industries over district production value (2009–2019) (million €)*

Year	District's production value	Ancillary industries	Year	District's production value	Ancillary industries
2009	2,197.5	9.44%	2015	3,150.9	11.39%
2010	2,574.7	10.61%	2016	3,113.3	12.16%
2011	2,747.9	10.54%	2017	3,260.4	12.59%
2012	2,755.5	10.44%	2018	3,207.9	12.67%
2013	3,040.0	10.64%	2019	3,083.4	13.13%
2014	3,149.0	11.17%			

Source: Own elaboration on Vicenza's CCIAA and UNIC data.

The close collaboration between the chemical firms, machinery manufacturers, and tanneries created synergies that led to increasingly more efficient and highly technological products. Over the years, ancillary sector firms exploited this know-how and the experience gained with district tanneries to internationalize. Belonging to the Arzignano district helped these firms on know-how and "brand" level: being a member of the district is seen by international customers as a signal of quality and expertise. According to professional associations, 80% of the production of tanning machinery in the district is destined for export. Italy[10] is the top global exporter of tanning machinery, and its share of the total global export of this product is 40%. Also, the export value of local tanning-chemistry firms considerably grew in the years taken into consideration (+120% from 2009 to 2018), especially when compared with the growth rate of imports (+27%). Unfortunately, because of the lack of year-by-year tanning-machinery export data,[11] it is not easy to analyze the district's total exports in detail. However, with a degree of approximation, 2019's overall Arzignano's leather district exports amount can be estimated at around 2.7 billion euros, corresponding to 6% of the Veneto region exports and 1% of the total Italian export for the year.

10.5   INNOVATION AND THE "AREA SISTEMA INTEGRATA D'INNOVAZIONE"

The Arzignano leather district represents a peculiar case of industrial district evolution. The review of its history and the data on its actual extension confirmed that the district has successfully exploited the possibilities offered by its dynamic structure to increase its importance in the leather market and evolved toward the Area Sistema described by Garofoli (1983). Moreover, the analysis suggests that the Arzignano district developed some peculiar traits that proved to be fundamental for the continuity of the district and its ability to overcome times of crisis and preserve its primary role at national and international levels.

The ever-growing foreign competition, the evolution of a good-quality tanning sector in developing countries, and several years of international crisis placed the district under massive pressure. Therefore, to give continuity to the district as a socio-territorial production organization, changes were needed, especially in terms of growth of integration and collaboration among firms and sectors, services development, and the role of leading companies and district associations.

Although external economies and productive flexibility remain the pillars on which the district operates, to deal with the new challenges imposed by the increased dynamism of the market, the district underwent further evolution that redefined interrelations among firms, both at the intersectoral and at the intrasectoral level. The district moved from specialization to flexibility. Its crucial success factor is not merely in the systemic and efficient dimension of production anymore but in dynamic entrepreneurship and innovation. Innovatively recombining endogenous resources allows the district to effectively respond to the world economy's changing technological and market conditions (Busato and Corò 2011).

When Garofoli examined the Area Sistema in 1983, the diversification of the local productive systems was in an initial phase. The system's complexity was growing parallel with the development of ancillary industries, primarily seen as supporting industries for the main specialization production. Garofoli already mentioned that these new sectors tended to have higher technological and economical levels (higher added value), increased innovation capacity and a higher degree of market control. However, at that point, those industries were only in the initial stage of their evolution.

In the Arzignano leather district, ancillary industries have now become mature sectors in the local system, with an excellent reputation and strong presence at national and international levels. They are co-primary industries and play a central role in the district innovation process and, thus, in creating its competitive advantage.

The characterization as Area Sistema no longer truly suits the reality of the Arzignano leather district. The local system evolved toward a more sophisticated local system configuration, an *area sistema integrata d'innovazione*, where innovation and knowledge creation play a central role in retaining the area's competitive advantage.

Thanks to synergies created by interactions between firms from different sectors, innovation is diffused and very rapid in the district. The frequent, face-to-face interactions among players enable them to generate a massive amount of tacit knowledge daily. This tacit knowledge grants the district its primary role in the global tanning sector: the district environment becomes an innovation breeding place that attracts external players who want to engage in the district synergies.

The value of the synergies created in the district is so high that we observe a peculiar phenomenon. Literature observed that the value of a territory specialization grows when external relations enrich the production contexts (Busato and Corò 2011). In the case of the Arzignano leather district, external players are the ones that tap into the district production context to enrich their products and exploit the acquired knowledge to compete in the international market, especially in ancillary industries, where a significant part of innovation occurs in the Arzignano system. Indeed, many companies from outside the district decided to open branches in the area while keeping their original plant in other locations. Such firms did so not only to commercialize their products locally but also to conduct in-loco R&D. Opening R&D subsidiaries in the district area provides another significant advantage: the possibility of rapidly accessing a specialized labor force to employ in these units, and at a lower cost.

Such a choice of location is consistent with many studies on proximity and innovation (Audretsch and Feldman 1996; Florida 2002; Balland, Boschma, and Frenken 2015; Stimson 2022). If the creation of added value is increasingly linked to the production of knowledge, the location choices of companies also increasingly depend on the possibility of accessing specific technological externalities. Such a path to innovation is more straightforward in areas with a concentration of knowledge resources.

In the leather industry, knowledge and the related technological competencies often result from an accumulation of tacit, highly peculiar skills from organizational routines, the experience acquired in manufacturing, and the interaction with customers and other manufacturers. In districts such as Arzignano, innovation is incremental; it consists of minor progressive adaptations, which allow keeping abreast of the market's changing needs and do not involve substantial investments in R&D as radical innovation would. Dynamic innovation and superior manufacturing methods can be facilitated by tacit forms of knowledge (Enright 2003; Davids and Frenken 2018; Carlino and Kerr 2015) embedded in the local context and, therefore, difficult to transfer elsewhere (Maskell and Malmberg 1999; Scherngell 2021). It is precisely this tacit knowledge, with its continuous developments, that allows the district to retain its competitive advantage against foreign competition. In the tanning sector, a significant part of the innovation comes from Italy, mainly from the Arzignano district, especially regarding bovine leather, which is the kind of hide in which the district is specialized. The high pace of this innovation is the factor that allows the district to maintain not only its competitiveness but also its leading role in the global leather market. The Arzignano leather district's economic success is rooted in this: while codifiable knowledge can easily be exported and imitated in other locations, tacit knowledge is more challenging to transfer (Pinch et al. 2003).

Many studies have emphasized the crucial role of networking and face-to-face interaction in innovation. Utterback (1974) suggested that oral, informal communications deliver a significant part of the critical information about market demands and technological possibilities that lead to innovation. Goddard (1978) points out that industry-specific information is subject to sharp distance decay and that a geographically concentrated structure allows for more interchange and exchange of such information. Moreover, even though communications are more rapid nowadays, and information systems are so advanced, it appears that diffusion of crucial information still works at its best when it happens among geographically close partners (Enright 2003; Cortinovis and van Oort 2022; Carlino and Kerr 2015). When discussing scientific or technological knowledge, geographical proximity and personal relations among researchers are even more crucial. Thanks to these, specific portions of knowledge created during the experimental stage that would otherwise never see the light of day are diffused. A straightforward example is errors: mistakes are inevitable in any innovation process; yet it is usually impossible to gain access to the knowledge around them. However, proximity with the people who made and learned from these mistakes in the first place also allows this knowledge to be transmitted, making it easier to discard some options beforehand, or to adjust the course of research accordingly, thus, optimizing the innovation process (Corò and Micelli 2007).

In the Arzignano district, the concentration of tanneries, suppliers, and buyers provides firms with short feedback loops that can lead to new ideas and innovations. Innovation usually emerges through cooperation between tanners and suppliers of specialized machinery and chemicals, who can rapidly develop customized solutions and test them directly with their very close customers.

The process of R&D thus often initiates from a request that directly comes from the tannery. Then, solutions are studied by the ancillary industries' laboratories and later tested in collaboration with the tannery itself, often even directly in the tannery plants. As aforementioned, it is an incremental innovation process: products and processes are upgraded through minor and unceasing adaptations based on customer feedback. These developments and their rapid pace are only possible thanks to the synergies created in the district by the interactions between firms from the different sectors.

The local concentration of production specializations (tanning, tanning machinery and tanning chemicals) reinforces the territory's capacity to innovate and allows more effortless exploitation of the technological and scientific knowledge developed by the ancillary industries' laboratories. Thanks to this, it is easier to access tacit and uncodified knowledge and allow imitation processes. Compared to a traditional district, the development and diffusion of technological knowledge are intensely emphasized by the relations among the different sectors. Over time, knowledge cumulates, and industry-specific skills are handed down from person to person. Thanks to this expertise transmission, industry-specific information becomes common knowledge within the district (Enright 2003), and the vitality of this environment attracts talented people. This allows firms to have a wide availability of high-skilled labor with low pooling costs. Furthermore, the flow of employees among different sectors is widespread in the Arzignano district, allowing an even better exchange of information and technology that contributes to the development of all the sectors.

The Arzignano leather district presents many similarities with one of the most promising concepts in the literature on strategy, innovation and entrepreneurship of the last twenty years, the *innovation ecosystem*. An innovation ecosystem consists of a group of local actors essential for innovation and the dynamic process in which they are involved. These players and processes, combined, lead to the development of solutions to different challenges (Oksanen and Hautamäki 2014). Innovation ecosystems are explicitly systemic, and innovation diffuses through a social system. Connections among the many innovation actors are regarded as crucial. However, while innovation ecosystems are not spontaneously evolving entities – they are designed by intention, and governance has a crucial role (Oh et al. 2016) – the Arzignano leather district naturally evolved: the role of public institutions in its initial phase was only minor. Indeed, public institutions became involved in the district's evolution only later in its history, particularly with the construction of the local water treatment plant ordered by the Valle del Chiampo municipal administrations in 1974. Nowadays, local authorities, industry associations, banks, foundations, chambers of commerce, and educational institutions play an important role in the district system. However, unlike innovation ecosystems, their role seems marginal compared to the productive system.

Nevertheless, recent developments seem to lead to a growing involvement of all the public stakeholders related to the district, mainly thanks to the efforts of the "Distretto Veneto della Pelle" consortium.

Bittencourt et al. (2019) pointed out how the inherent characteristics of industrial districts create the ideal conditions to encourage innovation and, thus, how they should be considered as local innovation systems, especially from the policy-maker's point of view. Corò and Micelli (2007) also highlighted how clusters are often considered policy instruments for innovation in other countries, but not Italy.

When considering the characteristics of the innovation ecosystem of the district, there are even further resemblances of the Arzignano district with the development model of Silicon Valley, as can be inferred by Kenney and Von Burg (1999) and Carlino and Kerr (2015). In the Arzignano district case, the specialized suppliers from the ancillary industries play the role of R&D generators. Indeed, in the tanning sector, where most innovation concerns the *tanning process*, innovation always involves either the chemicals used in the tanning process or the machinery that performs it.

R&D investments are imperative for established firms to remain competitive and maintain a leading role. However, especially in an environment that, by definition, breeds innovation, the pace of new opportunities for existing firms is so rapid that it becomes difficult for them to exploit all these openings. In some cases, firms miss them because they need to focus their attention and energies on maintaining the existing business. This is particularly true for the tanning sector, where innovation is peculiar because it always concerns, as mentioned before, the *tanning process*, thus, involving different contributions that cannot come only from inside the tannery R&D laboratories.

The cooperation among the different sectors provides the support needed to exploit innovations in the best possible way and focus on the main business simultaneously. In the light of this, the district is now configured as a local innovation system, an *area sistema integrata d'innovazione* (integrated industrial system of innovation), in which the principal advantage factor no longer lies only in the superior efficiency of manufacturing operations, but in the development of product culture, in the high speed of innovation and day-by-day knowledge creation. The ability of the local system to participate in global value chains is not merely through production capacity but with ideas, technologies, and abstract knowledge. This requires the development of investments in research and development, specialized training, and attracting talent (Busato and Corò 2011).

Innovation, as mentioned before, is an essential feature of the district and is vital to its success. However, evidence on R&D expenditure (Table 10.5) seems contradictory: in a district where much of the competitive advantage comes from constant innovation, the values of R&D investment are extremely low. Higher expenditure in this field would be expected (in 2019, it was only 0.23% of the total production value of the *area sistema integrata d'innovazione*).

Table 10.5   *R&D expenditures as a percentage of the total production value*

Year	% of R&D expenses
2009	0.07%
2010	0.05%
2011	0.05%
2012	0.08%
2013	0.12%
2014	0.11%
2015	0.14%
2016	0.13%
2017	0.16%
2018	0.17%
2019	0.23%

Source: Own elaboration on Vicenza's CCIAA data.

At first glance, these figures appear surprising and unsatisfactory; however, they do not necessarily reflect the actual amount of R&D expenditure. Indeed, as previously mentioned, most R&D processes are conducted informally in the district. They are often based on oral requests arising from face-to-face interactions among district players. Furthermore, leather tanning innovation is often a vertical process that encompasses different industries. For these reasons, accounting for actual R&D expenditures is not so easy and direct to calculate; a deeper dive-in would be necessary. Thus, especially regarding financial statements, many companies often do not specify these expenses as "R&D expenditure" and sort them among other general costs.[12] Even with the new governmental incentives[13] to stimulate companies to measure and disclose these R&D expenses, most innovation processes remain uncovered.[14] Nevertheless, as the dataset in Table 10.5 indicates, there has been a modest improvement in 2019 compared to 2009. Moving forward, new ways of detection and incentives would be necessary to quantify the R&D expenditure in this particular sector properly.

10.6   CONCLUSION

Throughout the analysis of the Arzignano leather district's main features and performances, this chapter highlighted the reasons behind its ability to withstand the increasing dynamism of the market and the challenges that come from it, while at the same time maintaining a primary role in the global tanning sector. Furthermore, the investigation of ancillary industries proved that they play an increasingly important role in the district and that their contribution to R&D and innovation is essential to the competitiveness of the productive system. Nowadays, we can affirm that the Arzignano leather district evolved towards a new local system configuration, an *area sistema integrata d'innovazione*, and that its competitive advantage lies in developing a product culture, the high pace of innovation and the day-by-day knowledge creation. This advantage is only possible thanks to the synergies created in the district by the interactions between firms from the different sectors. The frequent, face-to-face interactions among players enable them to generate a massive amount of tacit knowledge daily. This tacit knowledge grants the district its primary role in the global tanning sector: the district environment becomes a sort of innovation breeding place that ends up attracting external players who want to engage in the district synergies.

This work provides a framework that allows to understand the paradoxical success of the Arzignano leather district and the reasons behind it. While it is part of a wide range of research work on industrial districts, this chapter provides a new, extensive breakdown of the Arzignano district, on which it offers significant insights. Nevertheless, to better understand the implications of these results, future studies could take account of the exchanges among district players from a quantitative point of view, particularly regarding the R&D flows. Furthermore, it would be interesting to understand whether this framework is peculiar to the Arzignano leather district or the tanning sector, or if it could be applied to other resilient districts in today's globalized market.

NOTES

1. We call it *Italianate* industrial district to indicate that it has become an archetype itself and may become a model reproduced in other countries. The use of the term Italianate for the Italian districts is found in an old paper from Alberti (2007).
2. Six factors must be present to shape an Italianate industrial district and promote its evolution towards an Area Sistema. They are:
    a small and clearly demarcated *territory*;
    the presence of a *community*, sharing a homogeneous system of values in terms of work ethic, family values, a sense of belonging;
    a large number of *small and medium-sized enterprises*;
    the presence of *strong*, and as a rule informal, *links among the firms*, creating an atypical system of relations;
    widespread competency and know-how, mostly of a technical type, related to the dominant industry of the area;
    the involvement, not necessarily from the beginning, of *institutional players*.
    Besides Becattini (2002), who was the first to identify these elements in the 1980s, we refer to Gandolfi and Cozzi (1988), and to Tripodi (2000).
3. Indeed, in 2001 ISTAT identified 181 manufacturing industrial districts and in 2011 it found 141 of them – and some of them were new ones. Therefore, almost

one quarter of the districts active in 2001 did not survive the storms of the first decade of the 21st century in a structured form.

4.   For dematerialization of the district, they mean the end of the traditional industrial district, solidly rooted in its specific local area and in the almost physical contact between firms, replaced by the inclusion of the surviving district firms in global value chains that constitute the competitive space and the competitive unit in the era of globalization.

5.   This can be seen, among many, in the case of the Distretto del Mobile delle Murge (Furniture district in Northern Apulia).

6.   The area mentioned above is so-called with reference to the "triangle" Arzignano – Montebello Vicentino – Valle del Chiampo (Zampiva 1997).

7.   VICENZA: Alonte, Altavilla Vicentina, Altissimo, Arzignano, Brogliano, Castelgomberto, Chiampo, Cornedo Vicentino, Creazzo, Crespadoro, Gambellara, Lonigo, Montebello Vicentino, Montecchio Maggiore, Montorso Vicentino, Nogarole Vicentino, San Pietro Mussolino, Sarego, Trissino, Valdagno, Zermeghedo. VERONA: Cologna Veneta, Montecchia di Crosara, Roncà, San Bonifacio, San Giovanni Ilarione, Vestenanova, Zimella.

8.   Data from Vicenza's CCIAA. These municipalities are listed by the number of active local units.

9.   Unfortunately, data on previous years' profits are not available.

10.   Unfortunately, only data on the national level are available for this sector.

11.   The NACE code for tanning-machinery is too specific (five digits), and ISTAT does not provide export data to this level.

12.   To account for R&D expenditure, the balance sheet item "R&D and advertisement expenses" (intangible fixed asset) was considered. However, we can consider the amount to belong mostly to R&D, since the industry is of B2B nature, and has proved to be not prone to invest on advertisement, as pointed out in interviews with sector experts, such as local entrepreneurs.

13.   From 2015, the Italian government offers tax breaks to firms that invest in R&D, allowing them to enjoy a tax credit for part of their R&D expenditure (up to 50%).

14.   Recently, academics and rule-makers extensively pointed out the low level of R&D expenditure in Italy, compared with other countries. For example, in Italy the level of R&D expenditure over GDP only grew from 1% in 2000 to 1,39% in 2018, remaining well below the EU-28 average 2,03% expenditure. Italian expenditures level seems even lower when compared with Germany, where in 2018 the 3,13% of GDP was invested in R&D (data from OECD). This being said, it seems paradoxical that in many sectors (for example, as mentioned in this work, leather tanning) Italian firms are recognized as leaders worldwide for their innovation capability. In this sense, it would be very interesting to research and analyse further whether the role played by informal innovation in the Arzignano leather district can apply to other sectors and areas in Italy. If so, it could help to explain the difference among the official R&D expenditure records and the real situation of Italian firms, especially the ones in industrial districts.

BIBLIOGRAPHY

Alberti, Fernando 2007. *The concept of industrial district: main contributions*. INSME International Network for SMEs. http://www.insme.org/files/922.

Audretsch, David B., and Maryann P. Feldman. 1996. "R&D spillovers and the geography of innovation and production." *The American Economic Review* 86 (3): 630–640.

Balducci, Graziano. 2009. *Relazione del Presidente*. UNIC.

Balland, Pierre-Alexandre, Ron Boschma, and Koen Frenken. 2015. "Proximity and innovation: From statics to dynamics." *Regional Studies* 49 (6): 907–920.

Becattini, Giacomo. 1989. "Riflessioni sul distretto industriale marshalliano come concetto socio-economico." *Stato e Mercato* 25.

Becattini, Giacomo. 2002. "From Marshall's to the Italian 'industrial districts'. A brief critical reconstruction." In Quadrio Curzio, A., Fortis, M. (eds), *Complexity and Industrial Clusters: Dynamics and Models in Theory and Practice*, 83–106. Heidelberg, Physica-Verlag HD.

Bellandi, Marco, Monica Plechero, and Erica Santini. 2022. "Distretti industriali italiani in cambiamento e place leadership." *Economia e società regionale* 1/2022: 73–82.

Bettiol, Marco, Maria Chiarvesio, Eleonora Di Maria, and Stefano Micelli. 2022. "La trasformazione dei distretti industriali tra catene globali del valore e digitalizzazione." *Economia e società regionale* 1/2022: 83–95.

Bittencourt, Bruno Anicet, Vanessa Marques Daniel, Aurora Carneiro Zen, and Mariana Bianchini Galuk. 2019. "Cluster innovation capability: A systematic review." *International Journal of Innovation* 7 (1): 26–44.

Busato, Alessia, and Giancarlo Corò. 2011. "I distretti nella crisi: declino, adattamento o innovazione?" *Argomenti* 32: 74.

Carlino, Gerald, and William R. Kerr. 2015. "Agglomeration and innovation." *Handbook of Regional and Urban Economics* 5: 349–404.

Carminucci, Carlo, and Silvio Casucci. 1997. "Il ciclo di vita dei distretti industriali: ipotesi teoriche ed evidenze empiriche." *L'industria* 18 (2): 283–316.

Corò, Giancarlo, and Stefano Micelli. 2007. Industrial Districts as Local Systems of Innovation (June 2007). Ca' Foscari University of Venice Economics Working Paper No. 06/WP/2007.

Cortinovis, Nicola, and Frank van Oort. 2022. "Economic networks, innovation and proximity." In Torre, A., Gallaud, D. (eds) *Handbook of Proximity Relations*, 292–306. Cheltenham, UK and Northampton, MA, USA: Edward Elgar Publishing.

Davids, Mila, and Koen Frenken. 2018. "Proximity, knowledge base and the innovation process: Towards an integrated framework." *Regional Studies* 52 (1): 23–34.

De Marchi, Valentina, Gary Gereffi, and Roberto Grandinetti. 2017. "Evolutionary trajectories of industrial districts in global value chains." In De Marchi, V., Di Maria, E., Gereffi, G. (eds) *Local Clusters in Global Value Chains*, 33–50. Routledge.

Enright, Michael J. 2003. "Regional clusters: What we know and what we should know." In Bröcker, J., Dohse, D., Soltwedel, R. (eds) *Innovation Clusters and Interregional Competition*, , 99–129. Berlin, Heidelberg, Springer.

Feldman, Maryann P, and Scott W. Langford. 2021. "Knowledge Spillovers Informed by Network Theory and Social Network Analysis." *Handbook of Regional Science*: 957–970.

Florida, Richard. 2002. *L'ascesa della nuova classe creative*. Milano: Mondadori.

Fratocchi, Luciano, Alessandro Ancarani, Paolo Barbieri, Carmela Di Mauro, Guido Nassimbeni, Marco Sartor, Matteo Vignoli, and Andrea Zanoni. 2014. "Il back-reshoring manifatturiero nei processi di internazionalizzazione: inquadramento teorico ed evidenze empiriche." In *Atti del XXVI Convegno annuale di Sinergie: Manifattura tra processi di delocalizzazione e rilocalizzazione produttiva e internazionalizzazione*, 423–440. CUEIM Comunicazione.

Gandolfi, Valentino, and Gianni Cozzi. 1988. *Aree sistema: internazionalizzazione e reti telematiche*. Franco Angeli.

Garofoli, Gioacchino. 1983. "Le aree sistema in Italia." *Politica ed Economia* (11): 57–60.

Goddard, John B. 1978. "The location of non-manufacturing activities within manufacturing industries." *Contemporary Industrialization*. London: Longman: 62–85.

Grillitsch, Markus, and Magnus Nilsson. 2017. "Firm performance in the periphery: On the relation between firm-internal knowledge and local knowledge spillovers." *Regional Studies* 51 (8): 1219–1231.

Kenney, Martin, and Urs Von Burg. 1999. "Technology, entrepreneurship and path dependence: Industrial clustering in Silicon Valley and Route 128." *Industrial and Corporate Change* 8 (1).

Kiessling, Timothy, Jane Frances Maley, Miriam Moeller, and Marina Dabić. 2021. "Managing global knowledge transfer: Inpatriate manager embeddedness and firm innovation." *International Business Review*: 101868.

Maskell, Peter, and Anders Malmberg. 1999. "Localised learning and industrial competitiveness." *Cambridge Journal of Economics* 23, Special Issue on Learning, Proximity and Industrial Performance (2): 167–185.

Mosconi, Lorenzo. 2005. *Relazione del Presidente*. UNIC.

Oh, Deog-Seong, Fred Phillips, Sehee Park, and Eunghyun Lee. 2016. "Innovation ecosystems: A critical examination." *Technovation* 54: 1–6.

Oksanen, Kaisa, and Antti Hautamäki. 2014. "Transforming regions into innovation ecosystems: A model for renewing local industrial structures." *The Innovation Journal: The Public Sector Innovation Journal* 19, article 5 (2): 4.

Pinch, Steven, Nick Henry, Mark Jenkins, and Steven Tallman. 2003. "From industrial districts to knowledge clusters: A model of knowledge dissemination and competitive advantage in industrial agglomerations." *Journal of Economic Geography* 3 (4).

Russo, Gianni. 2015. *Relazione del Presidente*. UNIC.

Scherngell, Thomas. 2021. "The geography of R&D collaboration networks." *Handbook of Regional Science*: 869–887. Heidelberg: Springer Berlin.

Sikombe, Shem, and Maxwell A. Phiri. 2019. "Exploring tacit knowledge transfer and innovation capabilities within the buyer–supplier collaboration: A literature review." *Cogent Business & Management* 6 (1): 1683130.

Stimson, Robert J. 2022. "Proximity and regional development: An overview." In Torre, A., Gallaud, D. (eds) *Handbook of Proximity Relations*, 97–123. Cheltenham, UK and Northampton, MA, USA: Edward Elgar Publishing.

Tripodi, Carmine. 2000. "I sistemi locali di imprese: alcune riflessioni sulla riproducibilità del modello." *Sinergie* 52: 333–351.

Utterback, James M. 1974. "Innovation in industry and the diffusion of technology." *Scienze* 183 (4125): 658–662.

Zampiva, Fernando. 1997. *L'arte della concia: Ad Arzignano, nel Vicentino, nel Veneto e in Italia: dalle origini ai giorni nostri*. Vicenza: Egida.

11. Connecting innovation poles with lagging territories: how do collaborations with Europe and Asia influence innovation in Latin American cities?

Pablo Galaso and Sergio Palomeque

11.1 INTRODUCTION

Europe and Asia, together with North America, concentrate the main hotspots and clusters that lead innovation processes on a global scale. These clusters have dense local networks that facilitate the generation and diffusion of innovations in the territory (Porter, 1990; Vázquez Barquero, 2002; Vicente, 2022). At the same time, these territories are well connected to global knowledge networks, which allows them to maintain leadership positions in innovation processes at the global scale (Miguelez et al., 2019). The relevance of combining local networks with connections to global networks has been widely documented by different branches of the literature on clusters and innovation (e.g. Bathelt et al. 2004; Breschi & Lenzi, 2013, 2016; Coffano et al., 2017; Whittington et al., 2009; Capone et al., 2021).

The global linkages, in addition to generating impacts in the leading regions, may also cause spillovers to other less developed territories, favoring (or restricting) their innovation processes. Cities in developing countries tend to have weaker and more fragmented local networks, so they are particularly dependent on their connections to global networks (Bianchi et al., 2023). However, the effects of these global connections may differ depending on the region of the world with which underdeveloped territories are connected. This aspect, which has been understudied in the literature, is the focus of our chapter.

We address this problem by analyzing the connections between Europe, Asia, North America and the cities of Latin America, a developing region characterized by its technological backwardness and its peripheral position in global innovation networks (Delvenne & Thoreau, 2017). In particular, we are interested in analyzing whether there are differences in the influence of these global connections, depending on the region of the world with which Latin American cities are connected. In other words, whether the links with Europe have the same influence as those with Asia or North America. In addition, we seek to study how the combination of local networks in peripheral cities and their connections to the different central regions influence their innovation processes.

Our general hypothesis is that the effects on Latin American cities of maintaining links with cities in Europe, Asia and North America depend not only on the region of the world with which they are linked, but also on the topologies of the local network in the Latin American territory.

To test this hypothesis, we conducted an empirical study using patent data from the USPTO between 2006 and 2017. We identify the top 31 Latin American cities in terms of patenting, and study their collaboration networks at the local level and their links with global networks, differentiating between connections with Europe, East Asia and North America. To reconstruct networks, collaborations between patent owners are analyzed according to their geographic location. Using econometric models with panel data, we estimate the influence of local and global networks on innovation in Latin American cities (approximated by patenting levels). The models also allow analyzing the joint influence of the local and the global network, differentiating the regional orientation of the links.

Our findings show that the impact of global connections on innovation in Latin American cities is greater when local networks are well cohesive and present a small world structure. However, our models show clear differences in the impact of external links depending on the region of the world with which the city is linked. Thus, while links with Europe and North America can determine innovation in Latin American cities, their connections with Asian cities do not significantly influence local innovation. Furthermore, our study shows that the impact of global connections on innovation in Latin American cities is conditioned by the topology of the local network.

The study makes a novel contribution to the literature on local and global networks (e.g. Bathelt et al., 2004; Breschi & Lenzi, 2013, 2015), providing two original approaches to the problem. First, it explores the effects of the world's leading innovation regions on cities in lagging regions, such as Latin America, through global pipelines connecting the core and the periphery. Second, it differentiates the effect of these pipelines according to the region of the world with which the periphery is connected to (Europe, Asia or North America). These findings have also clear implications for future research on innovation networks in cities, indicating the relevance of analyzing not only the interaction between local and global networks, but also the different regions of the world that are connected by global networks.

The rest of the chapter is structured as follows. The next section develops a theoretical framework on local networks, global networks and innovation in peripheral territories. Subsequently, section 11.3 presents the methodological issues of the empirical study. Section 11.4 explains the results of the research. Finally, section 11.5 discusses the results and concludes the chapter.

11.2   THEORETICAL FRAMEWORK

Combining strong local networks, which connect actors based in the same territory, with links to global innovation networks is essential for the development of innovation. Local networks allow the rapid dissemination of knowledge and provide a reliable environment for the exchange and contrast of ideas (Uzzi & Spiro, 2005). The literature has used the term *local buzz* to describe the relevance of these local networks (Bathelt et al., 2004). On the other hand, links to global networks, also known as *global pipelines*, facilitate the influx of valuable new knowledge into the territory (ibid). Both types of networks (local and global) can complement each other in a way that substantially facilitates innovation processes in the territories. This has been widely documented from different branches of literature related to territorial development, clusters, geography of innovation, or business networks (e.g. Schilling & Phelps, 2007; Breschi & Lenzi, 2013, 2015, 2016; Coffano et al., 2017; Whittington et al., 2009; Capone et al., 2021).

Several territories in Europe and Asia (as well as in North America) have dense local networks and good connections to global networks, which enable them to lead innovation processes on a global scale. Some (few) of these global connections are directed towards territories in developing countries, including Latin America. These core–periphery connections have, logically, an impact not only on Europe and Asia, but also on cities in developing countries. In this chapter we will focus on this influence, that is, we will be interested in analyzing how the links with Europe and Asia (where the leading global innovation hotspots are located) influence the cities of developing countries.

Territories in developing countries present fundamentally different situations and challenges than those in developed countries (Yoguel & Robert, 2010). In these territories, local networks tend to be less dense, less rich and tend to have less impact on innovation processes, due to the fact that these processes are less collaborative. Moreover, innovation in underdeveloped territories is more dependent on external connections, on links with developed regions, from where the most relevant or cutting-edge knowledge is generated. At the same time, underdeveloped regions are more disconnected from global innovation networks. This reinforces the weakness of territories in underdeveloped countries: on the one hand, they are highly dependent on external links and, on the other, they are poorly connected and often occupy peripheral positions in global innovation networks (Miguelez et al., 2019; Bianchi et al., 2021).

Therefore, for cities in developing countries, connections with clusters and cities in other continents, in particular those that link them to global innovation hotspots, are crucial for developing innovations. These inter-continental links between the periphery and the core are useful for bringing into the peripheral territory novel information, frontier knowledge that often cannot be produced in developing countries. In addition, since global pipelines allow the introduction of information on new marketing opportunities and potential demand (Bresnahan et al., 2001), connections with leading innovation regions can be a source of opportunities to develop future key projects, which can lead to the generation of future innovations in lagging territories.

In the case of Latin America, as a developing region, local networks are weak, poorly connected, very fragmented, and therefore highly dependent on external connections (Bianchi et al. 2023; Montobbio & Sterzi, 2011). These external connections, moreover, tend to be extra-regional, due to the fact that there is little collaboration among Latin American territories (Bianchi et al. 2021).

But the impact on the periphery of these extra-continental connections is not homogeneous. On the one hand, this impact will depend on the region of the world with which the peripheral territory is connected. For example, for Latin American cities, links to Europe may have a different influence on innovation than connections to North America or Asia. In this regard, it is important to consider that Latin America has historically maintained strong cultural, political and economic relations with Europe and North America (Bértola & Ocampo, 2013). Meanwhile, the links with Asia, although growing substantially, are more recent and are mainly motivated by the economic expansion of China and India (Roett & Paz, 2016).

In this sense, the links that a peripheral city maintains with other cities in the core may be associated with different stages of the innovation process depending on the region with which these links are maintained. Thus, for example, for Latin America, connections with Europe and North America may include collaborations in research projects with greater involvement of local actors, projects in which some researchers based in the region may be playing a more active role in the research in Europe. On the other hand, with Asian countries, connections may be associated with projects where the involvement of local actors is lower, and this may result in a lower impact of connections with Asia compared to links with Europe.

In line with this idea, historical and cultural relations with different regions of the world may condition the links that are established to generate innovations and, therefore, may determine the impact that these links have on innovation processes. In particular, given Latin America's stronger relationship with Europe and North America, we expect connections with these two regions to have a greater impact on patent production in Latin American cities. In the case of Asia, due to the lesser linkage between Latin America and this region, we expect these connections to have less impact on innovation in Latin American cities.

These arguments lead us to state our first hypothesis as follows:

H1   Connections to Europe and North America will have a greater effect on innovation in Latin American cities than connections to Asia.

On the other hand, the connections of peripheral cities with central territories may also have a different impact depending on certain characteristics of the peripheral city. In particular, we argue that the topology of the local network can condition the way in which extra-continental connections affect innovation in Latin American cities.

The topologies of local networks in cities and regions can constitute a kind of collective capital of the territory that facilitates the dissemination of knowledge and encourages the cooperation of actors (Galaso, 2018). Thus, local networks can be associated with local capacities of the territory to take advantage of the resources it may obtain from its extra-regional links. Previous literature has documented how the effects of global connections depend on the territory having an adequate local network, a network that allows the knowledge that is introduced into the territory through global pipelines to be disseminated and used locally (Breschi & Lenzi., 2015; Capone et al., 2021; Coffano et al., 2017). In this sense, we argue that some topologies of the local network could make connections with Europe, Asia or North America particularly beneficial for innovation in Latin American cities, while other topologies may restrict the benefits of connections to the core.

This would imply that collaborating with one developed region or another (Europe, Asia or North America) is not good or bad per se, but depends on the topology of the local network in the Latin American city. There are several reasons that can support this idea. First, collaborations with certain regions of the world may specialize in certain technologies, sectors or research projects for which it is more beneficial to have certain types of local networks.

Previous literature has analyzed why several structural properties of local networks can facilitate or restrict innovation processes. For example, networks where their nodes are close to each other, form densely connected clusters and those networks that exhibit the so-called *small world* property (which, in turn, combines the properties of closeness and clustering), can allow the diffusion and contrast of knowledge, as well as the germination and emergence of novel ideas (Fleming et al., 2007; Crowe, 2007; Bettencourt et al., 2007). However, these structures may also end up generating a certain homogeneity of diffused knowledge, thus restricting innovation processes (Uzzi & Spiro, 2005; Breschi & Lenzi, 2016). On the other hand, the centralization of the network (i.e. the concentration of links in a few nodes), has been identified as an efficient network configuration at the local scale for the rapid diffusion of ideas (Crespo et al., 2016; Graf & Henning, 2009), although it can also lead to excessive dependence and concentration of power in a few actors, which could hinder innovation processes (Galaso & Kovářík, 2021).

Therefore, more centralized networks may be more conducive to developing projects that require strong coordination led by few actors. Or networks with high closeness, clustering or small world structures may be particularly beneficial for disseminating complex technologies, requiring densely connected groups of actors and short distances between nodes. In these cases, the topology of the local network would allow that connecting to one region or another may be beneficial for the development of the technologies, sectors or projects in which that region specializes.

According to these arguments, we can state the second hypothesis as follows:

H2   Linkages with Europe, Asia and North America will have different effects on innovation in Latin American cities depending on the topology of the local network of each Latin American city.

11.3   DATA AND METHODS

The data used are from patents registered at the USTPO and retrieved from the PatentsView database. This database contains disambiguated data that allows to identify inventors and patent owners. Patents where at least one inventor is located in a Latin American country are selected for the analysis.

From these data, we reconstruct co-patenting networks, that is, networks where nodes are patent owners and links are established when there are joint registrations of the same patent by (at least) two owners. Most patent owners are firms, but there are also research institutes, universities, governmental organizations and even individuals. This implies that the networks analyzed in this chapter can be considered as inter-organizational networks. Some of the selected patents are co-patented by an actor located outside Latin America and, therefore, the networks include not only Latin American cities, but also cities in other parts of the world. This allows us to observe the connections between Europe, Asia and North America and Latin American cities.

Some of the co-patents involve hardly any interaction between the owners, that is, no knowledge flows, no collaborative work. This lack of interaction is especially common in the case of patents with owners from different territories. Therefore, we aim to identify the most relevant inter-city links, those that represent real collaborative innovation processes. To this end, we apply the backbone extraction algorithm, which allows us to select statistically significant relationships between patent owners located in different cities based on the number of co-patents (Neal, 2014).

The period of analysis is between 2006 and 2017, during which the region substantially increased its patenting levels (Bianchi et al., 2020; WIPO, 2018). Four-year windows are used to study the evolution of the networks and a network is constructed for each window. In each of these windows, we will calculate a series of network statistics that allow us to understand the local collaboration structure of Latin American cities as well as their connections with Europe, Asia and North America.

The cities selected for analysis are identified using the backbone extraction algorithm, which determines which locations maintain statistically significant connections with other cities. As a result, we obtain an inter-city network that connects 104 Latin American cities and 450 cities in other regions of the world. Given that we aim to study how external connections influence innovation in Latin American cities, the econometric analysis is carried out only for cities in this region, specifically, for the 31 Latin American cities that remain in the network during the three periods analyzed. These 31 cities are distributed among seven countries, cover the main urban agglomerations of the region and constitute the Latin American centers where most of the innovation and patenting processes take place (see Table 11.1).

Although the rest of the cities identified in our analysis (73 in Latin America and 450 in other regions of the world) are not included in the panel analysis, they are part of the network and, therefore, their links are counted in the calculation of our independent variables that measure the external connections.

In order to estimate the effects of connections with Europe, Asia and North America on innovation in Latin American cities, we use panel data regressions. The dependent variable is the number of patents registered in each city for each period. This indicator, which has been widely used in previous literature (e.g. Bianchi et al. 2023; Fleming et al., 2007; De Noni et al., 2017; Yao et al., 2020), allows us to capture, at least partially, innovation processes at the urban scale and in a comparable way across – the heterogeneous set of – countries in the region.

The independent variables measure two fundamental aspects of collaborative networks: external connections and the topology of local networks. To measure the first aspect, we created three variables that count the number of links that actors in Latin American cities have with actors located in Europe, Asia and North America, respectively. Likewise, to analyze the orientation (regional vs. extra-regional) of external connections, we use the variable

Table 11.1   Selected cities

City	Country	Number of patents (2006–2017)
São Paulo	Brazil	596
Mexico City	Mexico	322
Rio de Janeiro	Brazil	270
Santiago	Chile	235
São José dos Campos	Brazil	167
Buenos Aires	Argentina	152
Monterrey	Mexico	94
Cadereyta Jiménez	Mexico	85
La Habana	Cuba	81
Bogotá	Colombia	55
Hermosillo	Mexico	50
Jundiaí	Brazil	47
Porto Alegre	Brazil	44
Campinas	Brazil	41
Camaçari	Brazil	28
Belo Horizonte	Brazil	27
Montevideo	Uruguay	25
Brasilia	Brazil	21
Medellín	Colombia	21
Corinto	Brazil	18
Ciudad Apodaca	Mexico	16
Florianópolis	Brazil	14
Heroica Veracruz	Mexico	14
Concepción	Chile	12
Santa Fe	Argentina	12
San Nicolás de los Garza	Mexico	11
Rosario	Argentina	10
Valparaíso	Chile	10
Araraquara	Brazil	5
Juiz de Fora	Brazil	5
Valparaíso de Goiás	Brazil	4

Source: Authors.

Extra-regional links, which measures the proportion of connections to cities outside the Latin American continent out of the total number of external connections.

Regarding local networks in Latin American cities, we are interested in analyzing four properties. First, the *closeness* or *cohesion* of the network, that is, the average social distance between each pair of actors in the network. Since our networks are fragmented into different components, we use the average reach indicator to measure this property. Second, we analyze the level of *clustering* calculating the network clustering coefficient, that is, the proportion of closed triads over the total number of triads. Third, we are interested in the *small world* property, that is, the combination of small average distances with high levels of clustering. According to the previous literature (e.g. Fleming et al., 2007; Schilling & Phelps, 2007; Galaso & Kovářík, 2021), we calculate the multiplication of the average reach and the clustering coefficient to measure the small world property. And, fourth, we study the *centralization* of the network, that is, the level of concentration of links in a few actors. In this case, we use the degree centralization indicator. Formal definitions of these four network indicators can be found in, for example, Jackson (2008). We have selected here these four topological properties to study local networks since they have been widely analyzed in the previous literature and have been shown to present significant impacts on innovation processes of cities and regions (see, e.g. Galaso 2018, for a review).

To control for other factors that may influence the patenting levels of cities, we include the following control variables in our models. First, the number of inventors and the number of patent owners located in each city allows us to control for city size and agglomeration effects of innovators in the territory. Second, counting the number of technologies (measured by the technological code of each patent) in which the city patents allows us to control for the technological specialization/diversification of cities. Third, to account for other unobservable factors reflecting heterogeneity in cities' propensity to patent, such as the evolution of the local economy or investments in research and technology, we include the number of patents filed during the previous period. These four control variables are strongly correlated, which can lead to collinearity problems. Therefore, we carry out a factor analysis that allows us to group these variables. Such analysis reveals that a single factor can replace all four variables, maintaining more than 90% of the variance. Hence, the models include *factor* as a control variable for the four aspects explained above.

The models include fixed effects that allow us to control for structural aspects of the cities, associated with the capabilities of the territory that can influence the propensity to patent such as, for example, the level of education, the institutional framework or the local industrial atmosphere. Furthermore, the dependent variable is lagged by one period. This implies considering that connections with Europe, Asia and North America (together with the other independent and control variables) in period *t* may facilitate (or constrain) innovation processes that will culminate in new patents during period $t + 1$. In turn, using lagged variables helps to mitigate possible endogeneity problems.

We use negative binomial models since they are best suited for estimations where the dependent variable is a count variable that takes strictly positive and integer values and is overdispersed, as in our case with the number of patents in each city. Similar literature, which employs the number of patents in the territories as the dependent variable, has widely employed this type of model (e.g. Fleming et al., 2007; Galaso & Kovářík, 2021; Owen-Smith & Powell, 2004; Schilling & Phelps, 2007; Yao et al., 2020).

11.4   RESULTS

Table 11.2 presents the results of the estimations. Each model includes the variables measuring the connection of the city to global networks, one variable measuring the structure of the local network, and the interaction between the latter and the global network variables.[1]

When analyzing the results, we can observe, first, that the variables measuring the topology of the local network show the relevance of these local structures in determining innovation in Latin American cities. In line with previous literature, we find that clustering and, especially, the closeness between local nodes (*Reach*) are positively associated with innovation, while the centralization of the local network seems to have a negative effect. The latter result suggests that the excessive concentration of linkages in a few actors and the homogenization of information arising from centralized structures could exert a negative influence on patent generation at the city level.

With respect to connections to the rest of the world, the proportion of extra-regional links does not seem to have a clear influence on innovation in Latin American cities, as we find both positive and negative associations. However, when we interact this variable with local network structure, we do observe interesting results. In particular, the models indicate that it is positive for innovation in the city to have a centralized local network and, at the same time, to be strongly oriented outside the region by maintaining a high proportion of extra-regional collaborations. This would imply that the possible negative effects of centralization (mentioned above) is mitigated when accompanied by a good openness towards global innovation networks.

When we analyze the connections with each region (i.e. Europe, North America, Asia), the first thing we observe is that there does not seem to be a clear effect of the links with any of the regions on the innovation of Latin American cities. But when interacting these variables with the topology of the local network, interesting results do emerge: we find that links to the same region can generate either positive or negative effects depending on the topology of the local network. Furthermore, the same local network topology can

Table 11.2   *Negative binomial regressions*

	Model 1	Model 2	Model 3	Model 4	Model 5
(Intercept)	2.419***	2.427***	2.432***	2.436***	2.436***
	(0.221)	(0.237)	(0.229)	(0.236)	(0.213)
Connections to global networks					
Extra-regional links	0.125*	-0.114**	-0.099*	-0.082	-0.051
	(0.064)	(0.051)	(0.052)	(0.05)	(0.045)
Europe	-0.014	0.099*	-0.044	-0.012	-0.069***
	(0.037)	(0.051)	(0.037)	(0.038)	(0.025)
North America	-0.150*	0.088	0.181*	-0.039	
	(0.087)	(0.089)	(0.093)	(0.08)	
East Asia	-0.417	0.102	-0.178**	-0.001	
	(0.254)	(0.066)	(0.084)	(0.079)	
Structure of the local network					
Reach	0.270***				
	(0.063)				
Small World		0.094			
		(0.075)			
Centralization			-0.137***		-.078**
			(0.048)		(0.036)
Clustering				0.113*	
				(0.067)	
Interactions					
Extra-regional: Reach	-0.072*				
	(0.04)				
Extra-regional: Small World		0.004			
		(0.039)			
Extra-regional: Centralization			0.126***		0.075**
			(0.042)		(0.033)
Extra-regional: Clustering				0.074	
				(0.049)	
Europe: Reach	-1.637**				
	(0.72)				
Europe: Small World		0.062**			
		(0.028)			
Europe: Centralization					0.078***
					(0.018)

	Model 1	Model 2	Model 3	Model 4	Model 5
North America: Reach	1.398**				
	(0.657)				
North America: Small World		0.216***			
		(0.06)			
North America: Centralization			-0.110***		
			(0.023)		
North America: Clustering				0.028	
				(0.022)	
Factor	-0.117***	-0.178***	0.014	-0.093**	-0.003
	(0.037)	(0.046)	(0.024)	(0.042)	(0.018)
AIC	459.921	475.955	467.533	486.36	468.33
BIC	485.447	501.48	490.932	509.76	487.474
Log Likelihood	-217.96	-225.98	-222.77	-232.18	-225.17
Num. obs.	62	62	62	62	62
Num. groups: name	31	31	31	31	31
Var: name (Intercept)	1.428	1.658	1.661	1.65	1.649

Note: *** $p < 0.01$; ** $p < 0.05$; * $p < 0.1$.
Source: Authors.

be associated with both positive and negative effects depending on the region of the world to which the city is linked.

In particular, we find that collaborations with North America are positive when Latin American cities have local networks with nodes close to each other and with small world structures, but negative in the case of centralized networks. In the case of Europe, the links with this region are positive if the cities are centralized and with a small world structure, but do not seem to be positive when the network has a high degree of closeness. Finally, the variable measuring connections with Asia presents very few observations, which reflects the low interaction of Latin America with this region. This also prevents the interaction of this variable with other network indicators, since it generates multicollinearity problems in the models.

In summary, the results of our models corroborate the greater influence of connections with Europe and North America compared to the weakness and low impact of links with Asia on innovation in Latin American cities, which supports our first hypothesis. On the other hand, our models show that the impact of these extra-continental connections depends not only on the region of the world to which Latin American cities are linked, but also on the structure of the local network, which confirms our second hypothesis.

11.5   DISCUSSION AND CONCLUSION

This chapter explores the influence on peripheral cities of their connections to the core of global innovation networks. In particular, it analyzes the effects on innovation in Latin American cities of their collaborations with Europe, Asia and North America, and considers how these effects are conditioned not only by the region of the world with which they are connected, but also by the structures of local networks.

The results show that links to Europe and North America have a stronger effect on innovation in Latin American cities than connections to Asia. We also find that these effects depend substantially on local network structures. Thus, while collaborations with Europe are beneficial for some types of local networks (centralized and with local nodes not very close to each other), links with North America are positive for other types of local networks (decentralized and with nodes close to each other).

These results have interesting implications for the literature on local vs. global networks and their effects on territories. In this sense, the chapter offers empirical evidence that shows which types of local networks are favorable (or not) to generate innovations when combined with global connections directed towards different regions of the world. In short, the chapter shows that there does not seem to be a uniform rule about how local networks should be or where global networks should be directed to foster innovations. On the contrary, the results indicate that there are different types of combinations between local network topologies and global pipelines that can be positive for innovation.

These results present interesting interpretations from different perspectives. For example, from a local development approach and, in particular, considering the specificities and capabilities of territories to generate innovations, our study suggests that different cities can achieve different results by combining their local interactions with connections to global networks. Also, from the point of view of global value chains (GVCs), an interpretation of our results could suggest that connections with different regions of the world may be associated with insertions in different stages of GVCs. Furthermore, this different insertion of peripheral cities may require different local capabilities approximated by their local network topologies.

The results of this research also have important policy implications. For developing cities, our study suggests that it is crucial not only to know which regions to connect with, but also to know how local actors collaborate and the topology of their local network. For territories in Europe, Asia and North America, the results show what effects they have on developing regions (such as Latin America). These effects can be taken into account when planning or implementing measures to promote partnerships with developing regions.

This work also opens up future lines of research. In particular, it would be interesting to include sectoral analyzes, considering, for example, to what extent the complementarity of productive specializations between different territories restricts or boosts the effect of collaborations between cities. Sectoral analysis would also allow to study how different sectors combine with different local network topologies, or even whether there is greater or lesser openness towards different regions of the world depending on the sector of activity in which the peripheral territories specialize.

It would also be interesting to break down the European, Asian and North American connections, analyzing different countries or territories within these developed areas. This would imply approaching a reconstruction of the global network of collaboration between cities. Analyzing this global inter-city network would allow, among other aspects, to investigate how core-periphery connections influence the central cities in order to know if these links are symmetrical or not.

Finally, it would be interesting to investigate further the causality of the relationships between local networks, connections with global networks and the development of innovations. For example, if a city has a local network with certain topologies, does this network enable it to connect with one region or another in the world, or does it enable a connection with a specific region to be positive for innovation? In addressing these questions, future research could make interesting contributions to the knowledge of local networks and global connections in innovation processes.

NOTE

1.   Models 3 and 4 do not include the interaction of the local network variable with the city's links to Europe. This is because this interaction presents perfect multicollinearity problems with the interaction between the local network variable and the links with North America. In model 5, this multicollinearity problem is solved for the interaction of the local network centralization with the links to Europe.

REFERENCES

Bathelt, H., Malmberg, A., & Maskell, P. (2004). Clusters and knowledge: Local buzz, global pipelines and the process of knowledge creation. *Progress in Human Geography*, 28(1), 31–56.

Bértola, L., & Ocampo, J. A. (2013). *El desarrollo económico de América Latina desde la Independencia*. Fondo de Cultura Economica.

Bettencourt, L. M., Lobo, J., & Strumsky, D. (2007). Invention in the city: Increasing returns to patenting as a scaling function of metropolitan size. *Research Policy*, 36(1), 107–120.

Bianchi, C., Galaso, P., & Palomeque, S. (2020). Invention and collaboration networks in Latin America: evidence from patent data. *Serie Documentos de Trabajo IECON*; 04/20.

Bianchi, C., Galaso, P., & Palomeque, S. (2021). Patent collaboration networks in Latin America: Extra-regional orientation and core-periphery structure. *Journal of Scientometric Research*, 10(1s), s59–s70.

Bianchi, C, Galaso, P., & Palomeque, S. (2023). The trade-offs of brokerage in inter-city innovation networks. *Regional Studies*, 57(2), 225–238.

Breschi, S., & Lenzi, C. (2013). Local buzz versus global pipelines and the inventive productivity of US cities. In T. Scherngell (Ed.) *The Geography of Networks and R&D Collaborations* (pp. 299–315). Springer, Cham.

Breschi, S., & Lenzi, C. (2015). The role of external linkages and gatekeepers for the renewal and expansion of US cities' knowledge base, 1990–2004. *Regional Studies*, 49(5), 782–797.

Breschi, S., & Lenzi, C. (2016). Co-invention networks and inventive productivity in US cities. *Journal of Urban Economics*, 92, 66–75.

Bresnahan, T., Gambardella, A., & Saxenian, A. (2001). 'Old economy' inputs for 'new economy' outcomes: Cluster formation in the new Silicon Valleys. *Industrial and Corporate Change*, 10(4), 835–860.

Capone, F., Lazzeretti, L. & Innocenti, N. (2021). Innovation and diversity: The role of knowledge networks in the inventive capacity of cities. *Small Business Economics*, 56(2), 773–788.

Coffano, M., Foray, D., & Pezzoni, M. (2017). Does inventor centrality foster regional innovation? The case of the Swiss medical devices sector. *Regional Studies*, 51(8), 1206–1218.

Crespo, J., Suire, R., & Vicente, J. (2016). Network structural properties for cluster long-run dynamics: evidence from collaborative R&D networks in the European mobile phone industry. *Industrial and Corporate Change*, 25(2), 261–282.

Crowe, J. A. (2007). In search of a happy medium: How the structure of interorganizational networks influence community economic development strategies. *Social Networks*, 29(4), 469–488.

De Noni, I., Ganzaroli, A., & Orsi, L. (2017). The impact of intra- and inter-regional knowledge collaboration and technological variety on the knowledge productivity of European regions. *Technological Forecasting and Social Change*, 117, 108–118. https://doi.org/10.1016/j.techfore.2017.01.003

Delvenne, P., & Thoreau, F. (2017). Dancing without listening to the music: Learning from some failures of the 'national innovation systems' in Latin America. In S. Kuhlmann & G. Ordóñez-Matamoros (Eds.) *Research Handbook on Innovation Governance for Emerging Economies: Towards Better Models* (pp. 37–58). Cheltenham, UK and Northampton, MA, USA: Edward Elgar Publishing.

Fleming, L., King, C., & Juda, A. I. (2007). Small worlds and regional innovation. *Organization Science*, 18(6), 938–954.

Galaso, P. (2018). Network topologies as collective social capital in cities and regions: A critical review of empirical studies. *European Planning Studies*, 26(3), 571–590.

Galaso, P., & Kovářík, J. (2021). Collaboration networks, geography and innovation: Local and national embeddedness. *Papers in Regional Science*, 100(2), 349–377.

Graf, H., & Henning, T. (2009). Public research in regional networks of innovators: A comparative study of four East German regions. *Regional Studies*, 43(10), 1349–1368.

Jackson, M. O. (2008). *Social and Economic Networks*. Princeton University Press.

Miguelez, E., Raffo, J., Chacua, C., Coda-Zabetta, M., Yin, D., Lissoni, F., & Tarasconi, G. (2019). Tied in: The global network of local innovation. Cahiers du GREThA (2007–2019), Groupe de Recherche en Economie Théorique et Appliquée (GREThA).

Montobbio, F., & Sterzi, V. (2011). Inventing together: Exploring the nature of international knowledge spillovers in Latin America. *Journal of Evolutionary Economics*, 21(1), 53–89. https://doi.org/10.1007/s00191-010-0181-5

Neal, Z. P. (2014). The backbone of bipartite projections: Inferring relationships from co-authorship, co-sponsorship, co-attendance and other co-behaviors. *Social Networks*, 39(1), 84–97. https://doi.org/10.1016/j.socnet.2014.06.001

Owen-Smith, J., & Powell, W. W. (2004). Knowledge networks as channels and conduits: The effects of spillovers in the Boston biotechnology community. *Organization Science*, 15(1), 5–21. https://doi.org/10.1287/orsc.1030.0054

Porter, M. E. (1990). The competitive advantage of nations. *Competitive Intelligence Review*, 1(1), 14–14.

Roett, R., & Paz, G. (Eds.) (2016). *Latin America and the Asian Giants: Evolving Ties with China and India*. Brookings Institution Press.

Schilling, M. A., & Phelps, C. C. (2007). Interfirm collaboration networks: The impact of large-scale network structure on firm innovation. *Management Science*, 53(7), 1113–1126. https://doi.org/10.1287/mnsc.1060.0624

Uzzi, B., & Spiro, J. (2005). Collaboration and creativity: The small world problem. *American Journal of Sociology*, 111(2), 447–504.

Vázquez-Barquero, A. (2002). *Endogenous Development: Networking, Innovation, Institutions and Cities*. Routledge, pp. 1–18.

Vicente, J. (2022). *The Economics of Clusters*. Cheltenham, UK and Northampton, MA, USA: Edward Elgar Publishing.

Whittington, K. B., Owen-Smith, J., & Powell, W. W. (2009). Networks, propinquity, and innovation in knowledge-intensive industries. *Administrative Science Quarterly*, 54(1), 90–122.

WIPO. (2018). *World Intellectual Property Indicators 2018*. World Intellectual Property Organization.

Yao, L., Li, J., & Li, J. (2020). Urban innovation and intercity patent collaboration: A network analysis of China's national innovation system. *Technological Forecasting and Social Change*, 160, 120185.

Yoguel, G. & Robert, V. (2010). Capacities, processes, and feedbacks: The complex dynamics of development. *Seoul Journal of Economics*, 23(2), 187–237.

12. Economic complexity and income inequality: evidence from Italian regions[1]

Roberto Antonietti and David Fanton

12.1 INTRODUCTION

The aim of this chapter is to investigate the relationship between income inequality and economic complexity at the regional level from 2004 to 2019. We focus on Italy, which is a well-developed and high-complexity country that did not receive much attention in the recent literature on this subject, but that represents an interesting case study because of its wide regional disparities and heterogeneity.

In the last twenty years, there has been a growing interest in the study of economic complexity. A quick search on Scopus reveals that the production of scientific products per year containing the words "economic complexity" in the title, abstract or keywords grew from 378 in 2002 to more than 3700 in 2022. Economists have used economic complexity to explain many contemporary issues, such as GDP dynamics and economic growth, sustainability, innovation, foreign direct investments, and public health dynamics (for a review, see Hidalgo 2021).

Recently, an open debate started on economic complexity as a possible determinant, or deterrent, of income inequality. Among the studies conducted at the country level, there is a strong consensus on the fact that higher levels of economic complexity correspond to lower levels of income inequality (Hartman et al. 2017). However, within-country analyses do not seem to confirm such evidence but find that in many cases economic complexity is related to a higher income dispersion at the regional level (Sbardella et al. 2017; Marco et al. 2022).

This work aims at providing an additional contribution on this subject focusing on the role of economic complexity in explaining recent income inequality dynamics at a regional level in Italy. To our knowledge, this is the first attempt to analyse empirically the complexity–inequality nexus within Italian regions.

In doing so, we try to make our analysis as robust as possible to endogeneity using panel fixed effects regressions and instrumental variables. Our estimates reveal that, *ceteris paribus*, a higher degree of economic complexity in a region corresponds to a higher level of income inequality. The only exception is the North-East of Italy, where the complexity–inequality relationship turns negative, and for which we provide some theoretical explanations based on institutional quality and technological diversification.

Our chapter contributes to two strands of literature. The first is on the economic effects of economic complexity at the sub-national level, providing further empirical support for its possible role in increasing income polarization. The second is the literature on the drivers of income inequality within regions, for which we offer a novel explanation based on the degree of sophistication of production and the underlying knowledge and capabilities required for its realization.

The rest of the chapter develops as follows. Section 12.2 presents a short overview of the concept of economic complexity. Section 12.3 discusses the most recent studies on economic complexity and inequality at the country (or between countries) level (12.3.1) and at the regional level (or within countries) (12.3.2). Section 12.4 presents our empirical analysis, from the data and variables description (12.4.1) to the presentation of the econometric strategy (12.4.2). Section 12.5 shows and discusses the results of our regression analysis. Section 12.6 concludes.

12.2   ECONOMIC COMPLEXITY

The origin of economic complexity comes from the late twentieth century and is based on the discussion of complex systems in natural science, such as mathematics and physics. The ambition was to change the neoclassical economic paradigm in favour of describing economic phenomena and their dynamic processes through the mathematics of stochastic processed computer simulation. In other words, there was a strong interest in using more sophisticated tools to apply in economics, taking knowledge from different fields of science (Fontana 2010).

Borrowing elements from economic geography, international trade theory, network science, and physics, Hidalgo and Hausmann (2009) propose a new conceptualization of economic growth and development theory, using international trade data. According to Hidalgo and Hausmann (2009), the reasons why divergences in countries' growth rates are observed should be blamed on the existence of non-tradable capabilities which are key determinants in the development of countries.

The novelty of this approach rests on the computation of indirect measures of these non-tradable capabilities. To better explain the underlying idea, the two authors use the Lego analogy. Think of a country or region that produces different outputs such as cars, computers, or clothes. To realize a single unit each country uses specific capabilities and resources, or some combinations of them. In the analogy, each product can be represented by a Lego model, while each bucket of Lego pieces represents a country, or a region, and each single Lego piece represents a capability. The higher the number, and variety, of Lego pieces in a bucket, the more complex the Lego model that can be created. This means that the more (and the more diversified) the capabilities in a country/region, the more sophisticated the goods and services that the country itself can produce (Antonietti and Burlina 2023). What the economic complexity method does, is retrieve the diversity and exclusivity (or non-ubiquity) of Lego pieces by looking at the Lego models, which means looking only at the final output that a country produces (Hidalgo and Hausmann, 2009).

The economic complexity index (ECI) is often calculated using international trade data but other types of information, such as data on patents, employment, value-added, and sales, can be used. Whatever the data at hand, the ECI is computed using the method of reflections.

The first step is to consider exports with a revealed comparative advantage (RCA), which means considering only products in which the country is specialized. This element can be extracted using the Balassa index of specialization RCA_{cp}, as follows:

$$RCA_{cp} = \frac{\frac{x_{cp}}{\Sigma_c x_{cp}}}{\frac{\Sigma_c x_{cp}}{\Sigma_{cp} x_{cp}}} \tag{12.1}$$

where x_{cp} is the export value of country c and product p. The Balassa index can give values greater or lower than one: country c is specialized in the production of product p if $RCA_{cp} > 1$. The second step is to define a binary specialization matrix M:

$$M_{cp} = \{1 \ if \ R_{cp} \geq R^* 0 \ if \ R_{cp} < R^* \tag{12.2}$$

where $R^* = 1$. Then, $M_{cp} = 1$ if country c has a revealed comparative advantage in the product p, $M_{cp} = 0$ otherwise. Thanks to this matrix, it is possible to derive the ubiquity, that is the number of countries that have a $RCA_p > 1$, and the diversity, that is the number of products in which a country has a $RCA_c > 1$. Stated differently, ubiquity is a measure of the sophistication of a product: if a product is competitively exported by a few countries, it means that the capabilities needed to produce it are rare and more complex, difficult to imitate, or sophisticated. On the other hand, if a country has high levels of diversity, it means that it has many capabilities to produce different (complex) products. Formally:

$$M_c = \sum_p M_{cp} = diversity \tag{12.3}$$

$$M_p = \sum_c M_{cp} = ubiquity \tag{12.4}$$

The final ECI is obtained by an iterative method of reflections that allows combining ubiquity and diversity, which means finding the eigenvalue of the following matrix:

$$\widetilde{M}_{cc'} \equiv \sum_p \frac{M_{cp} M_{c'p}}{M_c M_p} = \frac{1}{M_c} \sum_c \frac{M_{cp} M_{c'p}}{M_p} \tag{12.5}$$

The ECI is the second largest eigenvector K_c of the matrix M. To make it comparable across countries, the ECI is usually standardized as follows:

$$ECI_c = \frac{K_c - \underline{K}}{std(K)} \tag{12.6}$$

where $\underline{K}$ is the average value of K_c and $std(K)$ is the corresponding standard deviation. From Equation (12.6) it follows that countries with a level of economic complexity higher than the average are those with ECI>0, and vice versa. According to Hidalgo (2021), the ECI has some interesting properties. First, the complexity of a country does not necessarily increase by adding new activities but only if the newly added activity exceeds the average complexity, meaning that adding low-sophisticated goods does not increase the overall complexity of a country. Second, countries with similar complexity values have similar specialization models. Third, the ECI strongly correlates with traditional measures of technology sophistication, such as those based on R&D or patent intensity. However, unlike these traditional measures, the ECI does not need any ex ante information on which activities are classifiable as sophisticated, because the information comes directly *ex post* from the data. Finally, the ECI does not correlate with population and industry diversification, or concentration, which means that the ECI does not depend on the size of the country.

Since the seminal contribution by Hidalgo et al. (2007), it is clear that countries characterized by high levels of complexity are also those with high levels of GDP per capita. For example, if we look at the rankings on the Observatory of Economic Complexity (http://oec.world), we observe that the top-ranked countries are Japan, Germany, Sweden, Switzerland, USA, and the UK, whereas the least-ranked are Sudan, South Sudan, Chad, and Equatorial

Guinea. Such a positive link between economic complexity and aggregate economic growth is confirmed by many studies, such as Hidalgo and Hausmann (2009), Felipe et al. (2012), Ferrarini and Scaramozzino (2016), and Pugliese et al. (2017) at the country level, while recently Pintar and Scherngell (2022) provide additional evidence for European regions.

Less evident is, however, the relationship between the ECI and income inequality. Some studies have shown that higher economic complexity corresponds to more egalitarian income distribution between countries, while others have shown that, within countries or when endogeneity is properly addressed, higher economic complexity entails more unequal income distribution. The following section revises this emerging literature.

12.3   LITERATURE REVIEW

12.3.1   Economic Complexity and Income Inequality Between Countries

From a theoretical perspective, the production structure of a country can have both positive and negative effects on income inequality. First, it can positively or negatively affect the occupational choice of workers, binding their available options on education, human capital development, bargaining power or the possibility of having strong and effective unions. If technological development, industrialization, and an increasing level of complexity provide new jobs and new learning opportunities, then workers can benefit in terms of income per capita, also reducing inequality. On the contrary, if industrialization leads to the reduction of the unions' power, to increasing global competition that forces workers to accept low-wage jobs, then income inequality can increase (Hartmann et al. 2017).

The underlying idea is that the production of complex products requires a wide and differentiated set of skills, tasks, and knowledge, which are usually tacit and highly localized. The occupational structure of countries producing this kind of product is, therefore, relatively flat, because workers experience more job opportunities, higher bargaining power, higher class consciousness, and empowerment (Hartmann et al., 2017). The production of less sophisticated goods and services, on the other hand, requires low skills, raw materials, and extractive activities, providing limited job and earnings opportunities for workers, but higher returns for small groups of individuals who tend to adopt rent-seeking behaviours and increase income concentration in the hands of a few.

It can happen, however, that increasing economic complexity induces a higher income inequality. In a more complex productive structure with highly diversified products and tasks, the capabilities required and the type of jobs available will increase. Therefore, a high level of specialization is required and workers who can learn new tasks and can learn them quickly will have an advantage that turns into higher wages. On the contrary, workers that cannot follow the increasing complexity will be left behind (Hodgson, 2003).

From an empirical perspective, Hartmann et al. (2017) analyse more than 70 countries from 1962 to 2012. In their analysis, both economic complexity and GDP per capita show a negative relationship with income inequality. Moreover, the negative relationship between ECI and income inequality is stable across all the considered years. Through a series of pooled OLS regressions, they find not only that ECI is a negative predictor of income inequality but also that it is the most significant explanatory variable. Fixed-effect panel regressions reinforce this scenario, showing a strong and negative relationship between the two variables. Considering more than 120 countries from 1964 to 2013, Fawaz and Rahnama-Moghadamm (2019) use a spatial autoregressive model (SAR), to analyse if income inequality in a country depends on the income inequality and economic complexity of economically related countries. They find that trading with more economically complex countries is correlated with a reduction in income inequality.

Lee and Vu (2019) analyse more than 90 countries from 1980 to 2014 using both OLS and instrumental variable (IV) regressions. The former point out that economic complexity negatively affects income inequality, but this result is not robust to endogeneity: as shown by their dynamic panel data regressions, an increase in the ECI is associated with a higher level of income inequality.

Chu and Hoang (2020) study more than 80 countries from 2012 to 2017. They used an IV approach, using research and development intensity as an instrument in a dynamic model. Their results show that economic complexity positively affects income inequality. However, by calculating the marginal effect of the ECI on income inequality at different levels of other explanatory variables, they found that above a certain threshold of education, government spending and trade openness, more economic complexity helps to reduce income inequality. Similar results emerge in Sepehrdoust et al. (2021) who focus on a sample of developing countries between 2000 and 2019 and adopt a panel VAR approach.

Lee and Wang (2021), instead, look at 43 countries from 1991 to 2016. In their panel fixed effect model, they found that economic complexity reduces income inequality. Moreover, when splitting the sample between developed and developing countries, they found that for the former an increase in complexity corresponds to a decrease in inequality while for the latter the opposite holds, consistent with Sepehrdoust et al. (2021).

More recently, Pham et al. (2023) using two-stage GMM estimation for a sample of 99 countries from 2002 to 2016, find that both economic development and the shadow economy have non-linear effects on income inequality:

the relationship between economic complexity and income inequality has a U-shape, while the impact of the informal economy on income inequality follows an inverted U-shaped pattern.

Amarante et al. (2023) using a panel fixed effects estimator on a sample of approximately 190 countries from 1995 to 2018, find an inverted U-shape relationship between the ECI and income inequality, meaning that economic complexity reduces income inequality after achieving a certain threshold, which corresponds to the case of high-income economies.

Table 12.1 summarizes the main results of the between-country literature on ECI and inequality.

Table 12.1   Literature on ECI and inequality between countries

Authors	Methodology	ECI–inequality relation
Hartmann et al. (2017)	Pooled OLS, FE	Negative
Fawaz and Rahnama-Moghadamm (2019)	SAR	Negative
Lee and Vu (2019)	OLS, Dynamic panel data	Negative but only for developed countries, positive for developing countries
Chu and Hoang (2020)	IV-GMM, IV-2SLS	Inverted U-shaped
Sepehrdoust et al. (2021)	Panel-VAR	Inverted U-shaped
Lee and Wang (2021)	FE, FMM, IV-FMM	Inverted U-shaped
Pham et al. (2023)	GMM	Inverted U-shaped
Amarante et al. (2023)	FE	Inverted U-shaped

12.3.2   Economic Complexity and Income Inequality Within Countries

If between-country analyses generally agree on the sign of the relationship between income inequality and economic complexity, the empirical studies investigating this issue within countries are less uniform (see also Hartman and Pinheiro 2022 for a review). Sbardella et al. (2017), look at the relationship between wage inequality and economic complexity at the county level in the US from 1990 to 2014. The result of the non-parametric analysis is that higher levels of economic complexity correspond to higher levels of wage inequality. The explanation is that, in the 1990s, the US incurred a fast structural change induced by technological progress and globalization, where many workers moved from highly unionized manufacturing sectors to highly unregulated service sectors, which are also those that contributed to wage inequality the most. A fast-changing job distribution from manufacturing to knowledge-intensive business services determined not only a rise in product sophistication but also a rising income inequality.

Pinheiro et al. (2022) merge patent data from OECD REGPAT and macroeconomic data on employment and GDP per capita from the Structural Business Statistics of European regions provided by Eurostat, finding that low-income and low-complexity regions tend to be stuck on simple technologies and industries, with limited chances to diversify into more complex activities. Differently, high-income, or high-complexity, regions tend to develop more complex products, technologies, and jobs, raising their growth possibilities even more. The outcome of this process is a reinforcing income polarization across regions.

Gao and Zhou (2018) quantified the economic complexity of China's provinces analysing 25 years of firm export data from 1990 to 2015 for 31 provinces. They show that provinces with higher economic complexity, diversity, and relative income have less income inequality. Zhu et al. (2020) shift the analysis to China's prefecture-level regions (126 units) in 2013. They studied how regional export product/destination structures have shaped income inequality, not looking only at the complexity of the production structure but also at the export destination. They found that a higher level of economic complexity and a higher percentage of products exported to more complex countries/regions implies a lower level of inequality only for urbanized areas, while for rural area income inequality increases.

Bandeira Morais et al. (2021) analyse the income inequality-economic complexity nexus at the regional level in Brazil from 2002 to 2014. Their OLS and the random effects (RE) regressions stress that the ECI–inequality relationship has an inverted U-shape. When looking at regions with different levels of development, they observe that such an inverted U-shape holds only in highly developed regions, suggesting that a certain level of development needs to be reached before economic complexity starts to have an impact on inequality.

Marco et al. (2022) analyse the trilemma between income inequality, environmental degradation, and economic complexity at a sub-national level in 50 Spanish provinces from 2002 to 2016. Their estimates results show a trade-off between, income equality, environmental quality, and economic growth: in the end, a decrease in economic growth and a decrease in economic complexity leads to lower income inequality.

Gómez-Zaldívar et al. (2022) focus on 31 federal states in Mexico from 2004 to 2019. The result from RE regressions is strong and significant: states with more complex production structures show lower levels of inequality, suggesting that increasing the number of specializations leads to the creation of more job opportunities, and the resulting decrease in non-active population and unemployment rate in turn reduces income inequality. Table 12.2 summarizes the main results of the within-country literature on ECI and inequality.

Table 12.2   Literature on ECI and inequality within countries

Authors	Methodology	Country	ECI–inequality relation
Sbardella et al. (2017)	Non-parametric	USA	Positive
Pinheiro et al. (2022)	Correlations	EU	Positive
Gao and Zhou (2018)	Bivariate/multivariate	China	Negative
Zhu et al. (2020)	OLS	China	Positive in non-urbanized area
Bandeira Morais et al. (2021)	Pooled OLS, RE	Brazil	U-shaped
Marco et al. (2022)	Linear and non-linear	Spain	Positive
Gómez-Zaldívar et al. (2022)	RE	Mexico	Negative

12.4   EMPIRICAL ANALYSIS

12.4.1   Data and Variables

Taking stock of the literature discussed in Section 12.3.2, we empirically analyse the ECI–inequality relationship in Italy. Specifically, our dataset collects information for 19 Italian NUTS-2 regions and two autonomous provinces in NUTS-3 regions (*Provincia Autonoma di Trento* and *Provincia Autonoma di Bolzano*) for the years from 2004 to 2016. The final dataset is the outcome of the merge of different data sources: the Italian National Institute of Statistics (ISTAT), the European Statistical Office (EUROSTAT), and the Institutional Quality Index website developed by Annamaria Nifo and Gaetano Vecchione.

The choice to conduct the analysis at the NUTS-2 regional level is due to data constraints. Although the data on institutions and economic complexity are available at the NUTS-3 level, the information on income inequality from ISTAT and EUROSTAT is available only at the NUTS-2 regional level.

The dependent variable is the annual level of income inequality in Italian regions. We measure it through the Gini index including imputed rents ($GINI_{RENT}$) and the Gini index excluding imputed rents ($GINI_{NORENT}$),[2] which we extract from the Italian Statistics on Income and Living Conditions provided by ISTAT.

Figure 12.1 shows the annual trend of the two Gini indexes in Italy. As expected, the two measures show very similar dynamics, with the Gini index excluding the imputed rent being well above the Gini index that includes the imputed rent.

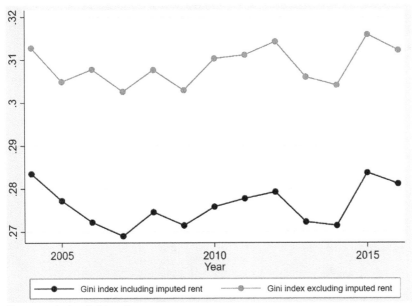

Source: Authors' elaboration.

Figure 12.1   Mean Gini index including and excluding imputed rent

Figure 12.2 shows the distribution of income inequality across the 21 Italian regions. Panels *a* and *b* refer to the $GINI_{RENT}$ index, while panels *c* and *d* to the $GINI_{NORENT}$ index. From the four maps, we observe three phenomena. First, as for Figure 12.1, both indicators provide the same information on the geography of income inequality both in 2004 and 2016. Second, in each of the two years, income inequality is more pronounced in Southern regions. Third, from 2004 to 2016 there are some changes in the mean level of income inequality across regions: for example, the Gini index increases in Liguria, Tuscany, Abruzzo, Apulia, and Sardinia, and it decreases in Trentino Alto Adige, Marche, Molise, and Veneto.

The ECI is available from Antonietti and Burlina (2023) and is computed on annual export data provided by ISTAT through the Coeweb archive at the NUTS-3 region and three-digit (manufacturing) industry level. The approach used is that of Hidalgo and Hausmann described in Section 12.2. The final index used for the econometric analysis is the NUTS-2 region average of the original ECI computed at the NUTS-3 region level.

In our empirical analysis, we also include a set of additional variables to test whether the ECI–inequality relationship is robust to the inclusion of confound-

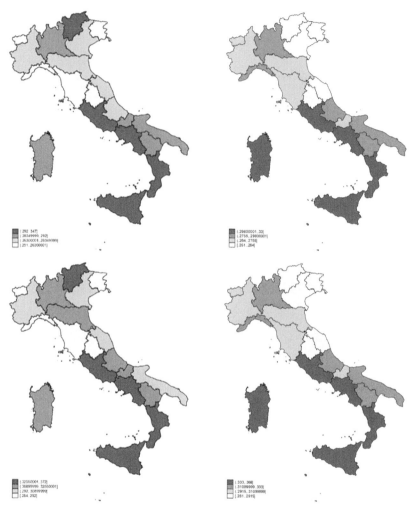

Notes: Top left: $GINI_{RENT}$ 2004; top right: $GINI_{RENT}$ 2016; bottom left: $GINI_{NORENT}$ 2004; bottom right $GINI_{NORENT}$ 2016.
Source: Authors' elaborations.

Figure 12.2   The geography of income inequality: 2004 and 2016

ing factors. Among them, we include variables that can influence income distribution within regions, such as the quality of regional institutions, the level of well-being, the size of the region, and the regional human capital endowment.

The quality of institutions at the regional level is measured by the Institutional Quality Index (IQI). This index is computed by Nifo and Vecchione (2014) and is available here https://sites.google.com/site/instit utionalqua lityindex/home. The IQI is a composite indicator based on five groups of elementary sub-indexes capturing the following types of institutions: (1) voice and accountability, which measures the citizens degree of participation in public elections, civic and social associations, the number of social cooperatives, the INVALSI test and the cultural liveliness measured in terms of books published; (2) government effectiveness, capturing the endowment of social and economic structures in Italian regions and the administrative capability of regional governments in terms of health policies, waste and environment management; (3) regulatory quality concerning the degree of openness of the economy, the rate of firms mortality, indicators of business environment and business density; (4) rule of law summarizing data on crime against persons or property, magistrate productivity, trial times, tax evasion and shadow economy; (5) corruption collecting data on crimes against the Public Administration, the number of local administrations overruled by the federal authorities and the Golden-Picci Index.

Table 12.3   Summaries statistics

	Mean	Std. Dev.	Min	Max
$GINI_{RENT}$	0.276	0.0248	0.225	0.356
$GINI_{NORENT}$	0.309	0.0256	0.256	0.396
ECI	-0.010	0.057	-0.251	0.165
IQI	0.586	0.245	0.0548	1
GDP per capita	28,442	7,768	16,036	43,733
Population	2,826,758	2,410,139	121,692	9,958,447
Population density	175.9	108.4	37.66	426.3
Human capital	0.094	0.019	0.054	0.159

The level of well-being of a region is proxied by its (real) GDP per capita (*GDPPC*), measured in 2015 prices, that we take from ISTAT regional statistics (*Conti economici territoriali*). Information on the total resident population (*POP*) is used to measure the size of each region, using data from ISTAT. We also use the information on population density (*POPDEN*), that is, total resident population per km^2, to capture the degree of urbanization of Italian regions, which can have a role in explaining the distribution of income, considering that the largest share of the population lives in urbanized areas. To measure the regional endowment of human capital (*HK*), we take the share of the population (aged 15 or more) with a tertiary education degree (at the

Bachelor and/or Master level) that we extract from the ASTI (*Atlante Statistico Territoriale delle Infrastrutture*) archive administered by ISTAT. Table 12.3 shows the main summary statistics of these variables.

12.4.2 Econometric Strategy

We begin our analysis by estimating the following model:

$$GINI_{RENTit} = \beta_0 + \beta_1 ECI_{i,t-n} + X'_{it-n}\beta_X + \mu_i + \delta_t + \varepsilon_{i,t} \tag{12.7}$$

where $GINI_{RENT}$ is our measure of income inequality in each NUTS-2 region i in year t. The focal regressor is *ECI*, which we include at time t-1, t-2, and t-3 to capture possible delays in the materialization of its influence on income inequality. The term X is a vector of additional control variables, including *IQI*, *GDPPC*, *POP*, *POPDEN*, and *HK*. Due to their high pairwise correlation, we include population and population density, as well as ECI and GDP per capita, separately in the estimates. Moreover, with the exception of *ECI*, we transform all the variables into natural logarithms so that we can interpret the corresponding estimated coefficient (β) as an elasticity. Finally, the terms μ_i, δ_t, and ε_{it} capture, respectively, region-specific unobservable fixed effects, time-specific fixed effects, and the stochastic error component.

Estimating Equation (12.7) through an OLS estimator can be subject to two main problems. The first is omitted variables. If there are unobserved endogenous regressors that are correlated with the other explanatory variables, then the OLS estimate of β_1 is biased. To mitigate this risk, we estimate Equation (12.7) using within-group transformation of all our variables and a panel FE estimator. The second problem is reverse causality, which arises if a higher income inequality, maybe reflecting a more uneven distribution of high-paid versus low-paid jobs, can determine the level of economic complexity in a region. To avoid this, we use an IV strategy. As a possible instrument, we select the level of diversification of the regional skill portfolio, that is, skill entropy.

To compute the variety in the labour force's skills, we follow Antonietti and Burlina (2023) and merge information from three additional datasets: the INAPP-ISTAT survey on occupations ("*Indagine Campionaria sulle Professioni*" – ICP), the ISTAT's Labour Force Survey (LFS) and ASIA (*Archivio Statistico Imprese Attive*) archive. The ICP provides information on the tasks, skills, attitudes to work, and working conditions for approximately 800 occupational titles, as classified by the International Standard Classification of Occupations (ISCO), obtained through a sample survey of 16,000 workers. The LFS provides information on the distribution of employees by one-digit occupational title. From the ICP we take the 35 available skills and calculate their average usage for each of the eight one-digit job titles to obtain the average skill level of each occupation in Italy. From the LFS we take the actual distribution of one-digit occupations across NUTS-2 regions in 2011, from which we calculate the regions' employment shares by type of occupation. These shares are used as weights in computing the average level of each of the 35 skills in every NUTS-2 region in 2011. To make this average skill level change over time, we use data from ASIA to calculate the annual rate of growth in total employment in each region, taking 2011 for reference, and we apply this growth rate to our average skill level indicators. We thus obtain 35 time-varying skill levels for each NUTS-3 region, and we use them to compute our final skill entropy indicator:

$$Skill\ entropy_i = \sum_{s=1}^{S} N_s log_2 \left(\frac{1}{N_s}\right) \tag{12.8}$$

where N_s is the average level of each skill s in the region i.

We surmise that a greater variety of skills and competencies should increase the possibility of (re) combining knowledge, increasing the likelihood of developing exclusive and sophisticated products and increasing the average degree of economic complexity of the region (Quatraro 2010; Antonietti and Burlina 2023). In other words, we assume that the effect of skill diversification on income inequality is not direct but indirectly passes through what these skills, which are embedded in occupations and employees, actually realize and produce, as captured by the ECI. A preliminary test for this is the pairwise correlation between skill entropy and $GINI_{RENT}$, which is -0.038 and not statistically significant, suggesting that between the two variables there is not a strong direct link. Moreover, to our knowledge, there is no literature finding theoretical or empirical support for this relationship.

Finally, we can also suspect that the error terms of our panel model are cross-sectionally independent. In fact, our regional data are likely to show a spatial correlation, which might further bias the OLS estimates. Providing a spatial regression analysis is beyond the scope of the chapter but we try to mitigate this issue as much as possible using Driscoll and Kraay's covariance matrix estimator for the FE estimates (Hoechle, 2007). This means correcting the standard errors to account for possible cross-sectional dependence in our covariates.

12.5   RESULTS

12.5.1   Baseline Results

Table 12.4   Economic complexity and income inequality: panel FE regressions

Dep. Var.	(1)	(2)	(3)	(4)	(5)	(6)
$GINI_{RENT}$	t-1	t-2	t-3	t-1	t-2	t-3
ECI	-0.037	0.206**	0.170**	-0.033	0.191**	0.157**
	(0.099)	(0.079)	(0.053)	(0.091)	(0.069)	(0.057)
POPDEN	0.177	0.356	0.326			
	(0.170)	(0.209)	(0.199)			
POP				0.213	0.335	0.204
				(0.136)	(0.164)	(0.154)
HK	-0.029	0.086	0.213**	-0.0130	0.102	0.207**
	(0.055)	(0.062)	(0.086)	(0.049)	(0.064)	(0.084)
IQI	0.005	-0.009	-0.005			
	(0.018)	(0.019)	(0.0075)			
GDPPC				-0.124	-0.089	0.079
				(0.126)	(0.134)	(0.125)
Region FE	✓	✓	✓	✓	✓	✓
Year FE	✓	✓	✓	✓	✓	✓
N. obs.	273	273	273	273	273	273
Within R^2	0.199	0.242	0.255	0.203	0.244	0.257

Notes: Driscoll and Kraay's standard errors in parentheses. *** significant at the 1% level; ** significant at the 5% level; * significant at the 10% level.

Tables 12.4 and 12.5 show the results of the panel FE and two-step IV-GMM regressions. In Table 12.4, Columns 1–3 population and GDP per capita are excluded from the set of regressors, while in Columns 4–6 we excluded population density and institutional quality. As explained in Section 12.4.2, these exclusions are due to the high correlation between, respectively, *POP* and *POPDEN* and *GDPPC* and *IQI*. We note, however, that the results remain the same across the specifications. More in detail, from Columns 1 and 4 we find that a one-year lagged ECI does not have any significant relationship with income inequality. From Columns 2–3 and 5–6, instead, we find that such a relationship becomes statistically significant and positive, meaning that, at the regional level, an increase in the level of economic complexity corresponds to an increase in income inequality two or three years later. Among the other

Table 12.5   Economic complexity and income inequality: IV regressions

	(1)	(2)
	First Stage	IV-GMM
Skill entropy$_{t-4}$	0.022***	
	(0.006)	
ECI$_{t-3}$		1.440*
		(0.786)
POPDEN	✓	✓
HK	✓	✓
IQI	✓	✓
Year FE	✓	✓
Region FE	✓	✓
N. obs.	252	252
Kleibergen-Paap F	11.25	
Endogeneity test (p-value)	0.108	
(Centred) R^2	0.860	0.741

Notes: Robust standard errors in parentheses. *** significant at the 1% level; ** significant at the 5% level; * significant at the 10% level.

regressors, only *HK* has a positive and significant coefficient, when measured at *t*-3. All the results do not change when we included different control variables, meaning that the nature and significance of the estimated coefficients of economic complexity are robust to the inclusion of confounding factors.[3]

The results are also confirmed in Table 12.5, where we use an IV-GMM estimator to mitigate potential reverse causality. Specifically, we instrument *ECI$_{t-3}$* with skill entropy at *t*-4. Column 1 shows the first-stage regression results, where we find that the estimated coefficient of our instrument is positive and statistically significant at the 1% level. The Kleibergen-Paap F statistic is larger than the commonly accepted value of 10, and the first stage R^2 is very high, demonstrating that the instrument is sufficiently strong. Column 2 shows the second-stage regression results, where we see that the *ECI* coefficient remains statistically significant at the 10% level. Moreover, we see that the exogeneity test does not reject the null hypothesis of exogeneity of *ECI*, which means that our panel FE estimates in Table 12.4 are more efficient.

Our results suggest that the degree of product sophistication is significantly related to income distribution and seem to confirm the within-country evidence supporting the role of economic complexity in rising inequality.

Table 12.6   ECI and income inequality by NUTS-1 region: panel FE regressions

	North-West			North-East		
	(1)	(2)	(3)	(4)	(5)	(6)
	t-1	t-2	t-3	t-1	t-2	t-3
ECI	0.252	0.411**	0.070	-1.025***	0.415	0.419
	(0.273)	(0.179)	(0.180)	(0.317)	(0.215)	(0.793)
NUTS-2 FE	✓	✓	✓	✓	✓	✓
Year FE	✓	✓	✓	✓	✓	✓
Observations	65	65	65	65	65	65
Within R²	0.327	0.389	0.342	0.356	0.324	0.329
	Centre			South and islands		
	(7)	(8)	(9)	(10)	(11)	(12)
	t-1	t-2	t-3	t-1	t-2	t-3
ECI	0.430	0.464***	0.199	-0.075	0.120	0.143
	(0.247)	(0.104)	(0.206)	(0.107)	(0.146)	(0.135)
NUTS-2 FE	✓	✓	✓	✓	✓	✓
Year FE	✓	✓	✓	✓	✓	✓
Observations	52	52	52	78	78	78
Within R²	0.590	0.594	0.601	0.222	0.259	0.289

Note: Driscoll and Kraay's standard errors in parentheses. $^*p < 0.05$, $^{**}p < 0.01$, $^{***}p < 0.001$.

12.5.2   Results by Macro Area

As a further step, we try to understand whether these results depend on the macro area (NUTS-1 region) in which the region is located, specifically North-West, North-East, Centre, and South (with islands).[4] Therefore, we repeat our panel FE regressions by NUTS-1 region, as in Table 12.6. Due to the limited number of observations for each area, we include only *ECI* and the NUTS-2 and year fixed effects as regressors.

From Table 12.6 we find an interesting result. Columns 1–3 and 7–9 show that a higher economic complexity corresponds to higher income inequality after two years in the North-West and in the Centre of Italy, whereas Columns 10–12 show that *ECI* does not affect $GINI_{RENT}$ in the South. Instead, from Columns 4–6, we observe a negative relationship between *ECI* and income inequality in the North-East.

Following Hartmann et al. (2017), Pinheiro et al. (2022), and Antonietti and Burlina (2023), we try to explain these dynamics by combining two elements, that is, institutional quality and technological diversification. To check for this, we consider two variables, *IQI* and an indicator of technological entropy computed as in Antonietti and Burlina (2023). Specifically, we consider the number of patent applications submitted each year from the OECD-REGPAT database, using the inventor's address to assign patents to regions. Using the International Patent Classification (IPC) to obtain the annual share of patents for every four-digit IPC code (P_g), we compute a measure of technological entropy measure as follows:

$$entropy_{tech_i} = \sum_{g=1}^{G} P_g \, log_2 \left(\frac{1}{P_g} \right) \tag{12.9}$$

where G is the total number of IPC codes g, and P_g is the share of patents for each four-digit IPC code.

Then, we plot the annual values of *IQI* and *entropy_tech* of each NUTS-2 region as in Figure 12.3, where the red lines identify the corresponding median values (computed for the whole 2004–2019 period). Interestingly, we note that all the NUTS-2 regions belonging to the North-East are in the top-right panel, where both institutional quality and technological diversification are above their median values. On the other side, Southern NUTS-2 regions are clustered in the bottom-left panel. Interestingly, many of regions in the North-West exhibit a level of average institutional quality above (or close to) the median but a relatively less diversified, or more specialized, portfolio of technologies.

In other words, institutions in the North-East are of higher quality as compared to other regions. This factor is important in the wage settings mechanism since better institutions allow for stronger unions and higher contractual power of the employees. More in detail (and not shown here), the specific institutional aspects in which North-Eastern regions outperform are voice and accountability, government effectiveness, regulatory quality, and rule of law.

Higher values of technological entropy, on the other hand, mean a higher potential for (re)combining technological knowledge (Quatraro 2010) and so generate new, and more complex, products and services. When combined, these two elements identify a situation where technological diversification creates more and more diversified job opportunities, while high institutional quality helps regulate labour and product markets to make the highest number of workers gain from such a rising economic complexity. On the contrary, lower chances for (technological) diversification combined with low-quality institutions may create a situation of job polarization, rent-seeking behaviours, and persistent inequality.

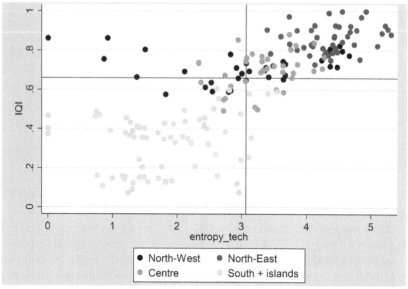

Source: Authors' elaborations.

*Figure 12.3   Institutional quality and technological diversification across
                 Italian regions*

12.6   CONCLUSIONS

The concept of economic complexity is gaining momentum in the academic
and policy debate on the drivers of economic growth and development. On
this issue, literature is flourishing around the link of economic complexity
with economic growth, environmental sustainability, human development,
and health. Not surprisingly, the economic complexity index has been found
as a very good predictor of long-term economic growth and GDP per capita in
many countries.

However, an important aspect that is attracting scholars and policymakers is related to the possible dark side of economic complexity, which is
income inequality. Recent empirical studies identify a negative, or inverted
U-shaped, relationship between economic complexity and income inequality
at the country level, indicating that higher complexity tends to favour a more
even distribution of earnings. Other studies conducted at the regional level,
however, do not share the same results but show that higher economic complexity can lead to a more unequal income distribution.

Our research fits this debate. The aim of this chapter is to investigate the
economic complexity–inequality relationship in Italian NUTS-2 regions, from

2004 to 2019. Merging different data sources, and combining panel fixed effects and IV-GMM regressions, we find that, on average, a higher level of economic complexity corresponds to a higher level of income inequality after two or three years. This result is robust to the inclusion of different confounding factors, such as region size, human capital, and quality of institutions. The reasons why we see an increase in income inequality when the economic complexity increases can be found in the characteristics of the workforce. Indeed, higher product sophistication may disproportionally benefit high skilled workers. In addition, higher complexity means higher development and technological/industry diversification, which corresponds to more job opportunities and thus a more differentiated income distribution. However, when complexity rises it is not automatic that it will influence workers' skills or learning opportunities.

This influence can only be obtained if the regional and national institutions are advanced enough, as combined with a sufficiently diversified technological landscape. This is the case of the North-East, where we find a level of institutional quality and patent diversification above the median. Instead, if the institutions are not sufficiently developed and/or knowledge sufficiently diversified, we may find situations where increasing complexity is associated with a worsening of disparities in the demand for skills and competences, with an elite of highly skilled and talented employees gaining the most on the one hand, and several low-skilled and marginalized workers on the other.

From a policy perspective, this evidence poses interesting challenges, especially for Smart Specialization and regional innovation policies. Technologically advanced and diversified regions have the chance to improve, and keep constantly high, their level of product sophistication, relying on a strong and diversified skill base and high quality of institutions. However, this comes at a cost, which is rising income inequality. Lagging regions, on the other hand, can remain locked-in low complex specializations and low-quality institutions. As suggested by Pinheiro et al. (2022), policies that can help peripheral regions explore new diversification opportunities, not necessarily in high-complexity activities, should try to remove the obstacles to credit and entrepreneurial attitude, while developing the local knowledge and education infrastructure in such a way that it can upgrade the local economy and help the region move into more complex activities. Another way is to favour skilled labour mobility across regions or increase the attractiveness to foreign investors.

NOTES

1.   Disclaimer: This chapter should not be reported as representing the views of the European Central Bank (ECB). The views expressed are those of the authors and

do not necessarily reflect those of the ECB. All errors are solely and exclusively attributable to the authors.
2. As a robustness test, we also use the income quintiles share ratio (S80/S20), calculated as the ratio of total income received by the 20% of the population with the highest income (the top quintile) to that received by the 20% of the population with the lowest income (the bottom quintile). This information is available from the "Living conditions in Europe – income distribution and income inequality" survey administered by EUROSTAT.
3. The results do not change if we use *GININORENT* and *S80/S20* as dependent variables. For reasons of space, we do not report the regression results here, but they are available on request.
4. Regions are distributed as follows. North-West: Aosta Valley, Piedmont, Liguria, and Lombardy. North-East: Trento, Bolzano, Veneto, Friuli-Venezia-Giulia, Emilia-Romagna. Centre: Tuscany, Umbria, Lazio, Marche. South and islands: Abruzzo, Molise, Campania, Apulia, Basilicata, Sicily, and Sardinia.

REFERENCES

Amarante, V., Lanzilotta, B., Torres, J. (2023). Inequality and productive structure: New evidence at the world level, WIDER Working Paper n. 2023-9, World Institute for Development Economic Research (UNU-WIDER).

Antonietti, R., Burlina, C. (2023). Exploring the entropy-complexity nexus. Evidence from Italy. *Economia Politica – Journal of Analytical and Institutional Economics*, 40, 257–283.

Bandeira Morais, M., Swart, J., Jordaan, J.A. (2021). Economic complexity and inequality: Does regional productive structure affect income inequality in Brazilian states? *Sustainability*, 13(2), 1006.

Chu, L.K., Hoang, D.P. (2020). How does economic complexity influence income inequality? New evidence from international data. *Economic Analysis and Policy*, 68, 44–57.

Fawaz, F., Rahnama-Moghadamm, M. (2019). Spatial dependence of global income inequality: The role of economic complexity. *The International Trade Journal*, 33(6), 542–554.

Felipe, J., Kumar, U., Abdon, A., Bacate, M. (2012). Product complexity and economic development. *Structural Change and Economic Dynamics*, 23(1), 36–68.

Ferrarini, B., Scaramozzino, P. (2016). Production complexity, adaptability and economic growth. *Structural Change and Economic Dynamics*, 37, 52–61.

Fontana, M. (2010). Can neoclassical economics handle complexity? The fallacy of the oil spot dynamic. *Journal of Economic Behavior & Organization*, 76(3), 584–596.

Gao, J., Zhou, T. (2018). Quantifying China's regional economic complexity. *Physica A: Statistical Mechanics and its Applications*, 492, 1591–1603.

Gómez-Zaldívar, M., Osorio-Caballero, M. I., Saucedo-Acosta, E.J. (2022). Income inequality and economic complexity: Evidence from Mexican states. *Regional Science Policy & Practice*, 14(6), 344–363.

Hartmann, D., Guevara, M.R., Jara- Figueroa, C., Aristarán, M., Hidalgo, C.A. (2017). Linking economic complexity, institutions, and income inequality. *World Development* 93, 75–93.

Hartmann, D., Pinheiro, F.L. (2022). Economic complexity and inequality at the national and regional level. arXiv preprint arXiv:2206.00818.

Hidalgo, C.A. (2021). Economic complexity theory and applications. *Nature Reviews Physics*, 3(2), 92–113.

Hidalgo, C.A., Hausmann, R. (2009). The building blocks of economic complexity. *Proceedings of the National Academy of Sciences*, 106(26), 10570–10575.

Hidalgo, C.A., Klinger, B., Barabási, A.L., Hausmann, R. (2007). The product space conditions the development of nations. *Science*, 317(5837), 482–487.

Hodgson, G.M. (2003). Capitalism, complexity, and inequality. *Journal of Economic Issues*, 37(2), 471–478.

Hoechle, D. (2007). Robust standard errors for panel regressions with cross-sectional dependence. *The Stata Journal*, 7(3), 281–312.

Lee, C.C., Wang, E.Z. (2021). Economic complexity and income inequality: Does country risk matter? *Social Indicators Research*, 154(1), 35–60.

Lee, K.K., Vu, T.V. (2019). Economic complexity, human capital and income inequality: A cross-country analysis. *Japanese Economic Review* 71, 695–718.

Marco, R., Llano, C., Pérez-Balsalobre, S. (2022). Economic complexity, environmental quality and income equality: a new trilemma for regions? *Applied Geography*, 139, 102646.

Nifo, A. and Vecchione, G. (2014). Do institutions play a role in skilled migration? The case of Italy. *Regional Studies*, 48(10), 1628–1649.

Pham, M.H., Truong, H.D.H., Hoang, D.P. (2023). Economic complexity, shadow economy, and income inequality: Fresh evidence from panel data. Preprint (Version 1) available at Research Square: https://doi.org/10.21203/rs.3.rs-2452093/v1.

Pinheiro, F.L., Balland, P.A., Boschma, R., Hartmann, D. (2022). The dark side of the geography of innovation: Relatedness, complexity and regional inequality in Europe. *Regional Studies*, doi: 10.1080/00343404.2022.2106362.

Pintar, N., Scherngell, T. (2022). The complex nature of regional knowledge production: Evidence on European regions. *Research Policy*, 51(8), 104170.

Pugliese, E., Chiarotti, G. L., Zaccaria, A., Pietronero, L. (2017). Complex economies have a lateral escape from the poverty trap. *PLOS ONE 12*(1): e0168540.

Quatraro, F. (2010). Knowledge coherence, variety and economic growth: Manufacturing evidence from Italian regions. *Research Policy*, 39(10), 1289–1302.

Sbardella, A., Pugliese, E., Pietronero, L. (2017). Economic development and wage inequality: A complex system analysis. *PloS ONE*, 12(9), e0182774.

Sepehrdoust, H., Tartar, M., Gholizadeh, A. (2021). Economic complexity, scientific productivity and income inequality in developing economies. *Economics of Transition and Institutional Change*, 30(4), 737–752.

Zhu, S., Yu, C., He, C. (2020). Export structures, income inequality and urban–rural divide in China. *Applied Geography*, 115, 102150.

13. The Italian National Strategy for Inner Areas: first insights from regions' specialization in cultural and creative industries

Andrea Porta, Giovanna Segre, and Josep-Maria Arauzo-Carod

13.1 INTRODUCTION

In recent years, culture, creativity and heritage, and their connection with tourism, are commonly seen as a development panacea, especially at the local administration level. In this sense, several local development policies have targeted solely tourism activities aiming at transforming them into magnets driving local growth (Bronzini, Ciani, & Montaruli, 2022; Petrei, Cavallo, & Santoro, 2020). When considering peripheral areas, this tendency is driven to excess, and becomes an idealistic solution to complex and rooted problems (Collins & Cunningham, 2017). Albeit the cultural dimension of territorial policies is still relatively unexplored (see for example OECD, 2018), there is an increasing awareness that cultural and landscape assets, even in peripheral areas, must be increasingly included in local administrations and communities' agendas and systemically connected to other territorial resources. This vision marks a shift toward better integrated policies, in direct relation with territories and societies, enhancing the existing potential but also fostering innovation, supporting the production of original cultural resources and cultural values, and activating new local value chains (Lysgård, 2016; Sacco & Segre, 2009).

In the Italian context, on which this chapter is focused, it is furthermore urgent to address the historically rooted unequal level of economic development (e.g., North vs South, mountains vs plain). Within this context, the Italian government in 2013 launched the National Strategy for Inner Areas (SNAI), openly declaring the aim of enhancing the cultural resources of the (lagged) peripheries[1] to foster economic growth and social cohesion. The desired development process described by the SNAI policy intervention needs a deeper understanding of the territorial distribution of the main sectors involved, those of the cultural and creative industries, the so-called CCIs.

The aim of the chapter is to contribute at building new knowledge on the geographical distribution and specialization of CCIs, highlighting their location, comparing the inner and central areas of the country as identified by the SNAI.

Being the strategy explicitly place-based, to assess the distribution of cultural sectors at the local level we apply a territorial approach, connecting and updating (using a very detailed dataset about firms in these industries) the statistical data on CCIs establishments and employees and the spatial classification of the Italian territory introduced by the SNAI in 2014.[2] As regions (NUTS 2) are responsible for applying the SNAI at the local level, the analysis is conducted at the regional scale.

The analysis refers to the well-established literature on culture-based local development and applies in particular the cultural districts perspective. The key factors considered crucial to foster local development, when cultural activities and industries are involved, rely on the close interaction between (1) cultural activities and assets and (2) non-cultural production chains, by means of institutional, social and economic networks (see Della Lucia & Segre, 2017; Santagata & Bertacchini, 2011). The results of the analysis are presented highlighting the concentration in the distribution of CCIs establishments and employees in the inner areas confronted by the ones in the centres.

Section 13.2 introduces the SNAI and the role given to culture within the strategy; Section 13.3 presents the data included in the analysis, the way in which they are organized and the methods applied; Sections 13.4 and 13.5 include the results of measuring and mapping the CCIs in inner areas of the Italian regions. In Section 13.6, the main conclusions are sketched, and further research lines and policy implications are discussed.

13.2　THE ITALIAN NATIONAL STRATEGY FOR INNER AREAS AND THE ROLE OF CULTURE

The definition and territorial classification of inner areas adopted in this chapter is the one systematized in the SNAI (for a broader definition of inner areas see Pezzi & Urso, 2016) launched in 2014, in the Italian context, by the Ministry of Territorial Cohesion and the ministries responsible for the coordination of EU funds, in a context of European place-based policies (Barca, 2009; Barca, McCann & Rodríguez-Pose, 2012; Servillo et al., 2016).

The first institutionalized definition of Italian inner areas can be found in the document "Methods and objectives for the effective use of EU funds 2014–2020",[3] in which these areas are defined and quantified as about three-fifths of the Italian territory, with a little less than a quarter of the population. Concretely, these areas are defined as the part of Italy that is "distant from centres of agglomeration and services and with unstable development trajectories but at the same time endowed with resources that central areas lack, "wrinkled", with demographic problems but at the same time strongly polycentric and with high potential for attraction" (see endnote 3, p.12). In this sense, the SNAI defines inner areas with the following parameters:[4]

(a)   They are far away from the main centres of supply of essential services (education, health and mobility);
(b)   They have important environmental resources and cultural resources;
(c)   They are a profoundly diversified territory, result of the dynamics of the various and differentiated natural systems and of the peculiar and secular processes of anthropization.

The SNAI highlights the marginalization process that, since the Second World War, has gradually affected a significant part of the Italian peripheral areas, causing a decrease in population, employment, land use for economic purposes and local supply of public and private services, as well as social costs affecting the whole country (such as those determined by hydro-geological instability and the degradation of the cultural and landscape heritage). A large part of these areas coincides with mountainous and rural territories, characterized by a historical disadvantage compared to urban areas, as they are far away from services, lack large urban areas and have fewer labour market opportunities (for a European overview see Rodríguez-Pose, 2018).

Starting from this overall picture, the SNAI, by considering territorial diversity as a national distinguishing feature, attempts to overcome existing territorial dichotomies (i.e., urban vs. rural, centre vs. periphery, and mountain vs. plain), and considers inner areas as a new subject and actor for strategic development, moving from being excluded and disadvantaged territories to laboratories of sustainable development. In relation to the entire national territory, these areas are interpreted as resources, an element of support and a complement to the country's development (Strategia nazionale per le Aree interne, 2017, p.14). The SNAI is based primarily on the definition of policies for the activation of latent or unused territorial capital, which includes natural and cultural capital, the social energy of the local population and potential residents, productive systems, and local know-how.

The spatial identification of the inner areas departs from a polycentric consideration of Italy, a country characterized by a network of municipalities or aggregations of municipalities (service supply centres) around which areas characterized by different levels of spatial peripherality gravitate. According to this spatial structure, the territorial classification adopted by the strategy consists of two main phases:

1. Identification of the A – Poles, B – Intermunicipal poles and C – Belt (these three categories are considered the centres), according to criteria of capacity to offer essential services (education, health services, public transport);
2. Identification of the remaining municipalities in three categories: D – Intermediate areas, E – Peripheral areas, F – Ultra-peripheral areas (these three categories are considered inner areas).

The final spatial classification (applied to the territorial context of 2014 in terms of local units in Italy) is therefore mainly influenced by two factors: (i) the criteria used for the selection of the essential services; and (ii) the choice of the distance thresholds to measure the degree of peripherality of municipalities. In this regard, the classification of the municipalities was obtained on the basis of an indicator of accessibility calculated in terms of minutes of travel time from the nearest pole according to the existing transport infrastructures (for a critical view see Vendemmia, Pucci, & Beria, 2021). In this sense, the resulting categories are calculated using the second and third quartiles of the distribution of the index of distance in minutes to the nearest pole, equal to approximately 20 and 40 minutes (intermediate and peripheral areas respectively). A third category, over 75 minutes, equal to the 95th percentile, was then created to identify the ultra-peripheral territories. The inner areas identified, resulting from the sum of intermediate, peripheral and ultra-peripheral areas, represent about 53% of the Italian municipalities (4.261), with 23% of the population residing in a portion of the territory that exceeds 60% of the total. In order to proceed with the pilot application of the strategy, a further selection of 72 "project areas" took place within this classification, comprising 1077 municipalities, 2,072,718 inhabitants, covering a total of 51,366 square kilometres or 16.7% of the national territory.[5] These areas, with the guidance of the regions, elaborated partnership projects and development strategies at the local level, having access, for the implementation phase, to the funds allocated by the strategy.

The SNAI, although still ongoing and without evidence of its efficacy so far, marks a shift from a welfare-type policy to a place-based policy, based on the potential of the high value resources (e.g., cultural ones) that characterize the areas and that constitute a vulnerable but precious heritage to activate local development processes. Indeed, the place-based approach aims at rebalancing the territory, working on social exclusion and under-use of local resources and, regardless of the strategy's impact on cohesion policies, the tested logic has had an important influence at national and international level (Cotella & Vitale Brovarone, 2021).

Taking into account that today there is a spread of studies and research on the valorization of the cultural and creative potential of rural areas as places where it is possible to experiment with a new idea of quality of life and social cohesion (see, for instance, De la Barre, 2012; Lysgård, 2016; Weaver, 2018; Collins & Cunningham, 2017), the SNAI constitutes in this perspective a laboratory of sustainable development, which, at least in theory, works through a bottom-up planning, centred on culture, people and communities, supported by a planned and transformative political vision of the territory (Punziano & Urso, 2016). But how is this transferred in the strategy? What is the actual role of culture in rural (lagged) areas?

Looking at the application of the strategy, according to the 2020 report of the Italian Agency for territorial Cohesion[6] (Lezzi, 2018) a total amount of 1,167.13 million euros have been allocated for inner areas (658 million for Southern Italy and 508 for Northern Italy). Considering the distribution of these funds among the different sectors of intervention of the SNAI, two main categories were considered: services (which received 44% of funds and include Mobility/Transport; Health and School) and local development (which received 56% of funds and include Nature, Culture and Tourism; Agriculture; Firms; Energy; Digital services and infrastructures; Territory disaster risk reduction; Forests; Jobs and competences; Efficiency of the Public Administration). Within those, the two most covered sectors are Mobility/Transport (255 million euros), with 22% of the total amount, corresponding to the interventions aimed at roads' renovation as established in some strategies of areas belonging to less developed regions; and Nature, Culture and Tourism (208 million euros), with 18% of the total amount, concretely including the valorisation of the natural and cultural heritage, having as an indicator of results: "Increase the number of tourists and visitors to the area's cultural and natural heritage" (p.25), limiting then the measured and expected impacts mainly to the tourism sector.

According to the application of the strategy so far, culture, as a development driver, seems mostly related to tourism, considering mainly the attractive function of cultural heritage, and not the broader added value of cultural sectors in fostering innovation, as widely demonstrated in the literature, especially at the urban level (see for example Boix et al., 2016; Coll-Martínez, Moreno-Monroy, & Arauzo-Carod, 2019). This role of culture, only partially aligned with the initial aim of the SNAI, is attributed to culture not by the central state, which allocated most of the resources needed for the services, but by regions and local administrations, which are directly responsible for the strategies. As Cotella and Vitale Brovarone highlight (2021), regions play a central role in the institutional set-up of the SNAI and its development process varies strongly from one region to another, due to a heterogeneous set of factors (e.g., the willingness to be involved, the planning capacity, the "culture" of horizontal cooperation, etc.). It is therefore interesting to investigate the actual cultural economic fabric and the resources of the inner areas of the regions, considering the funds allocated and the tourism-centred role given to culture.

Although in Italy there is a reasonable amount of research focusing on CCIs at the national level (see, for instance, Symbola (2021) annual report), at the local level for inner areas (see Battino & Lampreu, 2017 for Sardinia; Scrofani & Petino, 2019 for Sicily; Meini & Di Felice, 2017; Vitale, 2018 for Molise), and using local labour systems (see Crociata, Pinate & Urso, 2022), there is limited empirical evidence at the regional level focusing on a geographical and sectorial overview of CCIs establishments in inner areas. Consequently, this is the gap we are contributing to fill with this chapter.

13.3   DATA AND METHODS

To describe the actual profile of cultural sectors in the regions and related inner areas, we followed six methodological steps:

1. Definition of the sectorial perimeter of the CCIs to be considered.
2. Selection of the data on CCIs establishments and employees.
3. Selection of the data and definition of the spatial perimeter, according to the classification of Italian municipalities adopted by the SNAI.
4. Creation of a relational database merging the data of steps 2 and 3.
5. Data analysis at the regional and CCIs level.
6. Mapping of the data.

We started with the definition of the most representative cultural industries (step 1), using the Italian mercantile register and the classification of a firm according to five-digit ATECO code (Italian version of standard NACE codes). The CCIs sectors classification we adopt in this chapter integrates the Italian model of the economy of culture introduced by Walter Santagata (Santagata & Bertacchini, 2011) articulated in three pillars and twelve sectors: (a) cultural heritage (museums, architecture, performing arts, contemporary arts and photography), (b) material culture (fashion, wine and food, design and craft), and (c) media and new media (movies, TV and radio, printing, software, advertising). The three-pillar model is constructed according to cultural output and cultural and creative input approaches like the concentric circles model (Throsby, 2000), taking into account Italian specificities, namely considering the network of economic and social relations both between the different institutional actors and economic subjects within a single local supply chain and between the different industries that make up the macro sector of cultural and creative activities (see Lazzeretti & Capone, 2015 and Sacco & Segre, 2009, for additional details). Given the necessity of having clear boundaries for the CCIs, although in the Italian context food and tourism are strictly related with culture and included in the country-level analysis proposed by Santagata, we decided to limit the overview to the core cultural sectors commonly included at the international level (Boix et al., 2016), excluding activities such as food production, restaurants, travel agencies and accommodation. This decision was made with the aim of drafting a clear picture of the establishments located in inner peripheries, following the general specificities effectively defined by Collins and Cunningham (Collins & Cunningham, 2017), for two main reasons: (i) the establishments included in the food sector, and related ATECO codes, are fuzzy and not always clearly linked with culture, especially considering local resources (for example: can a pizza restaurant located in the mountains of Trentino Alto Adige be considered a cultural establishment as it is in Naples?), and (ii) having in mind the limited number of establishments located in inner peripheries, the inclusion of food and tourism activities could have created some bias in the results. According with previous strategy, we proceeded then in the deconstruction of the three pillars model, focusing on the cultural core, considering the focus on peripheral areas, and we finally selected the following five macro sectors: Cultural heritage; Performing arts; Fashion; Design and craft; Media and new media.

As for the data selection on CCIs (step 2), the main source of this work is the dataset on Italian firms and establishments managed by IRCrES-CNR. The dataset contains detailed information (at the establishment level) on firms and establishments' location; sectors of activity (ATECO code); establishments' structure and typology; number and structure of workforce for each establish-ment. We are using the last available dataset (2018), which corresponds to the pre-COVID-19 pandemic situation, and contains data on a total number of 4,829,555 active establishments in Italy, 511,591 of which are included in the selected CCIs sectors.

The spatial perimeter (step 3), according to the classification of Italian municipalities adopted by the SNAI, was defined using the data available on the Italian Cohesion Agency website[7] and merged, using QGIS software, with the shapefiles of Italian municipalities available on the ISTAT (Italian national statistics institute) website. Some major discrepancies between the munici-palities included in the shapefile, the establishments' dataset (2018) and the municipalities considered in the SNAI classification (2014) were identified. Due to the four years gap between the datasets several municipalities were in fact the subject of change (e.g., change of name, change of surface, elimination, merging with another, etc.). This problem was solved using QGIS, through the conversion tables of the ISTAT municipalities classification database, and the map of inner areas was updated to the list of municipalities of the year 2018.

In order to facilitate and conduct the analysis we then created a relational database of the Italian establishments (step 4), using SQL open-source clients called SQuirreL and SQlite (Harrington, 2016), including the following tables:

I.   Spatial location (municipality level) of the establishments according to the territorial classification of Italian municipalities adopted by the SNAI (source: own elaboration on ISTAT and SNAI 2014);
II. Identification data at the establishment level (source: IRCrES 2018);
III. Structure data at the establishment level (source: IRCrES 2018);
IV. Selected CCIs sectors and subsectors (source: ATECO classification, own elaboration).

The analysis (step 5) was aimed at drafting a description and a picture of the CCIs structure, number and location at the regional level. First, the aggregated numbers were calculated at the regional level (centre and inner areas), in order to give a first measure of the field. Specialization indexes[8] were then applied to the different sectors, considering establishments and employees, at the various scales. Finally, the data were spatially located and mapped using QGIS open-source software (step 6).

13.4   MEASURING CCIs IN INNER AREAS

13.4.1   Cultural and Creative Industries' Size of Establishments and Employment

A first insight into CCIs at the Italian level shows that they constitute 10% of the total number of establishments in Italy (511,591), and that they are located mainly in central areas (87% of them, that correspond to 443,569 establishments) rather than in inner areas (13% of establishments – 67,995). As for their relative weights, CCIs account for 11.3% of establishments in central areas and 7.6% in inner areas. A focus on the regional level shows a clear difference in the location of CCIs in Northern, Middle and Southern Italy, with the latter hosting a small portion of the Italian CCIs. Still, these are small differences considering the percentage of CCIs located in inner areas, being Southern Italy characterized by higher conditions of peripherality. In this regard, the region with the highest percentage of CCIs (considering the total and the establishments located in centres) is Lombardy, followed by Lazio and Tuscany (driven by the main cities Milan, Rome and Florence). Considering CCIs establishments located in the inner areas of the regions, the highest percentage of the total is located in Lazio, followed by Veneto and Lombardy.

Table 13.1   CCIs establishments and employees in Italian regions by territorial position, 2018

Regions		% Total establishments		% Total CCIs establishments		% Total employees		% Total CCIs employees	
		Centre	Inner	Centre	Inner	Centre	Inner	Centre	Inner
North	Piedmont	10.6%	7.4%	7.6%	4.1%	8.4%	6.9%	8.6%	5.1%
	Aosta Valley	10.9%	7.1%	0.2%	0.5%	5.6%	3.2%	0.1%	0.3%
	Lombardy	12.8%	8.5%	23.8%	10.0%	9.0%	6.9%	24.9%	12.0%
	Trentino Alto Adige	12.4%	8.7%	1.5%	5.3%	7.8%	4.8%	1.4%	4.6%
	Veneto	11.7%	9.2%	9.4%	10.2%	9.6%	9.3%	11.4%	16.8%
	Friuli Venezia Giulia	11.2%	9.1%	2.0%	1.6%	6.6%	5.1%	1.8%	1.4%
	Liguria	9.0%	6.0%	2.6%	0.9%	4.7%	3.5%	1.6%	0.7%
	Emilia Romagna	11.0%	7.6%	8.9%	4.7%	6.9%	4.1%	8.3%	3.5%
Middle	Tuscany	14.9%	9.6%	10.6%	5.2%	15.1%	10.2%	13.4%	7.0%
	Umbria	11.3%	9.9%	1.4%	2.5%	9.4%	8.6%	1.5%	2.6%
	Marche	11.2%	10.4%	3.0%	2.9%	12.0%	15.2%	4.1%	5.9%
	Lazio	12.5%	8.1%	10.7%	11.9%	7.9%	4.6%	8.6%	8.5%

Regions		% Total establishments		% Total CCIs establishments		% Total employees		% Total CCIs employees	
		Centre	Inner	Centre	Inner	Centre	Inner	Centre	Inner
South	Abruzzo	10.2%	8.0%	1.7%	4.0%	7.6%	5.9%	1.4%	4.1%
	Molise	9.3%	7.1%	0.2%	1.3%	5.3%	4.3%	0.1%	0.9%
	Campania	8.7%	6.7%	6.4%	5.5%	7.1%	4.7%	5.7%	3.9%
	Apulia	8.5%	7.5%	4.0%	7.8%	6.5%	8.1%	3.4%	8.8%
	Basilicata	11.3%	6.9%	0.3%	2.6%	7.3%	3.3%	0.3%	1.6%
	Calabria	7.8%	5.7%	1.1%	4.7%	4.4%	3.9%	0.6%	2.9%
	Sicily	7.8%	5.7%	3.2%	9.5%	4.5%	3.9%	1.9%	6.4%
	Sardinia	9.8%	6.2%	1.3%	5.0%	4.8%	3.6%	0.7%	3.1%
	Total (Italy)	**11.3%**	**7.6%**	**100%**	**100%**	**8.5%**	**6.1%**	**100%**	**100%**

Source: Own elaboration on data provided by IRCrES-CNR.

The picture changes looking at employees in CCIs at the Italian level, as they constitute around 8% of the total number of employees in Italy (14,623,370). Specifically, 11.7% of CCIs employees are located in inner areas and 88.2% in central areas, constituting respectively 6.1% and 8.5% of the total number of employees. These findings confirm that central areas host a higher share of the workforce than inner areas, although this percentage is lower when dealing with establishments. At the regional level, there is a clear difference in the number of CCIs employees in Northern, Middle and Southern Italy, with the latter hosting a small portion of the Italian CCIs employees. In this sense, the region with the highest percentage of CCIs employees (in relative terms) is Tuscany, followed by Marche and Veneto. If we look at the distribution of the total CCIs employees, then the highest percentage is in Lombardy, followed by Tuscany and Veneto: it is interesting to highlight that both Lombardy and Tuscany are characterized by the presence of large cities like Milan and Florence, attracting employees, while in Veneto there is a presence of mid-sized cities. In some regions the percentage of CCIs employees of the total number of employees is higher in inner areas than in central areas, as in the case of Marche and Apulia. This can be explained by the weight of the fashion sector in the first, and cultural heritage in the second, as described in the next paragraph. Considering the percentage of the total number of CCIs employees, in some regions it is higher in inner areas than in central ones (e.g., Veneto in Northern Italy, and whole Southern Italy, except Campania and Molise). This suggests that in inner areas employees are less specialized and more distributed among regions, small cities and sectors than in the centre, where the role played by metropolitan cities like Milan and Florence is evident.

13.4.2   CCIs Fundamental Sectors Breakdown

Looking at the considered CCIs sectors (see Table 13.2) and their percentage within the total number of CCIs, Cultural heritage establishments are the most numerous (30.5% in centre, 35.2% in inner areas), followed by Media and new media (22.8% in centre, 20.7% in inner areas), Performing arts (21.6% in centre, 18.6% in inner areas), Design and crafts (15.1% in centre, 16.2% in inner areas) and Fashion (10% in centre, 9.3% in inner areas). The large number of establishments in the cultural heritage sector, especially in inner areas, is due to the high number of professionals, like architects, which, due to the specificities of the sector and business organization, are characterized by one-person companies, counting then as one establishment according to the Italian legislation and in our database. If we consider the regional context, the difference between Northern, Middle and Southern Italy is evident. In the South, the majority of establishments are in the cultural heritage sector (up to 51% in inner areas of Basilicata), while the fashion sector is underrepresented.

Table 13.2   CCIs establishments in Italian regions by sector, 2018

	Region	Design and Craft		Media and New Media		Fashion		Cultural Heritage		Performing Arts	
		Centre	Inner	Centre	Inner	Centre	Inner	Centre	Inner	Centre	Inner
North	**Piedmont**	18.3%	17.1%	23.8%	21.3%	5.4%	7.1%	31.2%	34.1%	21.3%	20.4%
	Aosta V.	13.8%	15.2%	21.3%	25.5%	3.1%	5.2%	41.1%	37.4%	20.7%	16.8%
	Lombardy	15.2%	17.0%	24.5%	18.6%	6.9%	12.1%	27.3%	31.3%	26.1%	20.9%
	Tr. Alto A.	13.5%	20.6%	25.2%	20.1%	1.9%	3.0%	37.8%	35.2%	21.7%	21.1%
	Veneto	20.0%	18.7%	20.3%	16.7%	11.1%	17.5%	29.8%	28.3%	18.9%	18.7%
	Friuli V. G.	18.2%	19.1%	24.6%	22.8%	2.8%	4.2%	31.0%	26.6%	23.4%	27.2%
	Liguria	13.2%	16.0%	23.8%	22.0%	2.9%	3.0%	37.7%	35.9%	22.5%	23.2%
	Emilia Rom.	14.3%	17.3%	22.9%	20.4%	10.0%	8.2%	29.2%	27.7%	23.6%	26.4%
Middle	**Tuscany**	17.3%	24.0%	16.1%	18.3%	28.2%	14.2%	23.0%	24.1%	15.4%	19.5%
	Umbria	16.7%	16.2%	22.0%	19.2%	13.8%	17.5%	30.2%	28.0%	17.3%	19.0%
	Marche	19.5%	16.7%	19.7%	14.3%	15.7%	31.6%	29.0%	24.0%	16.0%	13.4%
	Lazio	9.5%	12.5%	27.0%	25.0%	2.6%	3.5%	32.7%	34.5%	28.3%	24.5%

	Region	Design and Craft		Media and New Media		Fashion		Cultural Heritage		Performing Arts	
		Centre	Inner	Centre	Inner	Centre	Inner	Centre	Inner	Centre	Inner
South	Abruzzo	11.6%	13.8%	20.7%	19.3%	13.1%	8.1%	38.4%	43.0%	16.1%	15.7%
	Molise	13.5%	14.5%	22.4%	17.3%	4.7%	7.8%	45.1%	46.4%	14.3%	13.9%
	Campania	12.9%	11.5%	21.8%	20.9%	15.4%	10.4%	33.1%	42.5%	17.0%	14.7%
	Apulia	13.3%	17.1%	23.0%	21.3%	12.5%	12.5%	35.5%	36.0%	15.6%	13.1%
	Basilicata	14.1%	9.5%	25.5%	19.4%	1.9%	5.2%	40.8%	51.4%	17.7%	14.4%
	Calabria	11.2%	13.0%	25.9%	23.2%	3.6%	4.5%	44.1%	46.2%	15.3%	13.2%
	Sicily	12.3%	15.6%	25.8%	23.6%	2.5%	4.1%	41.0%	42.3%	18.5%	14.3%
	Sardinia	11.5%	16.9%	22.7%	22.2%	2.3%	3.6%	43.7%	38.9%	19.8%	18.4%
	Total (Italy)	**15.1%**	**16.2%**	**22.8%**	**20.7%**	**10.0%**	**9.3%**	**30.5%**	**35.2%**	**21.6%**	**18.6%**

Source: Own elaboration on data provided by IRCrES-CNR.

This is an industry with a particular location profile across regions, as in Tuscany it holds 28% of CCIs establishments in the centre, and in Marche is 31% of the CCIs located in inner areas, doubling the percentage related to the centre of the same region. Apparently, it is more represented than in the centre, in the inner areas of Veneto, Lombardy, and almost any other region (with smaller numbers).

The picture slightly changes when analysing employees working in the CCIs sectors. As for the central areas, the Media and new media employees are the most numerous (31%), followed by Fashion (25.8%), Design and crafts (16.7%), Cultural heritage (15.6%) and Performing arts (10.7), while in inner areas the employees working in Fashion (35.4%) are the most numerous, followed by Design and crafts (20%), Cultural heritage (17.6%), Media and new media (17.4%) and Performing arts (9.6%).

Previous differences can be explained looking at the mean number of employees, with the fashion sector being characterized by larger numbers (up to 20 for one establishment). Conversely, sectors like Cultural heritage and Performing arts are mostly represented by individual professionals, as highlighted in the previous paragraph.

13.5   MAPPING CCIs SPECIALIZATION IN INNER AREAS

13.5.1   Cultural and Creative Industries Specialization

Starting with the average specialization in CCIs establishments, looking at the classification of the municipalities at the national level, in general it is possible to affirm that central areas are specialized (index 1), while inner areas are not (index 0.7). In fact, if we look at the micro classification only the category A – Pole (biggest cities) is specialized (index 1.2, followed by B – Intermunicipal pole (index 0.9), C – Belt (0.9), and for inner areas, D – Intermediate (index 0.7), E – Peripheral (index 0.6), F – Ultraperipheral (index 0.5).

Moving to the scale of interest of this chapter, in terms of regional specialization in CCIs establishments the most important ones are Lazio, Marche, Umbria, Abruzzo, Tuscany, Friuli Venezia Giulia, Veneto, Lombardy and Trentino Alto Adige, all of them belonging to Northern and Middle Italy. As Figure 13.1 illustrates, there are regions such as Abruzzo, Umbria, Marche and Friuli Venezia Giulia where inner areas are specialized whilst centres are not. A first insight about this pattern suggests that a role is played by the fact that in these regions there are many small or medium sized cities, which are not as attractive as metropolitan areas such as Milan or Rome.

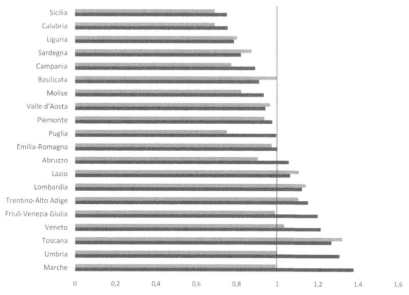

Source: Own elaboration on data provided by IRCrES-CNR.

Figure 13.1   Regions' specialization in CCIs establishments, 2018

To better understand the previous patterns, the specialization levels and the inner areas are presented together. From Figure 13.2 we can notice how the municipalities specialized in CCIs (at the establishments' level) are mostly located in Northern and Middle Italy, especially around the main cities such as Milan, Rome, Turin, Florence and Venice. It is also interesting to note that there are some concentrations of specialized municipalities which follow the spatial distribution already measured by the literature on Italian industrial and cultural districts, confirming the strength of our data and methods. The same spatial concentration is not visible in the inner areas, where the specialized municipalities are more and more scattered moving from North to South.

We have calculated the same specialization index of the employees working in CCIs sectors and the results are aligned with the ones of the establishments.

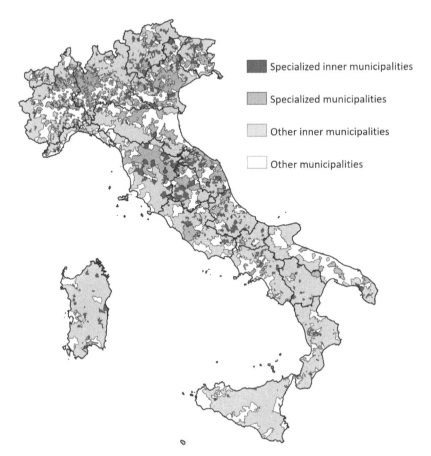

Source: Own elaboration on data provided by IRCrES-CNR.

Figure 13.2   Municipalities' establishments specialization in CCIs, 2018

13.5.2   CCIs Sectors Specialization

Moving to the analysis at the CCIs sectors level, we used the specialization index to identify the municipalities and areas where the considered industries are more represented than at the national level. In doing so, we considered establishments (Figure 13.3) and employees, including the inner areas layer. The analysis shows some interesting results, especially looking at the spatial distribution of each sector.

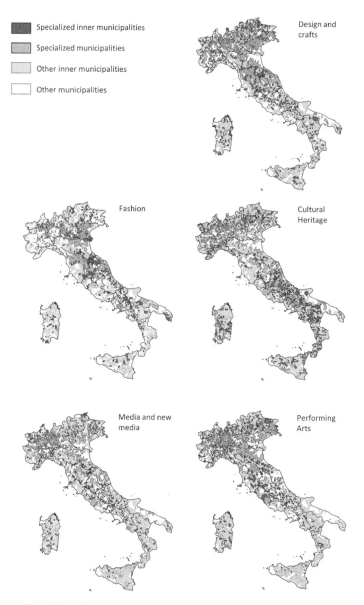

Source: Own elaboration on data provided by IRCrES-CNR.

Figure 13.3 *Municipalities' establishments specialization in CCIs sectors, 2018*

Some preliminary considerations can be drawn for each sector as follows:

Performing arts: it is possible to notice that, considering both establishments and employees, municipalities are concentrated around the main cities of Northern and Middle Italy (Milan, Rome, Florence, Venice, etc.). If we look at inner areas, we can observe a lot of specialized municipalities are scattered from North to South (even in mountainous areas where this pattern is not expected), underlining a location choice that deserves further research. This is especially evident regarding the index applied to employees' specialization.

Media and new media: As expected, the sector is characterized by a lower number of specialized municipalities in inner areas, as the industry is traditionally urban based. The only evident concentration refers to the establishments' specialization around Milan, whilst there are few specialized municipalities when measuring at employment level.

Cultural heritage: This is the sector with the highest number of specialized municipalities in Southern Italy and inner areas, more than in the Northern and Middle regions, both for establishments and employees. This outcome can be explained by the relative weight of the sector in areas characterized by lower numbers in CCIs industries, but probably also by the importance of this sector, strictly linked to the built heritage, with a high number of professionals and one-person companies (architects in particular).

Fashion: This is the sector where the concentration of specialized municipalities is more evident. As already noticed in previous paragraphs, it is possible to recognize the historically rooted industrial districts in Middle and Northern Italy (Veneto, Tuscany, Emilia Romagna and Marche in particular), but also in Apulia (more evident when considering employees). Considering inner areas, apart from the municipalities around the main concentrations in Central and Northern Italy, there is also a scattered pattern of municipalities in Southern Italy, worthy of further research.

Design and crafts: There is a concentration of specialized municipalities (noticeably at the establishments level) in this sector, particularly in Middle and North Eastern Italy, being crafts historically linked with an agglomeration tendence. Despite this, unlike in the fashion sector, we can see that there are some specialized municipalities in inner areas, especially in the Alps (Northern Italy) and Apennines mountains (Middle and Southern Italy), probably due to the strong link of crafts with the natural and cultural resources of these areas.

13.6 CONCLUSIONS

This chapter analysed the CCIs establishments' and employees' specialization in the inner areas of Italian regions, contributing to the existing literature with a sectorial and geographical overview based on the overall policy and on the first results of the Italian National Strategy for Inner Areas.

The creation of an original database bridging the data on the CCIs with the territorial classification according to the SNAI contributes at the existing literature, showing that CCIs play an important role in some of the Italian inner peripheries and that are spatially distributed following specific patterns different for each considered sector.

Looking at the distribution of CCIs and their specializations across Italian regions and municipalities the rooted difference between North, Middle and South of Italy, as well as the widely recognizable cultural and industrial districts characterizing Italian economic development is confirmed.

Considering the scope of our work, the overall picture drafted in the chapter raises the question of the actual alignment of the SNAI with the cultural economic fabric of the territories. On the one hand it is evident that a difference exists in the distribution of CCIs in inner areas and centres, being the latter generally more specialized. On the other hand, the economic dimension of culture is so far treated by the SNAI mainly in relation with tourism, leaving the strategic decisions to regions and local administrations. The spatial pattern of CCIs in different sectors should be taken into account by specific policies targeted at the local level, promoting specific cultural and creative activities according to their actual presence and territorial vocation, and not in general.

There are, however, limitations. Since we focused on 2018, both for CCIs data and territorial classification, our conclusions are based only on a single year (even though 2018 was the most recent dataset available at the time of the analysis). Furthermore, the following update of the SNAI was launched in March 2022, with a classification of the included areas updated in 2020. Nevertheless, although we refer to a single year the database is rich enough to get a complete picture of the spatial distribution of CCIs across central and inner areas.

Some issues beyond the scope of this work are left for further analysis. First, this chapter does not consider the correlations both among the different CCIs sectors and the different areas classified in the SNAI. Looking at the spatial distribution of establishments, employees, and the specialized municipalities, for a wide-ranging understanding of the economic role of culture and creativity in the inner peripheries, further research on local indicators of spatial autocorrelation could be necessary. Second, considering the strict relation between culture and tourism declared in the strategy (and crucial for the Italian development), food and tourism sectors could be taken into account and their analysis deepened, especially in their intersection with the other CCIs. Third, having shown the importance of territorial specificities in the definition and application of the SNAI, it would be appropriate to deepen the analysis of the results and projects developed in the pilot areas, especially for the evaluation of the actual results and possible improvements of the strategy in future years.

NOTES

1. Through the chapter inner areas and peripheral areas are used as synonyms.
2. Institutional website: https://www.agenziacoesione.gov.it/ strategia -nazionale -aree-interne/ (accessed January 2022).
3. Note MCT 3387 27 December 2012. https://www.reterurale.it/flex/cm/pages/ ServeAttachment .php/ L/ IT/ D/ 4 %252Fe %252Fb %252FD .a 1a6c84e636 0aeb60fe6/P/BLOB%3AID%3D10538/E/pdf (accessed January 2022).
4. This definition is included in the document "Strategia nazionale per le Aree interne: definizione, obiettivi, strumenti e governance": https://www.miur.gov.it/ documents/20182/890263/strategia_nazionale_aree_interne.pdf/d10fc111-65c0 -4acd-b253-63efae626b19 (accessed January 2022).
5. For the list of the 72 areas see: https://www.agenziacoesione.gov.it/ strategia -nazionale-aree-interne/ (accessed January 2022).
6. See https://www.agenziacoesione.gov.it/wp-content/uploads/2021/11/Relazione -CIPESS-2020_finale.pdf (accessed January 2022).
7. See https://www.agenziacoesione.gov.it/ strategia -nazionale -aree -interne/ la -selezione -delle -aree/ https://www.agenziacoesione.gov.it/strategia -nazionale -aree-interne/la-selezione-delle-aree/ (accessed January 2022).
8. Specialization indexes were calculated following the function:
   $S_{ji} = (E_{ij} / E_j) / (E_i / E) > 1$
   i = CCI sector
   j = municipality (or other territorial scale)
   E_{ij} = number of establishments (or employees) of the sector i in the space j
   E_j = total number of establishments (or employees) in the space j
   E_i = total number of establishments (or employees) in the sector i
   E = total number of establishments (or employees) in Italy
   The municipality/other scale specializes in a sector when the index is higher than one.

REFERENCES

Barca, F. (2009). An agenda for a reformed cohesion policy: A place-based approach to meeting European Union challenges and expectations. Independent report prepared at the request of Danuta Hübner, Commissioner for Regional Policy (April)

Barca, F., McCann, P., & Rodríguez-Pose, A. (2012). The case for regional development intervention: Place-based versus place-neutral approaches. *Journal of Regional Science, 52*(1), 134–152. https://doi.org/10.1111/j.1467-9787.2011.00756.x

Battino, S., & Lampreu, S. (2017). Strategie di valorizzazione e promozione in chiave caso in sardegna. *Annali Del Turismo, VI*, 83–105

Boix, R., Capone, F., De Propris, L., Lazzeretti, L., & Sanchez, D. (2016). Comparing creative industries in Europe. *European Urban and Regional Studies, 23*(4), 935–940. https://doi.org/10.1177/0969776414541135

Bronzini, R., Ciani, E., & Montaruli, F. (2022). Tourism and local growth in Italy. *Regional Studies, 56*(1), 140–154. https://doi.org/10.1080/00343404.2021.1910649

Coll-Martínez, E., Moreno-Monroy, A. I., & Arauzo-Carod, J. M. (2019). Agglomeration of creative industries: An intra-metropolitan analysis for Barcelona. *Papers in Regional Science, 98*(1), 409–431. https://doi.org/10.1111/pirs.12330

Collins, P., & Cunningham, J. A. (2017). *Creative Economies in Peripheral Regions.* Palgrave Macmillan. https://doi.org/10.1007/978-3-319-52165-7

Cotella, G., & Vitale Brovarone, E. (2021). The national strategy for inner areas. A place-based turn for Italian regional policy. *Archivio Di Studi Urbani e Regionali, 129,* 22–46. https://doi.org/10.3280/ASUR2020-129002

Crociata A., Pinate A. C., & Urso G. (2022). The cultural and creative economy in Italy: Spatial patterns in peripheral areas. *GSSI Discussion Paper Series in Regional Science & Economic Geography, 2022–02,* 1–51

De la Barre, S. (2012). Creativity in peripheral places: Redefining the creative industries. *Tourism Planning & Development, 9*(4), 441–443. https://doi.org/10.1080/21568316.2012.726258

Della Lucia, M., & Segre, G. (2017). Intersectoral local development in Italy: The cultural, creative and tourism industries. *International Journal of Culture, Tourism, and Hospitality Research, 11*(3), 450–462. https://doi.org/10.1108/IJCTHR-03-2016-0032

Harrington, J. L. (2016). Relational Database Design and Implementation: Fourth Edition. *Relational Database Design and Implementation: Fourth Edition.* Morgan Kaufmann. https://doi.org/10.1016/C2015-0-01537-4

Lazzeretti, L., & Capone, F. (2015). Narrow or broad definition of cultural and creative industries: Evidence from Tuscany, Italy. *International Journal of Cultural and Creative Industries, 2*(2), 4–19.

Lezzi, B. (2018). *Relazione annuale sulla Strategia nazionale per le Aree Interne.* 1–70. https://www.agenziacoesione.gov.it/wp-content/uploads/2020/07/Relazione_CIPE_ARINT_311218.pdf

Lysgård, H. K. (2016). The "actually existing" cultural policy and culture-led strategies of rural places and small towns. *Journal of Rural Studies, 44*(June), 1–11. https://doi.org/10.1016/j.jrurstud.2015.12.014

Meini, M., & Di Felice, G. (2017). Mappare le risorse delle aree interne : potenzialità e criticità per la fruizione. *Bollettino Della Associazione Italiana Di Cartografia, 2017*(161), 4–21. https://doi.org/10.13137/2282-572X/

OECD. (2018). *Culture and Local Development.* http://books.google.com/books?id=eOuJ9_U2absC&pgis=1%0Ahttp://www.oecd-ilibrary.org/urban-rural-and-regional-development/culture-and-local-development_9789264009912-en

Petrei, F., Cavallo, L., & Santoro, M. T. (2020). Cultural tourism: An integrated analysis based on official data. *Quality and Quantity, 54*(5–6), 1705–1724. https://doi.org/10.1007/s11135-019-00929-y

Pezzi, M. G., & Urso, G. (2016). Peripheral areas: Conceptualizations and policies. Introduction and editorial note. *Italian Journal of Planning Practice, 6*(1), 1–19

Punziano, G., & Urso, G. (2016). Local development strategies for inner areas in Italy: A comparative analysis based on plan documents. *Italian Journal of Planning Practice, 6*(1), 76–109

Rodríguez-Pose, A. (2018). The revenge of the places that don't matter (and what to do about it). *Cambridge Journal of Regions, Economy and Society, 11*(1), 189–209. https://doi.org/10.1093/cjres/rsx024

Sacco, P. L., & Segre, G. (2009). Creativity, cultural investment and local development: A new theoretical framework for endogenous growth. *Advances in Spatial Science, 56,* 281–294. https://doi.org/10.1007/978-3-540-70924-4_13

Santagata, W., & Bertacchini, E. (2011). Creative atmosphere: Cultural industries and local development. *Accounting & Finance, 4.* https://doi.org/10.1111/j.1467-629X.1980.tb00220.x

Scrofani, L., & Petino, G. (2019). Le attività culturali e creative per il rilancio turistico delle aree interne in Sicilia . Il caso studio dell ' Ypsigrock Festival Cultural and creative activities for touristic development of the inner areas. *Bollettino Della Associazione Italiana Di Cartografia, 9733*(166), 28–42. https://doi.org/10.13137/2282-572X/

Servillo, L., Russo, A. P., Barbera, F., & Carrosio, G. (2016). Inner peripheries: Towards an EU place-based agenda on territorial peripherality. *Italian Journal of Planning Practice, 6*(1), 42–75

Strategia nazionale per le Aree interne. (2017). *Accordo di partenariato 2014–2020*. https:// www .agenziacoesione .gov .it/ wp -content/ uploads/ 2019/ 09/ accordo _di _partenariato_sezione_1b_2017.pdf

Symbola. (2021). *Io sono cultura 2021*. https://symbola.net/wp-content/uploads/2021/07/Io-sono-Cultura-2021.pdf

Throsby, D. (2000). *Economics and Culture*. Cambridge University Press. https://doi.org/10.1017/CBO9781107590106

Vendemmia, B., Pucci, P., & Beria, P. (2021). An institutional periphery in discussion. Rethinking the inner areas in Italy. *Applied Geography, 135*(July), 102537. https://doi.org/10.1016/j.apgeog.2021.102537

Vitale, C. (2018). La valorizzazione del patrimonio culturale nelle Aree Interne. Considerazioni preliminari. *Aedon. Rivista Di Arti e Diritto on Line, 3*. https://doi.org/10.7390/92256

Weaver, D. (2018). Creative periphery syndrome? Opportunities for sustainable tourism innovation in Timor-Leste, an early stage destination. *Tourism Recreation Research, 43*(1), 118–128. https://doi.org/10.1080/02508281.2017.1397838

Index